D1266073

Orchids

Text by *Jack Kramer*

Foreword by Anthony West

Photographs by Guy Burgess, Joyce R. Wilson, and others

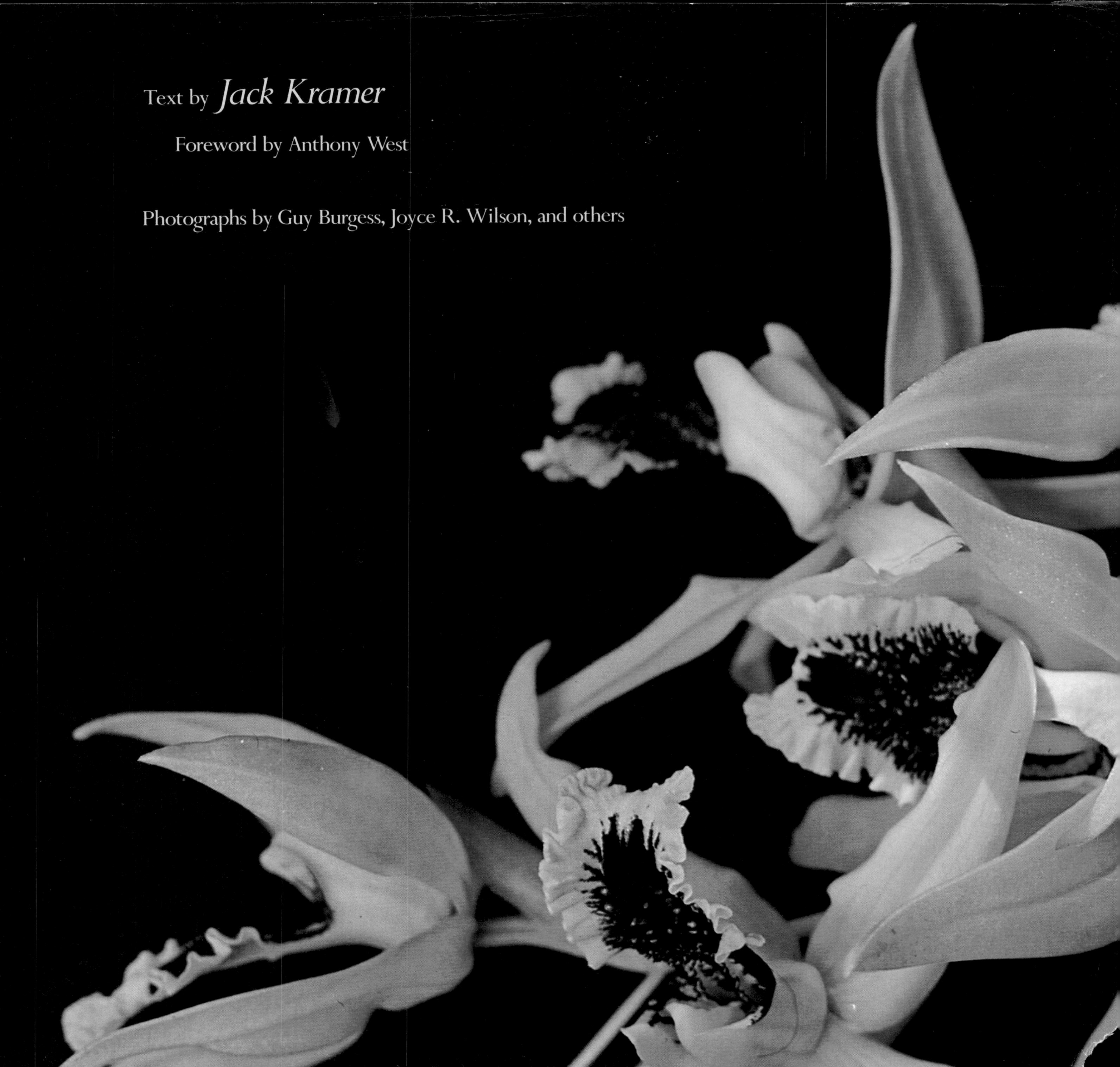

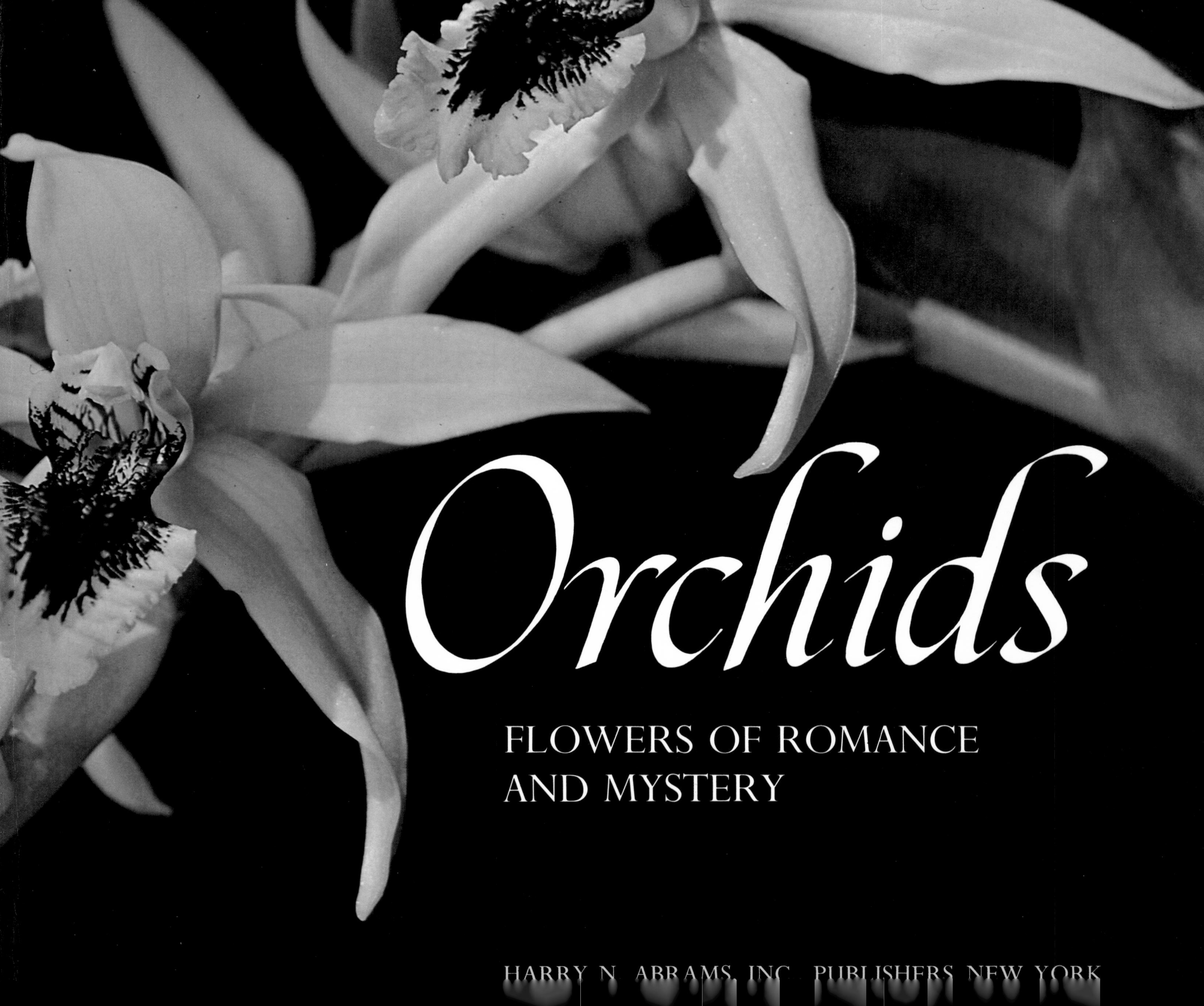

Orchids

FLOWERS OF ROMANCE AND MYSTERY

HARRY N. ABRAMS, INC. PUBLISHERS NEW YORK

NAI Y. CHANG, *Vice-President, Design and Production*

JOHN L. HOCHMANN, *Executive Editor*

MARGARET L. KAPLAN, *Managing Editor*

BARBARA LYONS, *Director, Photo Department, Rights and Reproductions*

WILSON GATHINGS, *Editor*

PATRICIA DUNBAR, *Designer*

Library of Congress Cataloging in Publication Data

Kramer, Jack, 1927-
Orchids, flowers of romance and mystery.

Bibliography: p.
Includes index.
1. Orchid culture. 2. Orchids. I. Burgess, Guy, ill. II. Wilson, Joyce R., ill. III. Title.
SB409.K716 635.9'34'15 74-30476
ISBN 0-8109-0270-2

Library of Congress Catalogue Card Number: 74-30476
Published by Harry N. Abrams, Incorporated, New York, 1975

Printed and bound in Japan.

Contents

ACKNOWLEDGMENTS

Grateful acknowledgment is made to the following institutions for permitting use of reproductions of holdings in their collections:

Academy of Science, Botanical Library, San Francisco; American Orchid Society, Inc., Botanical Museum of Harvard University, Cambridge, Mass.; Art Institute of Chicago; Bancroft Library, University of California, Berkeley; East Asiatic Library, University of California, Berkeley; Freer Art Gallery, Washington, D.C.; Hunt Botanical Library, Philadelphia; Massachusetts Horticultural Society, Boston; Metropolitan Museum of Art, New York; Museum of Fine Arts, Boston; Royal Botanical Gardens of Kew, Richmond, Surrey, England.

My personal thanks go to the following individuals who gave freely of their time and knowledge:

Hermann Pigors, Oak Hill Gardens, Dundee, Ill.; Frank Fordyce, Rod McLellan Orchids, South San Francisco; Elizabeth C. Hall, Horticultural Society of New York and New York Botanical Garden; Margaret Ilgenfritz, Ilgenfritz Orchids, Monroe, Mich.; R. Desmond, Library of the Royal Botanical Gardens of Kew, Richmond, Surrey, England; Paul C. Hutchison, Escondido, Calif.; Anton Christ, University of California Botanic Gardens, Berkeley; George Lawrence, Hunt Botanical Library, Philadelphia; Henry Teuscher, Montreal Botanical Gardens; Gordon W. Dillon and Merle Reinnika, American Orchid Society, Inc., Cambridge, Mass.; and a special note of appreciation to my editor on the job, Wilson Gathings, of Harry N. Abrams, Inc.

Many of the photographers who worked with me went far beyond the call of duty to capture on film the plants I wanted represented. Joyce R. Wilson of California shot and reshot orchids almost on a weekly basis for many months. Guy Burgess of Colorado provided a select group of very fine orchid photographs to further enhance the book. Hermann Pigors of Oak Hill gardens in Dundee, Ill., contributed many excellent photographs from his slide library. Andrew R. Addkison of Jackson, Miss., kept a record on film of the orchids in my collection; some of his best shots are included. To all these people, my gratitude for their enthusiasm, interest, and patience.

FOREWORD

Orchids

A FOREWORD BY ANTHONY WEST

Orchids are the most extraordinary of flowers, with their smoky and sometimes strangely impure colors, their ultrasophisticated and often sinister shapes, and their remarkable scents. There is almost always a suggestion of otherworldliness about them; it is as if they were visitors from outer space, the butterflies or moths of some unknown planet attached to a sun from another galaxy, frozen in mid-flight, silently waiting a magic word that will set them free to flutter away.

Many of the more than twenty thousand members of this enormous family are hauntingly and unforgettably beautiful, while others, startling in their mimicries, their appearance of an altogether animal vitality, their suggestions of carnivorousness, are almost repellent. There are people who are even frightened of them and who can never quite overcome a lingering suspicion that the most ordinary purple airline orchid may not have it in its power to sink its fangs into any flesh carelessly exposed to it, to cling there, fattening itself like a leech. This was a favorite fantasy of the last century when the craze for hothouse orchids was at its height, and there must be a dozen variants of the story of the orchid collector attacked and drained of his blood by his latest acquisition. It was thought for a long time that the orchids that trapped insects in stomach-like vessels, filled with a liquid in which the insects were at length dissolved, were eating and digesting them. But this was an error; and though orchids do many remarkable things, none of them is in fact a carnivore.

Highest Efficiency and Adaptability

Most of the remarkable things orchids do are connected with sex. The orchids are, indeed, specialists in reproductive techniques, and they have raised their performances to a level of refinement and elegance reached by few other flowers. At some remote stage in their evolution, a chance mutation knocked them out of the main line of floral development and made them unique. Its consequence was a simplification of their sexual organs so drastic and so effective that it might have been the product of an inspired design decision consciously aimed at achieving the highest possible levels of efficiency and adaptability.

In place of the usual arrangement of distinct reproductive organs—ovaries, pistils, and stamens (each consisting of filament and anther)—the orchids have a single structure, capped with one anther, called the column. The internal arrangements of this structure are such that in most cases a single pollination will fertilize an enormous number of seeds. Since these are light enough and small enough to be distributed by the wind, and since a single flower may produce hundreds of thousands of them, it is not surprising that orchids are found wherever plants will grow.

Paradoxically, and as if in compensation for this basic organic simplification, the orchids have developed an enormous variety of elaborately distorted floral structures. Although these are in themselves essentially simple, all orchids having flowers made up of three petals and three sepals, the deformations that the majority of them have undergone, in order to adapt themselves to the special needs of their environments and their pollinators, are so great that their simplicity is hard to recognize.

The starting point of these deformations is the specialization of one of the three petals as a species of landing strip for pollinators. This elaborated petal, called the labellum, is the distinguishing feature of the flowers of all the members of the family, but it often takes a trained botanist with a good deal of experience to know it for what it is.

In the case of the grass pink (calopogon), the small field orchid that is the simple New England equivalent of the paphiopedilums shown, the labellum has become an ingenious mechanical device baited with a cluster of imitation stamens, apparently loaded with pollen. When a bee lands on the attractive platform placed handily in front of this lure, it finds itself on a fringed flap that gives way and drops it on its back onto the head of the column. The wild paphiopedilums don't offer their victims—mostly flies—visual lures. They offer them a range of softly funky odors attuned to their low appetites.

This is, however, beginners' stuff so far as the victimization and manipulation of pollinators by orchids can go. The flowers of many of the more sophisticated orchids of the tropical jungles and rain forests twist as their buds form and open in such a way as to set up complex patterns of stress and tension. When the pollinator alights on what is in effect a spring-loaded surface, the result is not unlike springing a mousetrap. In some cases the flower seems to grasp its visitor and to process it so deftly that it is hard to believe that it has no idea of what it is doing. The flowers of one species of orchid first drug or intoxicate their pollinators and then lure them onto a lubricated chute or slide that delivers them helpless and often upside down to a point where pollen can be conveniently attached to them or removed from them.

Practical Jokers

In the extreme case of the group of orchids bearing the name *Coryanthes,* part of the labellum has become a vase, the column has developed two glands capable of distilling water in sufficient quantities partially to fill it, and the spring-loaded petals and sepals have been so organized as to drop the pollinator into the enclosed pool. The victim of this practical joke then has the choice of staying where he is and drowning or of crawling to safety through a tunnel of love, which opens temptingly before him, an arrangement closely resembling the pelvis-like feature that is to be seen in the Phalaenopsis Palm Beach. If he does this, he will find himself being processed like a car in an automated car wash, and he will finally emerge with a load of pollen attached to an inaccessible part of his abdomen by an adhesive paste.

The ingenuity, and the Rube Goldberg elaboration, of such common orchid mechanisms for manipulation is fully matched by the sophistication of their visual and chemical deceptive devices. The cluster of imitation stamens used as a lure by the grass pink has already been mentioned, but that again is beginners' stuff. Many orchids offer their pollinators artificial bribes, some of them so alluring that they are preferred to the real thing. This is the case with the *Cryptostylis,* an orchid genus distributed fairly widely throughout the general area of Southeast Asia. They lure male wasps with a flash of color resembling the colors of the abdomens of the wasp females, but the real damage is done with an intoxicating odor that smells, if one may so put it, more like the female than the female does.

Sometimes the orchid beats out its rival by good timing, as does the member of the genus *Ophrys,* whose labellum simulates the female, complete with shining eyes, of a species of solitary bee whose males hatch out some weeks before its females. The flowers of this orchid open as the male bees appear, so that its dummy females enjoy freedom from competition with the real thing for a useful period.

Besotting Male Flies

But the most extraordinary case of all is that of the orchid that shares a territory covering the uplands of Colombia and Peru with a species of fly whose females notify its males of their availability for mating in a rather special way. They settle on leaves exposed to direct sunlight, and when they hear the sound made by the wing beats of a passing male, they agitate their abdomens in such a way that the shiny, almost mirror-like surfaces surrounding their genital orifices send out flashing calls. The orchid concerned exploits this situation with a certain cynicism. It offers the passing male an almost perfect model of the rear end of the female, complete with the reflective surfaces surrounding the center of interest, poised on what appears to be a small cluster of leaves; when a puff of wind ruffles the foliage to which the orchids are attached, out go the flashing signals and down come the besotted males who proceed to copulate with the nodding flowers.

What is so extraordinary in these cases of deception, whether by appearance or by smell, is the high degree of specificity that is achieved. The orchids do not simply attract particular kinds of pollinators, such as bees, wasps, butterflies, moths, flies, beetles, and even birds, but more often than not limit themselves to the members of a single variety belonging to a single species.

How a flower comes to be so wholeheartedly selective of its pollinators is hard to explain—but the why of selectivity is another matter. If a given variety of a flowering plant can only be pollinated by a specific pollinator, the chances of hybridization by crossbreeding between varieties are much reduced, and the chances of surviving as a discrete identity are much increased. In the whole orchid family there is an extraordinarily delicate balance between he evolutionary advantages to be derived from the extreme facility with which new varieties can be developed by hybridization and equally great facility with which they can develop mechanisms for preserving the new identities once they have been produced.

It should be mentioned that orchids fascinated Charles Darwin for this reason, and that they have provided Darwin's critics with an enormous amount of antievolutionary argument ever since he pointed out their importance and interest in the study of their reproductive devices that he published in 1877.

The principal source of opposition to Darwinian thinking in this field was the idealistic school of botany, most of whose members were German and most of whom shared Johann Goethe's dislike of ''all this chatter about marriage'' in connection with flowers. These delicate gentlemen couldn't bear to think that a lily, a rose, an orchid, or even a common daisy could be anything as dismal as *ein geistloser Kopulationsmechanismus* (a spiritless mating apparatus).

These people pointed, among other instances, to the

stunningly beautiful Javanese orchid, one of the dendrobiums, whose flowers resemble a cloud of butterflies hovering along the line of a branch. They flower, dazzlingly and marvellously, for from five to six minutes. How could such a brief explosion of beauty satisfy any useful purpose, they asked, and they went on to assert that it could only be accounted for in aesthetic terms, either as an expression of a kind of Bergsonian *joie de vivre,* a display of the élan vital, or as a display of decadence of the art for art's sake variety. Here was one flower that had to be flowering purely for flowering's sake.

But while thousands of orchids are brief flowers, thousands of others have the most enduring of blossoms. The range extends from the five minutes of the Javanese orchid to an astonishing nine months for the improbable *Grammatophyllum multiflorum,* the longest lasting of all flowers. A great many of the potentially longer living flowers last for just as long as they remain unpollinated—they may be able to last for two or three months, but they are apt to collapse with a dramatic suddenness once they have set seed. This is because fertilization sets off chain reactions that cause the generation of substances toxic to the floral structure. This is a fairly common arrangement in the world of flowers, but some of the short-lived orchid blossoms liquidate themselves in an unusual manner. As their buds open, the flowers are already secreting an enzyme that has the capacity to dissolve the cell walls of the fabric of the petals and sepals. The fully opened flowers are already beginning to digest themselves, and after the set interval of two to three days, each blossom collapses into a gelatinous mass.

Orchids have been grown for well over a thousand years in China, where they were painted and written about as early as the eleventh and twelfth centuries. The characteristic Chinese orchid of the older centers of culture is sweetly scented and has predominately white or greenish flowers, which hover delicately among grass-like or brushlike leaves. Many Westerners who see such orchids as they are represented in classical Chinese drawings or paintings fail to recognize them and take them for romantically idealized members of the narcissus or jonquil families. They were developed from the wild varieties available to Chinese plant hunters in wilderness areas near such centers as Soochow, where the growers of the Middle Kingdom concentrated. The only places in China where orchids of the kinds sought after and admired by Western growers and collectors were grown were in the extreme south, in such towns as Kweilin and Canton. But here, as in central China and the north, the orchids grown by the Chinese were those natural to the region and rarely, if ever, exotic imports from overseas.

In contrast to all this, the growers and collectors of the West are either indifferent to or contemptuous of the hundreds of small but astonishingly lovely orchids that grow on their doorsteps. They speak slightingly of them as botanicals and leave them strictly alone. They are only interested in exotics from faraway places, and the story of both European and American growing is inseparable from that of the development of the ability to maintain artificial climates in greenhouses and conservatories which is part of the history of the industrial revolution and its technology.

The great takeoff in the technique of orchid growing in hothouses that launched a mania for orchid collecting in the last half of the last century could not have happened until just that moment in history, not only because it had not been possible to create and maintain artificial climates in weatherproof enclosed spaces until then but also because it had not been possible to bring the delicate exotics from the tropics swiftly enough.

The eighteenth century's plant-handling techniques were exemplified by the arrangement of tubs shielded from the weather by a canvas awning on the poop deck of Captain Bligh's *Bounty* in which he attempted to take his breadfruit trees across the Pacific Ocean. Between Captain Bligh's day, in the mid-eighteenth century, and the eighteen thirties, when the Duke of Devonshire's head gardener, the great Paxton, perfected the modern greenhouse, an enormous amount had been learned about transporting live plants. Plant collectors employed by rich gardeners had by then been ransacking the world for novelties for over a century, but nineteen out of every twenty growing specimens sent home were still being lost enroute as late as the 1820s. The rate of loss was more or less reversed when steamships came in. From the 1850s on, European growers could have any plant they could pay for.

In phase one of the history of Western orchid growing, it was a competitive sport for rich men. In the eighties and nineties, the mark of arrival, beyond keeping your own carriage, beyond having a town house and country place, a shoot in Scotland, or a string of race horses, was having an orchid house—and having in it something from the heart of Brazil, or darkest

New Guinea, or upper Burma, that they hadn't got at Chatsworth, or in the Rothschilds' orchid houses at Tring Park.

This era ended, literally with a bang, one dark day in 1917 when the Duke of Devonshire pushed down the plunger of a detonator and set off the explosive charges that had been placed all round the foundations of Paxton's greenhouse on his Devonshire estate. The beautiful glass temple of extravagance shattered and vanished in a matter of seconds—the days in which a private individual could burn seven tons of coal a day to keep his tropicals warm had gone by.

The depression of 1929 completed the process that began during World War I, and the guardianship of the orchid has now passed to the commercial grower. In a way this has not been a bad thing. The pursuit of rarities and eccentricities is no longer a factor with the orchid grower who concentrates on beauty of form and color as his predecessors did not. And if there has been a slowing down of the search for new orchids in the jungles and in the wild places of the world, there has been a more than compensatory advance in the art of creating new varieties by hybridization. Lovelier and more exquisitely colored varieties of these most fascinating flowers are constantly being created. There are those who feel that this second phase, in which the question of salability is the ultimately determining factor, may lead to the establishment of commercial types—commonplace in form and of conventional color—as the norm of available orchids. But this has not happened yet, and in any case the more than twenty thousand wild varieties are still producing their own random hybrids all over the world and constantly adding to the endless repertory of the family's unique marvels.

Orchids

AND MYSTERY FLOWERS OF ROMANCE

Cattleya
C. bowringiana
British Honduras, Guatemala

Introduced into England in 1884, this beautiful epiphytic orchid immediately captured a following that has never deserted it. A showy species, it grows to about 40 inches tall. Its canelike pseudobulbs are crowned by large clusters of flowers. (Photograph courtesy of Guy Burgess.)

Introduction

The first orchid I ever saw was the corsage my mother was given on special occasions, generally once a year on her birthday. It was a gaudy bright lavender flower of the genus *Cattleya,* perfected by man to excel in size and color.

While most of us think of the cattleya as *the* orchid, few people realize that some thirty thousand species of orchids grow wild all over the world—from Alaska to the antipodes. In the last ten years many of these have become house plants, and today orchids are, like African violets, indoor favorites.

The wonderful world of flowers is almost limitless, and members of the family Orchidaceae are outstanding for their drama, color, and form. It has taken us over one hundred years to explode the myth that orchids could not survive unless they were sealed under glass like rare gems in treasure houses. Today, we know that orchids can be grown as easily as any other plant—perhaps even more easily because many of them have water-storage vessels (pseudobulbs) to keep them alive if we sometimes forget to tend them (presupposing that they receive adequate light and the proper growing temperature).

Now that orchids are attaining the status of popular indoor plants, it is time to learn something about them—where they come from, how they grow in nature, why some grow on mountainsides, others on trees or on the ground. It is time to find what has made them so appealing and desirable through the years, and to investigate the myths and superstitions that have led to the mystique of the orchid.

In spite of their beauty and desirability, orchids are perhaps the most misunderstood of flowers. But when we separate fact from fancy, we discover their true and fascinating stories. First, let us eliminate a few of the more popular fantasies. Orchids are not carnivorous or parasitic; they have no malefic methods of propagation, no secret devices to enhance their beauty. Orchids are merely the result of nature performing at her best—creating the dazzling array of colors, shapes, and textures that make these flowers among the most beautiful known.

There are many books on how to grow orchids but few books on the plants themselves. I shall concentrate here on the plant and its background. Included are the best possible photographs, in black and white and in color, which show the true beauty of the plants as they really are—the exquisite texture, the incredible form, the dramatic character of the flower. I only wish that photographs could catch scent, because some orchids have such a lovely fragrance.

Most of the orchids in this book are from my collection, covering fifteen years, and were photographed in my garden room. Mainly, they are species orchids, free from the hand of man, rather than the hybrid cattleyas and cymbidiums, which most people recognize on sight.

It was difficult to select some two hundred plants from the many thousands I have grown over the years. The final decision was based not so much on the availability of the orchid but on its beauty. Some are rare, many are common; some simply did not photograph well, others did. Often a flower I especially wanted to show did not bloom in time; or when it finally bloomed, the photograph was not satisfactory. In all, some four hundred plants were photographed over a period of four years. The best of the collection is shown in this book. If your favorite orchid is missing, it is not by deliberate act but because of limitations of space or time.

Botanical names of orchids are changed occasionally as taxonomists continue their research, and plants that have been classified for years in one genus are sometimes relegated to another. No doubt there will be changes in botanical nomenclature by the time this book goes to press.

The genus *Cypripedium* (lady's-slipper orchids) for years included *Paphiopedilum, Phragmipedium,* and sometimes *Selenipedium*. Today, many authorities consider these as entirely different genera. They are so treated in this book.

I have tried to place the plants in their genera as they are accepted by most growers and as they are listed in suppliers' catalogues. I have used the names widely accepted, without trying to define the borderline species that still puzzle taxonomists.

Through the years I have grown hundreds of orchids and written several books on how to grow them. As I discovered the secrets of caring for the plants, I began to wonder why they so captivated and intrigued me—and countless others. (Even nongardeners have a fondness for orchids.) What is the lure of orchids? Their history reveals stories of adventure as exciting as the flowers themselves. Knowing their stories has given me a greater appreciation of the plants, and I hope, through this book, to enhance your enjoyment of the Orchidaceae.

Jack Kramer
Mill Valley, California

These small plants hardly resemble the exotic orchids we know today, yet they are members of the family Orchidaceae, and in Otto Brunfels's *Kreuterbuch* (1546) they are designated as Satyrion. (Photograph courtesy of Hunt Botanical Library.)

Early Knowledge and Studies of Orchids

In antiquity and during the Middle Ages, orchids, like many other plants, were used chiefly for their supposed medicinal properties, especially as aphrodisiacs. Mediterranean orchids were small, temperate-zone species, barely resembling the large and colorful corsage flowers we know today.

The word *orchis,* from which the whole family received name, was first used for this purpose by the Greek philosopher Theophrastus (c.372–c.287 B.C.), a pupil of Aristotle. Theophrastus is sometimes called the father of botany. In his manuscript *Enquiry into Plants, orchis* (meaning testis) referred to the underground tuberous roots of the Mediterranean orchis, which are similar in shape to testicles.

For the next three hundred years orchids remained unnoted in the plant world, but they were mentioned again in the first century A.D. by Dioscorides, a Greek physician in Asia Minor, who collected information on medicinal plants while serving as surgeon in Nero's

Insignificant flowers grace this orchid, still called Satyrion because of the myth that connected orchids with Satyrs, sylvan spirits noted for lecherousness. This representation is from Otto Brunfels's *Kreuterbuch* of 1546. (Photograph courtesy of Hunt Botanical Library.)

Roman army. In his chief work, *Materia medica,* he describes some five hundred plants, designating two of them *orchis,* from Theophrastus' work. Because the orchis tubers resembled testicles, he hypothesized that the plants influenced sexuality. For sixteen centuries Dioscorides' *Materia medica* dominated botanical thought, as the wisdom of the ancient Greeks remained accepted without question.

The Doctrine of Signatures, a popular philosophical-medical theory during the Middle Ages that relied heavily on superstition and myth, perpetuated the belief that orchids were synonymous with fertility and virility. Preparations from certain tubers were said to be effective in stimulating sexual desire, helping to produce male children, and so on.

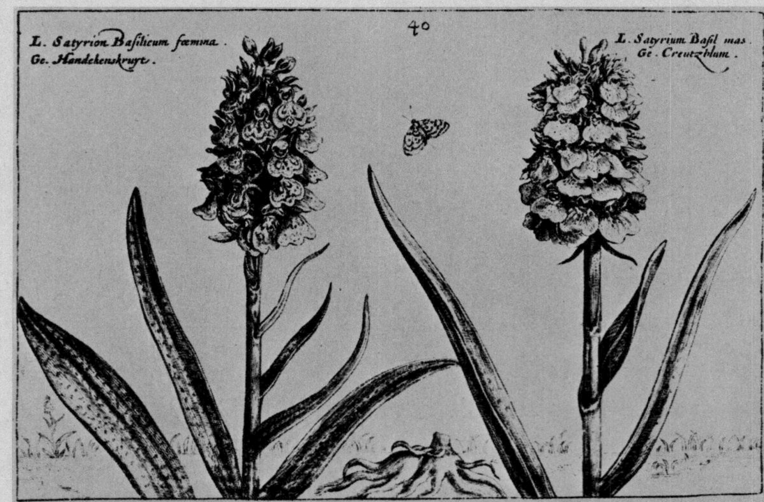

The name Satyrion, an early one for this orchis relative, persists as can be seen in this illustration from Crispijn van de Passe's *Hortus Floridus* of 1614. (Photograph courtesy of the University of California.)

The writings of Hieronymus Bock ("Tragus"), 1489–1554, furthered the orchid's reputation for arousing sexual appetites. He based his work on the theory that all living things originated from lifeless matter; orchis (since it was assumed that they were seedless plants) sprang from the seminal secretions that dropped from mating animals. In 1665 his theory was "confirmed" by the German Jesuit Athanasius Kircher in his *Mundus subterraneus;* he called orchis *satyria* and alleged that they grew in the ground at places where animals bred. (In the herbals of the time orchis do appear under the name Satyrion.)

The first reference to orchids in the Western hemisphere is in the Badianus codex, an Aztec herbal of 1552. It depicts vanilla as being used as a flavoring, as a perfume, and in making a concoction called *tlilxochitl,* a lotion for health. The herbals of the Middle Ages and later—notably those of John Gerard and John Parkinson, published in 1597 and 1629, respectively—considered plants important only for their usefulness to man. In Gerard's *Herball,* orchids are called the female Satyrion because legend purported they were associated with satyrs. The plants were believed to be the food of satyrs and responsible for helping to arouse them to excesses. In 1640 Parkinson, London apothecary and royal herbalist for Charles I, in his *Theatrum botanicum,* said of orchids (which he called Cynosorchis) that they stimulated lust. Just as men lived in the belief that human destinies depended upon the stars, they also believed that plants exercised powers over the welfare of man because certain leaves, flowers, and seeds resembled parts of the human anatomy. Thus, if a plant had a leaf that resembled a human liver, it was said that it was intended as a remedy for hepatic disease. If the flower was heart-shaped, it would cure cardiac complaints.

164 THE FIRST BOOKE OF THE

8 The ſmall yellow Satyrion hath leaues ſpread vpon the ground, at the firſt comming vp; the ſlender ſtalke riſeth vp in the middeſt, of halfe a hand high. The flowers grow ſcatteringly towarde the top, reſembling the flies laſt before mentioned, darke or ruſtie of colour: the ſtones or bulbes are very round.

7 *Orchis Myodes Luteum.* Yellow Satyrion.

8 *Orchis Myodes minor.* Small yellow Satyrion.

✱ The deſcription.

9 Birdes Orchis hath many large ribbed leaues, ſpred vpon the ground like vnto thoſe of Plantaine: among the which riſe vp tender ſtalkes couered euen to the tuft of the flowers with the like leaues, but leſſer, in ſuch ſort that the ſtalkes cannot be ſeene for the leaues. The flowers grow at the top not ſo thicke ſet or thruſt togither as the others, purple of colour like in ſhape vnto little birds, with their wings ſpred abroad readie to flie. The rootes be like the former.

10 Spotted Birdes Satyrion hath leaues like vnto the former, ſauing that they be daſht or ſpotted heere and there with darke ſpots or ſtreakes, hauing a ſtalke couered with the like leaues, ſo that the plants differ not in any point, except the blacke ſpots which this kind is daſht with.

11 Butterflie Satyrion hath leaues riſing immediately foorth of the ground like vnto the blades or leaues of Leekes, but ſhorter: among the which riſeth vp a ſlender naked ſtalke two handfuls high: on the top whereof be white flowers, reſembling the ſhape or forme of a ſmall bird readie to flie, or a white butterflie with hir winges ſpread abroad. The rootes are round and ſmaller than any of the former.

12 Souldiers Satyrion bringeth forth many broad large and ribbed leaues, ſpred vpon the ground like vnto thoſe of the great Plantaine: among the which riſeth vp a fat ſtalke full of ſap or iuice, clothed or wrapped in the like leaues euen to the tuft of flowers, wherupon doe grow little flowers reſembling a little man, hauing an helmet vpon his head, his hands and legs cut off; white vpon the inſide, ſpotted with many purple ſpots, and the backe part of the flower of a deeper colour tending to rednes. The rootes be greater ſtones than any of the kinds of Satyrions.

9 *Orchis*

The similarity of the orchid's underground tubers to testes is shown in this illustration from John Gerard's *Herball* (1597). Here the plant is given botanical clarification as orchis, but the common name, Satyrion, is also cited. (Photograph courtesy of the University of California.)

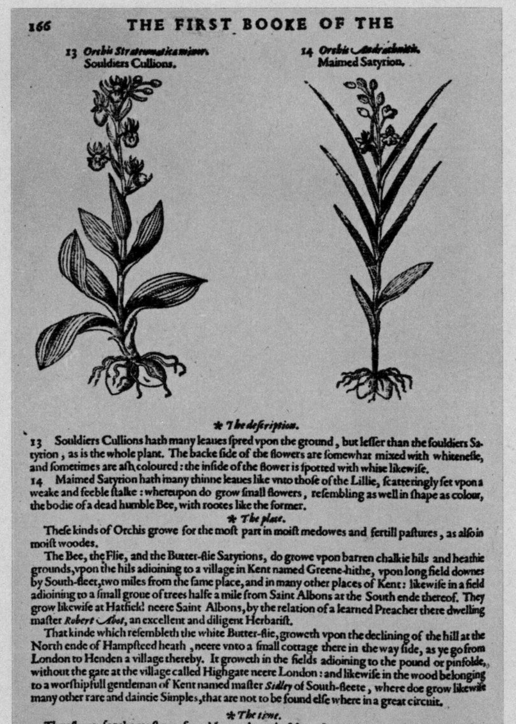

166 THE FIRST BOOKE OF THE

13 *Orchis Stratiomatica minor.* Souldiers Cullions.

14 *Orchis Andrachnitis.* Maimed Satyrion.

✱ The deſcription.

13 Souldiers Cullions hath many leaues ſpred vpon the ground, but leſſer than the ſouldiers Satyrion, as is the whole plant. The backe ſide of the flowers are ſomewhat mixed with whiteneſſe, and ſometimes are aſh coloured: the inſide of the flower is ſpotted with white likewiſe.

14 Maimed Satyrion hath many thinne leaues like vnto thoſe of the Lillie, ſcatteringly ſet vpon a weake and feeble ſtalke: whereupon do grow ſmall flowers, reſembling as well in ſhape as colour, the bodie of a dead humble Bee, with rootes like the former.

✱ The place.

Theſe kinds of Orchis growe for the moſt part in moiſt medowes and fertill paſtures, as alſo in moiſt woodes.

The Bee, the Flie, and the Butter-flie Satyrions, do growe vpon barren chalkie hils and heathie grounds, vpon the hils adioining to a village in Kent named Greene-hithe, vpon long field downes by South-fleet, two miles from the ſame place, and in many other places of Kent: likewiſe in a field adioining to a ſmall groue of trees halfe a mile from Saint Albons at the South ende thereof. They grow likewiſe at Hatfield neere Saint Albons, by the relation of a learned Preacher there dwelling maſter *Robert Abot*, an excellent and diligent Herbariſt.

That kinde which reſembleth the white Butter-flie, groweth vpon the declining of the hill at the North ende of Hampſteed heath, neere vnto a ſmall cottage there in the way ſide, as ye go from London to Henden a village thereby. It groweth in the fields adioining to the pound or pinfolde, without the gate at the village called Highgate neere London: and likewiſe in the wood belonging to a worſhipfull gentleman of Kent named maſter *Sidley* of South-fleete, where doe grow likewiſe many other rare and daintie Simples, that are not to be found elſe where in a great circuit.

✱ The time.

They flower for the moſt part from May to the end of Auguſt.

✱ The

This illustration from Gerard's *Herball* (1597), in its depiction of the testes-like tubers, makes evident why orchids have been regarded as sexual symbols. (Photograph courtesy of the University of California.)

PLATE 1 ▶
Cypripedium
C. calceolus var. *parviflorum*
North America, Europe, northern Asia

One of our native, wild terrestrial orchids, it is fast disappearing. Found from Quebec and Newfoundland sout to Georgia, west to New Mexico and Arizona, it is also found in Europ and northern Asia. A typical lady's-slipper orchid, it is almost impossibl to transplant and grow in cultivation. (Photograph courtesy of Guy Burgess

It was not until the eighteenth century that botanical science was born and the first attempts at classification were made. The great Swedish botanist Carolus Linnaeus introduced systematic botany with his *Genera plantarum,* published in 1737. He placed orchids and other plants in classes founded on the number and positions of the stamens and pistils of the flowers. In 1753 he described eight orchid genera (retaining the name orchis) in his *Species plantarum,* which is still a reference source for botanical nomenclature. In 1763 another treatise by Linnaeus named a hundred different species, but all were placed in the same genus, *Epidendrum.*

Orchids in China and Japan

The Chinese and Japanese were avid gardeners from the earliest times, appreciating plants for their beauty and fragrance as well as for their utility. The orchid had no particular importance as a medicinal plant but was grown for its fragrance and was also a favorite subject of painters.

Orchids were called *lan* by Confucius (c.551–479 B.C.); he compared the flowers to the perfect or super-

CONTINUED ON PAGE 109

This delicate rendering of orchids on a rock (ink on paper) is by Gyokuen Bompo (1344–c.1420). The orchids depicted are probably cymbidiums. (Photograph courtesy of Freer Gallery of Art.)

PLATE 2
Cypripedium
C. calceolus var. *pubescens*
North America, Europe, northern Asia

A close-up of the flower. See following plate for description. (Photograph courtesy of Hermann Pigors.)

PLATE 3
Cypripedium
C. calceolus var. *pubescens*
North America, Europe, northern Asia

A native species with large flowers, it has sepals and petals of red-brown mixed with yellow. Occasional native stands are still found. (Photograph courtesy of Hermann Pigors.)

◀ PLATE 4
Cypripedium
C. reginae
Quebec and northern New England to Manitoba;
Georgia, Tennessee to Missouri

This orchid, commonly called showy lady's-slipper, is one of our lovliest wild species. Most often found in regions where limestone is predominant in soil, it has flowers of white and pink, varying to pinkish-white and mauve. (Photograph courtesy of Hermann Pigors.)

PLATE 5
Phragmipedium
P. Grande (hybrid)

This hybrid was produced in 1880 by crossing *P. longifolium* and *P. caudatum*. It bears large flowers, one following the other in a succession of bloom for several months. (Photograph courtesy of Hermann Pigors.)

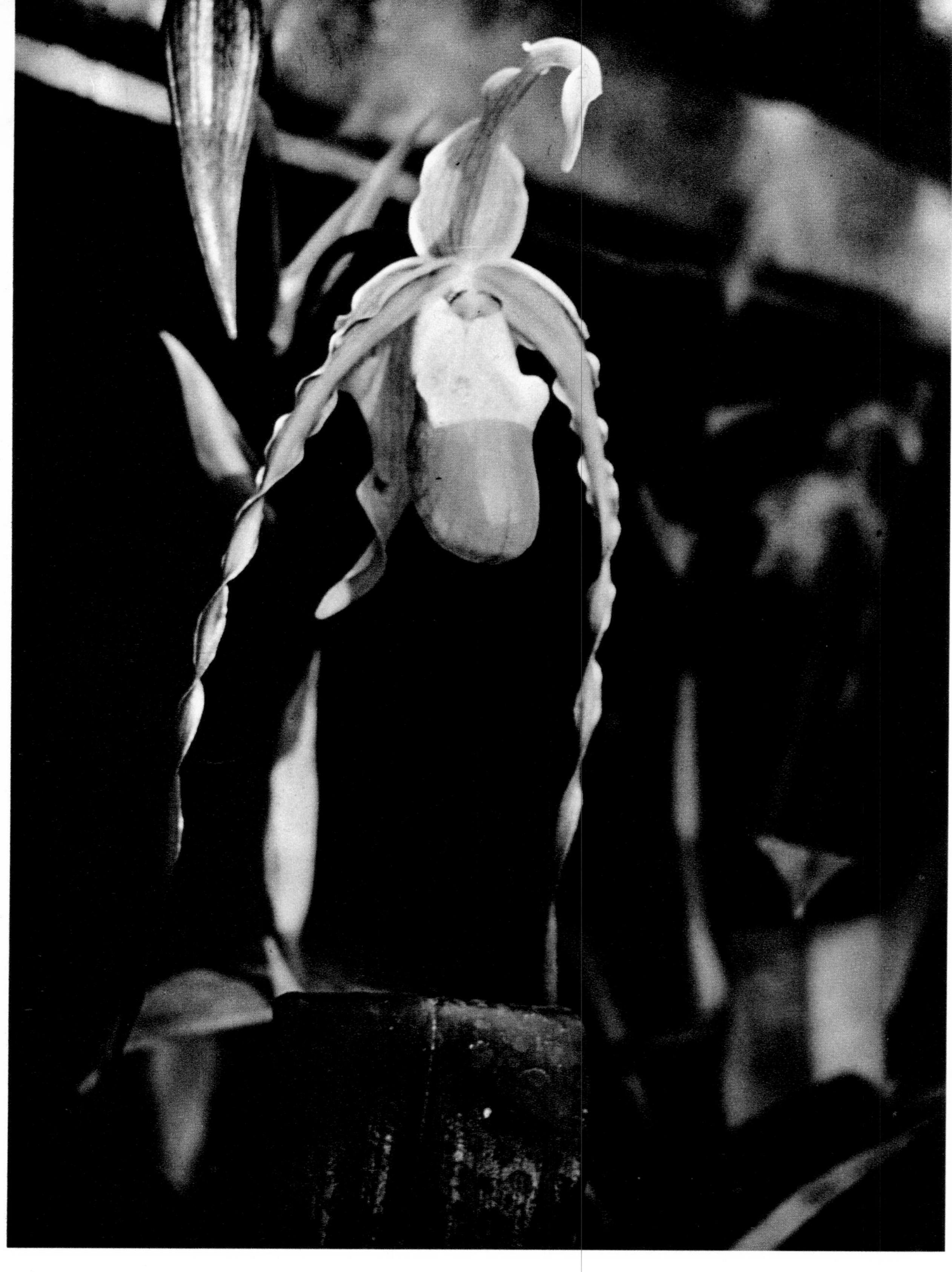

PLATE 6
Phragmipedium
P. Grande (hybrid)

A close-up of the flower. See black-and-white plate 5 for description. (Photograph courtesy of Hermann Pigors.)

PLATE 7
Phragmipedium
P. longifolium
Costa Rica, Panama, Colombia

Through the years this orchid has been classified in the genera *Selenipedium, Paphiopedilum,* and *Cypripedium*. The plant has a typical lady's-slipper lip. The flowers are waxy, long-lasting, and handsomely colored. The lip is greenish-white with reddish spurs. (Photograph courtesy of Joyce R. Wilson.)

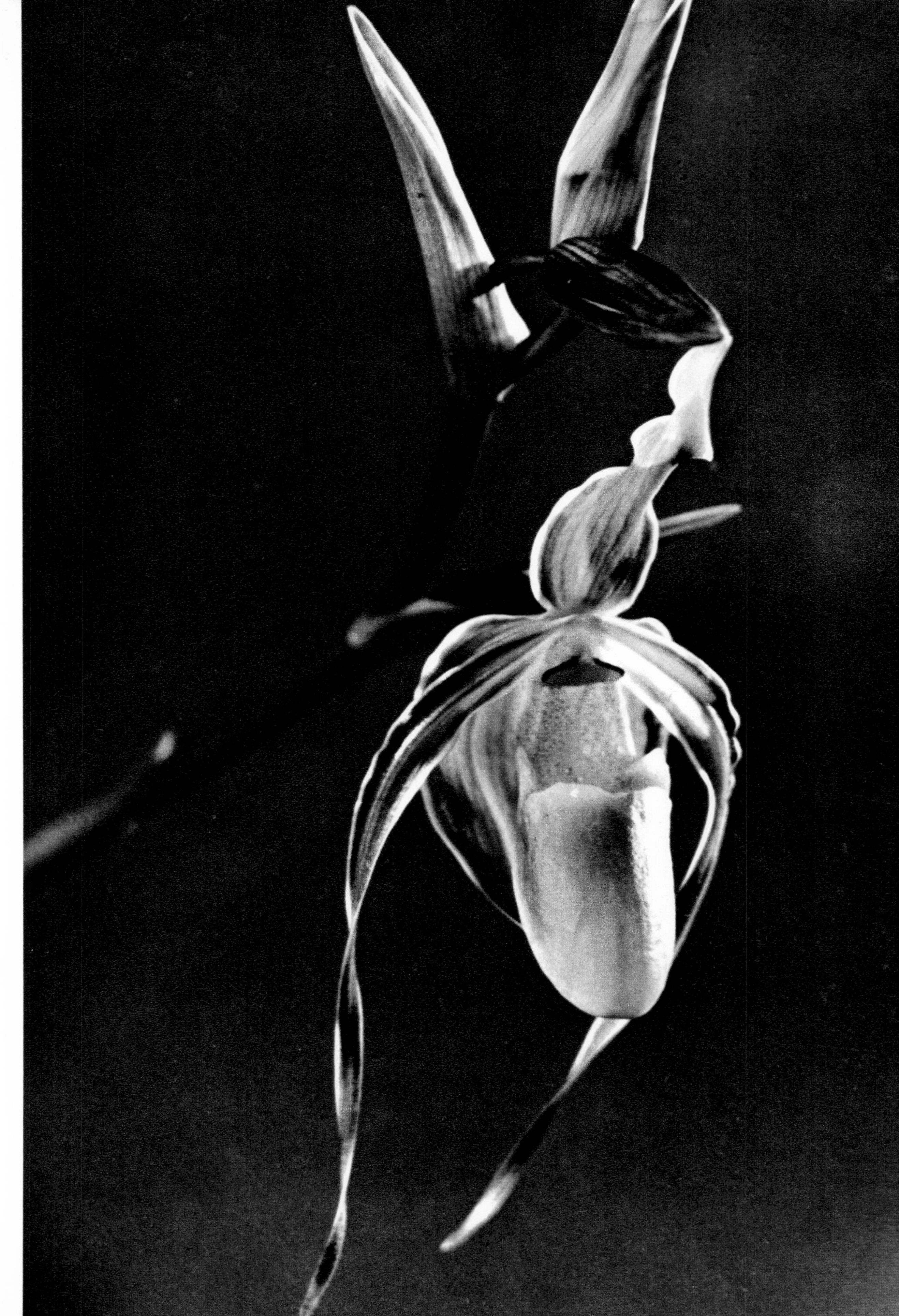

◀ PLATE 8
Phragmipedium (*Selenipedium*)
P. Sedeni (hybrid)

This cross was made in England in 1873 by Sir Harry Veitch between *P. schlimii* and *P. longifolium*. An exquisite orchid, it has reddish tones on a white background. Sometimes phragmipediums are cultivated under the genus name *Selenipedium,* but this is a misnomer. In fact, selenipediums are phragmipediums. (Photograph courtesy of Joyce R. Wilson.)

PLATE 9
Paphiopedilum
P. callosum (left)
P. sublaeve (center)
Thailand, Vietnam

P. callosum has medium-size growth, up to 16 inches high. Its flowers—multicolored, exotic—are about 4 inches across. Discovered by Alexandre Regnier in Siam or Cochin China, it was introduced by him in 1885. *P. sublaeve* has a more diminutive, fragile flower, but its colors—dark green, magenta-purple, and greenish-yellow—are similarly opulent. The plant on the right is a natural hybrid between the two species. (Photograph courtesy of Hermann Pigors.)

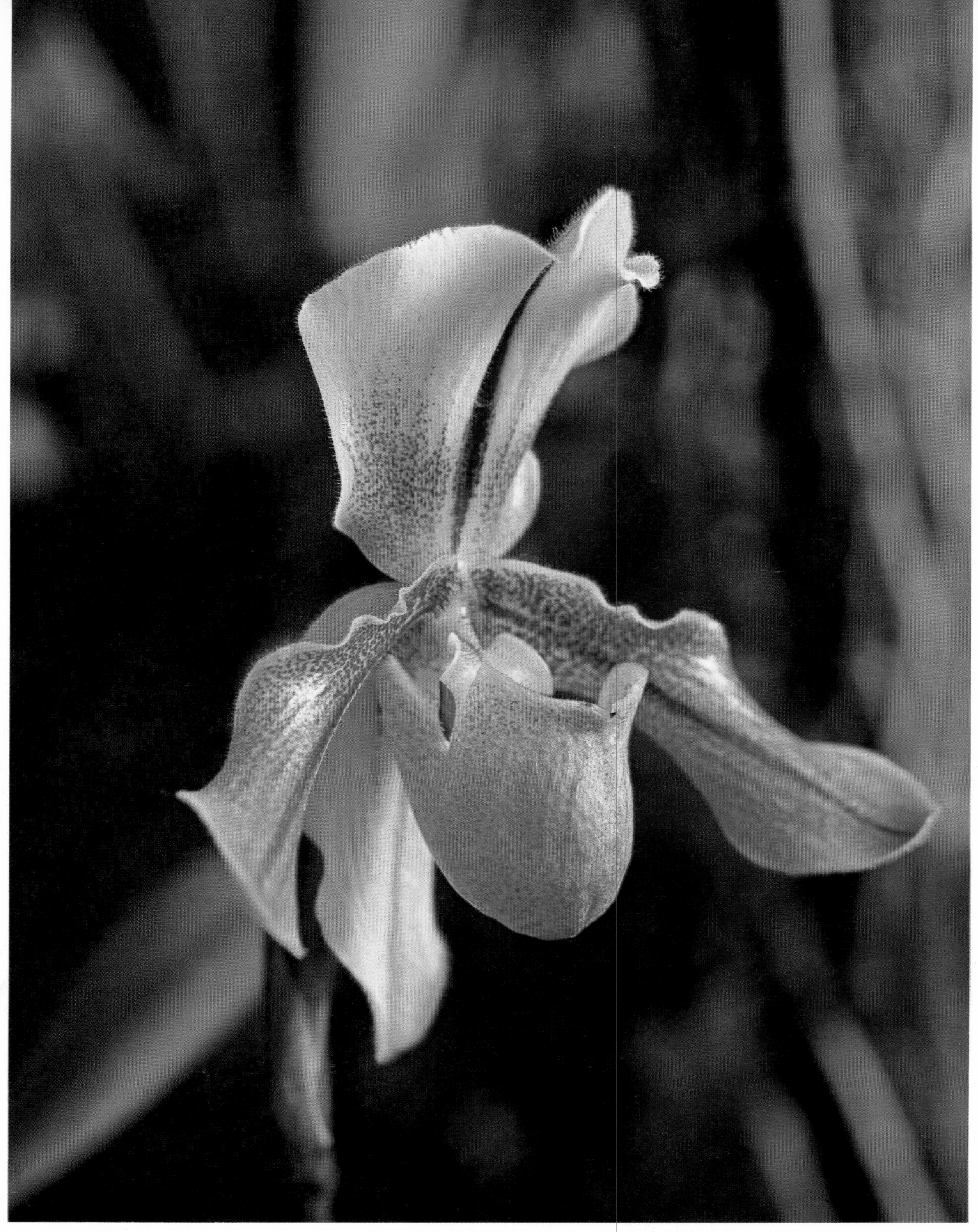

PLATE 10
Paphiopedilum
P. hybrid

This terrestrial orchid of unknown parentage has an extremely beautiful flower, with heavy waxen petals. It is possibly a cross between *P. spicerianum* and *P. villosum*. (Photograph courtesy of Guy Burgess.)

PLATE 11 ▶
Paphiopedilum
P. insigne
India, Assam

This is a popular, well-known orchid that has many varieties. The species was discovered by Dr. Nathaniel Wallich in northeast India. A terrestrial plant, it flowered for the first time in Liverpool Botanic Gardens in 1820. (Photograph courtesy of Guy Burgess.)

PLATE 12
Paphiopedilum
P. fairieanum
Assam

This orchid has a bright 2-inch flower with purple-and-white lip; the rosettes are of green leafy foliage. It was first noticed in 1857, when flowers were sent to Sir William J. Hooker, of the Royal Botanical Gardens at Kew, from the garden of a Mr. Reid of Burnham, Somerset, and the nursery of a Mr. Parker at Upper Holloway, England. (Photograph courtesy of Guy Burgess.)

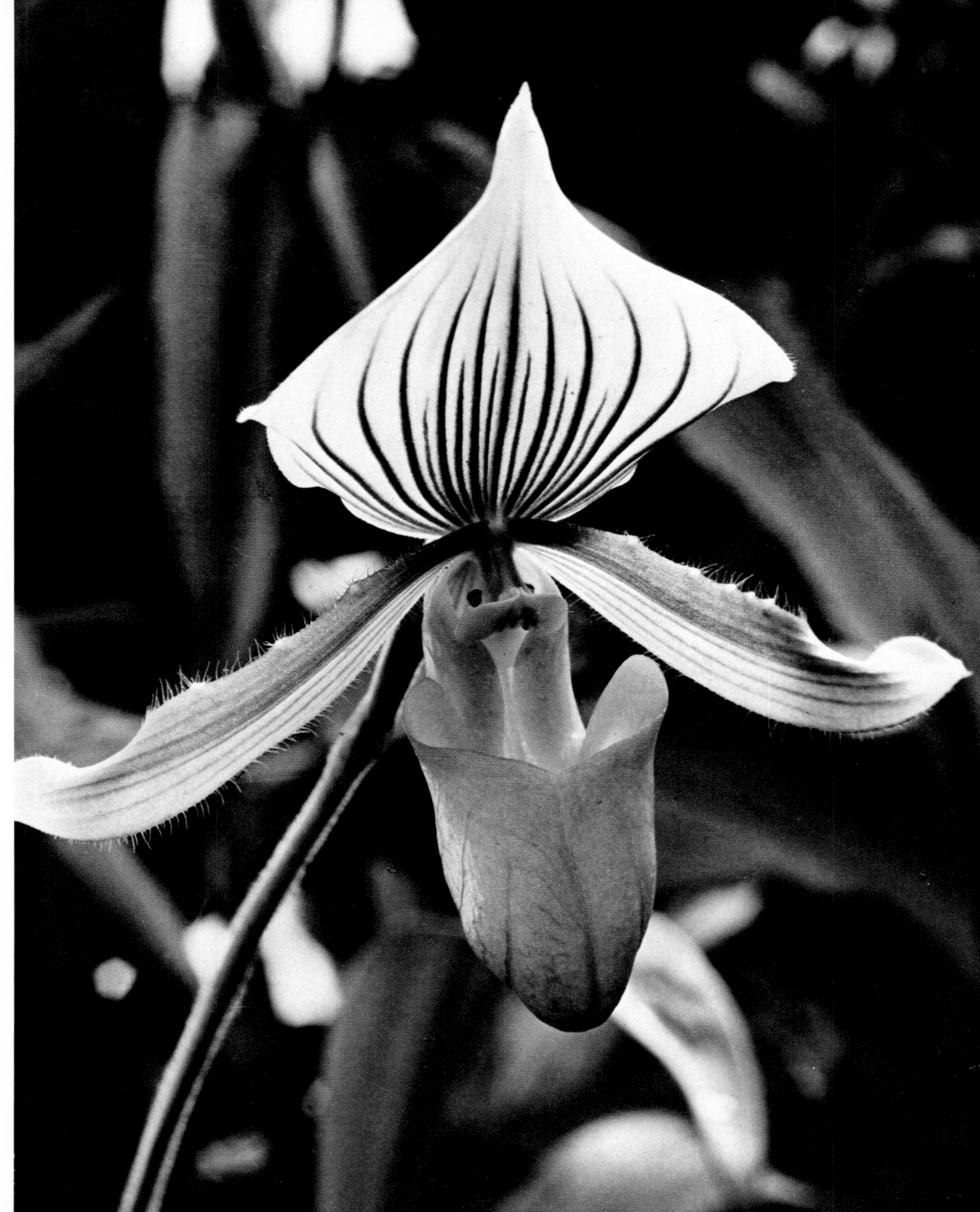

PLATE 13
Paphiopedilum
P. Maudiae (hybrid)

This hybrid is distinguished by its tiger-like markings. The original cross was made in 1900 between *P. callosum* and *P. lawrenceanum*. It is still a very popular orchid. (Photograph courtesy of Guy Burgess.)

PLATE 14
Paphiopedilum
P. insigne var. *sanderae*
Assam

Variety *sanderae* is superior to the species in color and form. Quite a large orchid, it is about 4 inches across. See plate 11. (Photograph courtesy of Hermann Pigors.)

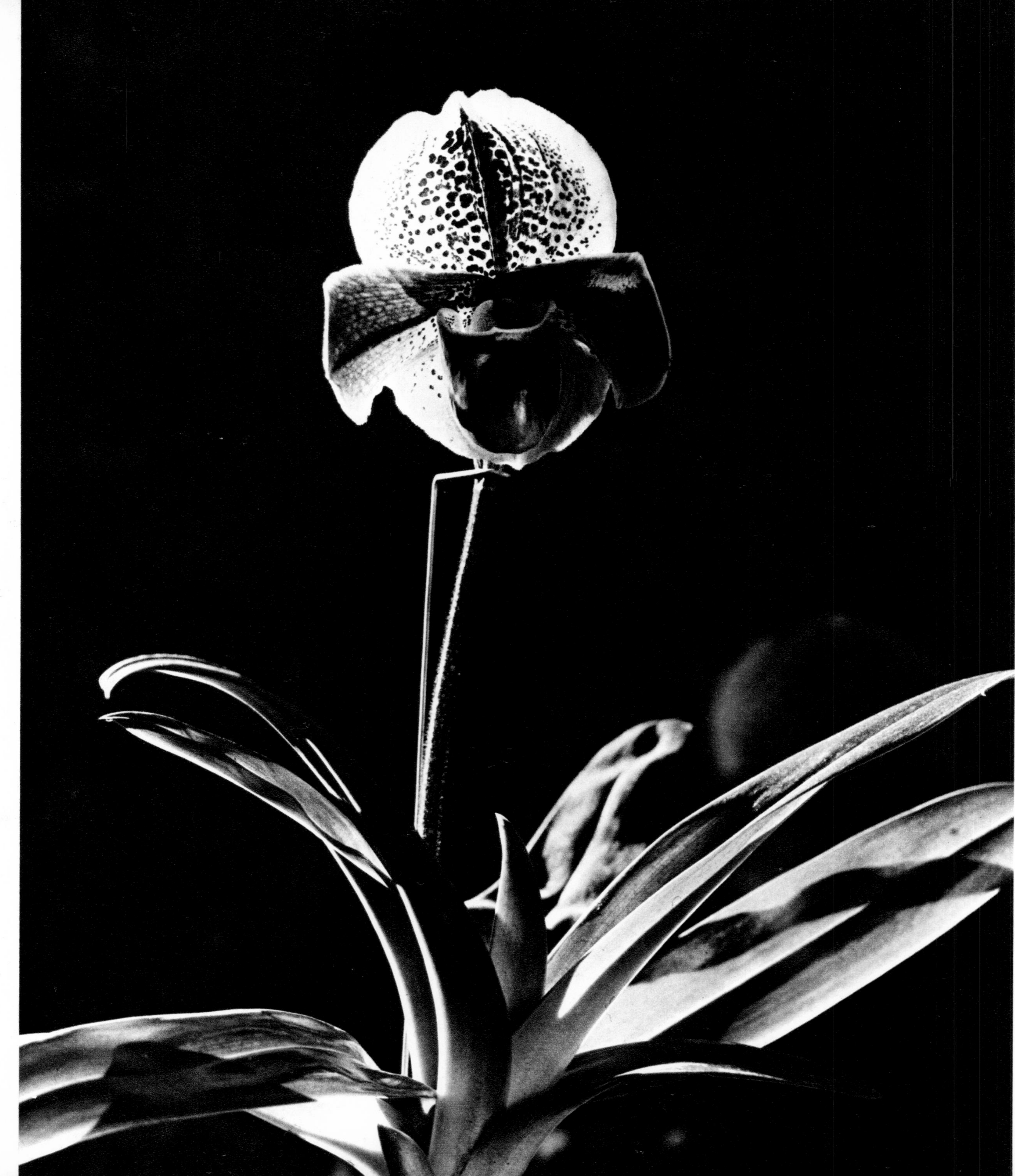

◀ PLATE 15
Paphiopedilum
P. Milmoore (hybrid)

This terrestrial orchid is popular with collectors and is noted for its long-lasting flowers, which remain fresh for six to eight weeks. A dependable yearly bloomer, it is greenish-brown with brownish-black spots. Its parents are P. Mildred Hunter and P. Farnmoore. (Photograph courtesy of Joyce R. Wilson.)

PLATE 16
Paphiopedilum
P. parishii
Burma, Thailand

The flowers of this orchid, about 3 inches in diameter, are pale yellow with green veins. The species was discovered by the Rev. C. Parish in the Moulmein district in 1859. Living plants were introduced for the first time by the English firm of Messrs. Low and Co. in 1868. (Photograph courtesy of Hermann Pigors.)

PLATE 17
Paphiopedilum
P. praestans
New Guinea

This outstanding orchid, with leaves to 12 inches long, has flowers about 4 inches in diameter, whitish streaked with red-purple. The twisted petals are yellow-green with red-brown veins and black warts. (Photograph courtesy of Andrew R. Addkison.)

PLATE 18 ▶
Paphiopedilum
P. Pitt River (hybrid)

This colorful orchid is distinguished by its excellent form. The flowers are large, sometimes 6 inches across, with centers that vary in color from dark greenish-black to pale green. P. Pitt River blooms for over three weeks. It is a cross between P. Pittlands and P. Burleigh Mohur. (Photograph courtesy of Joyce R. Wilson.)

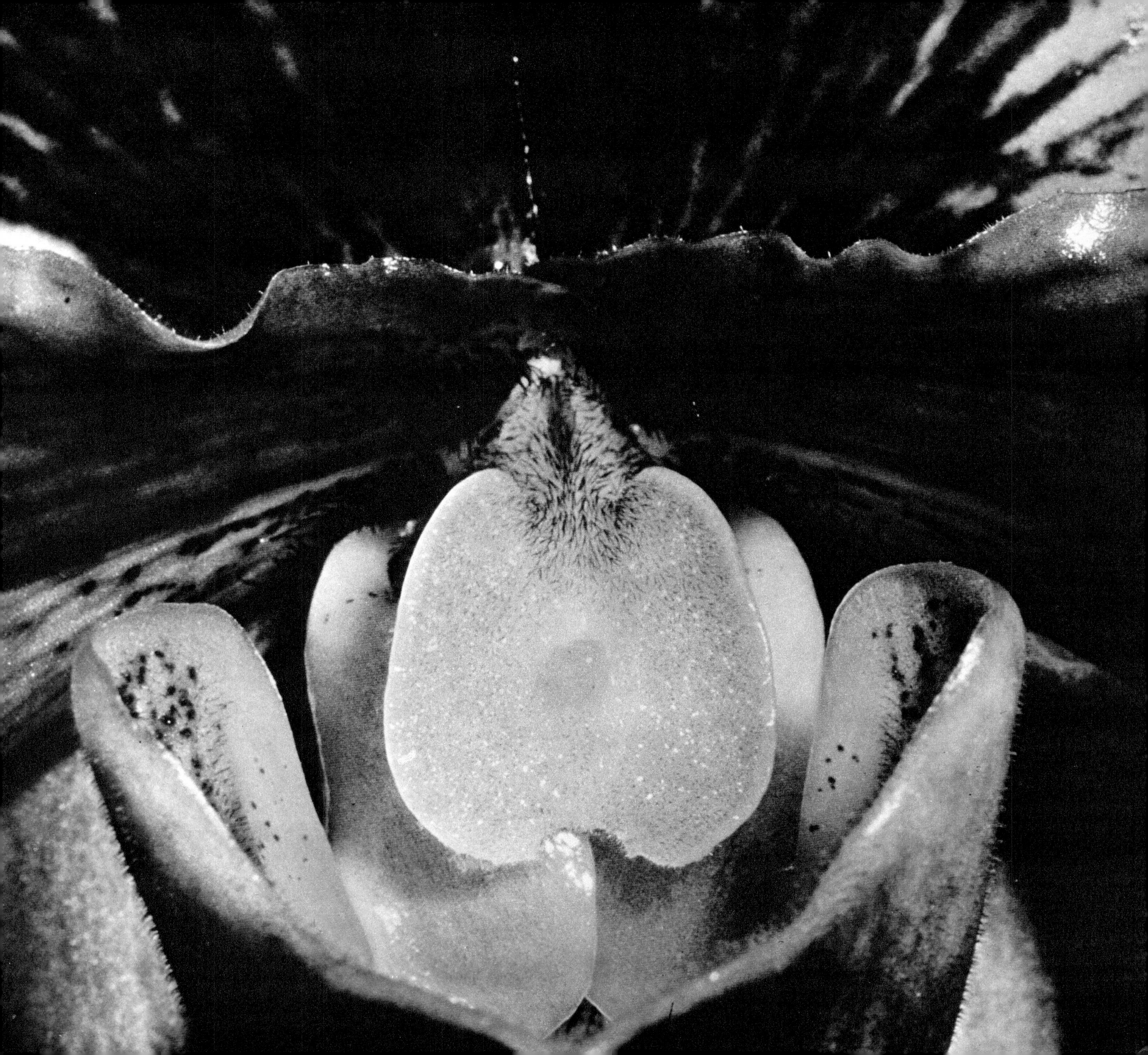

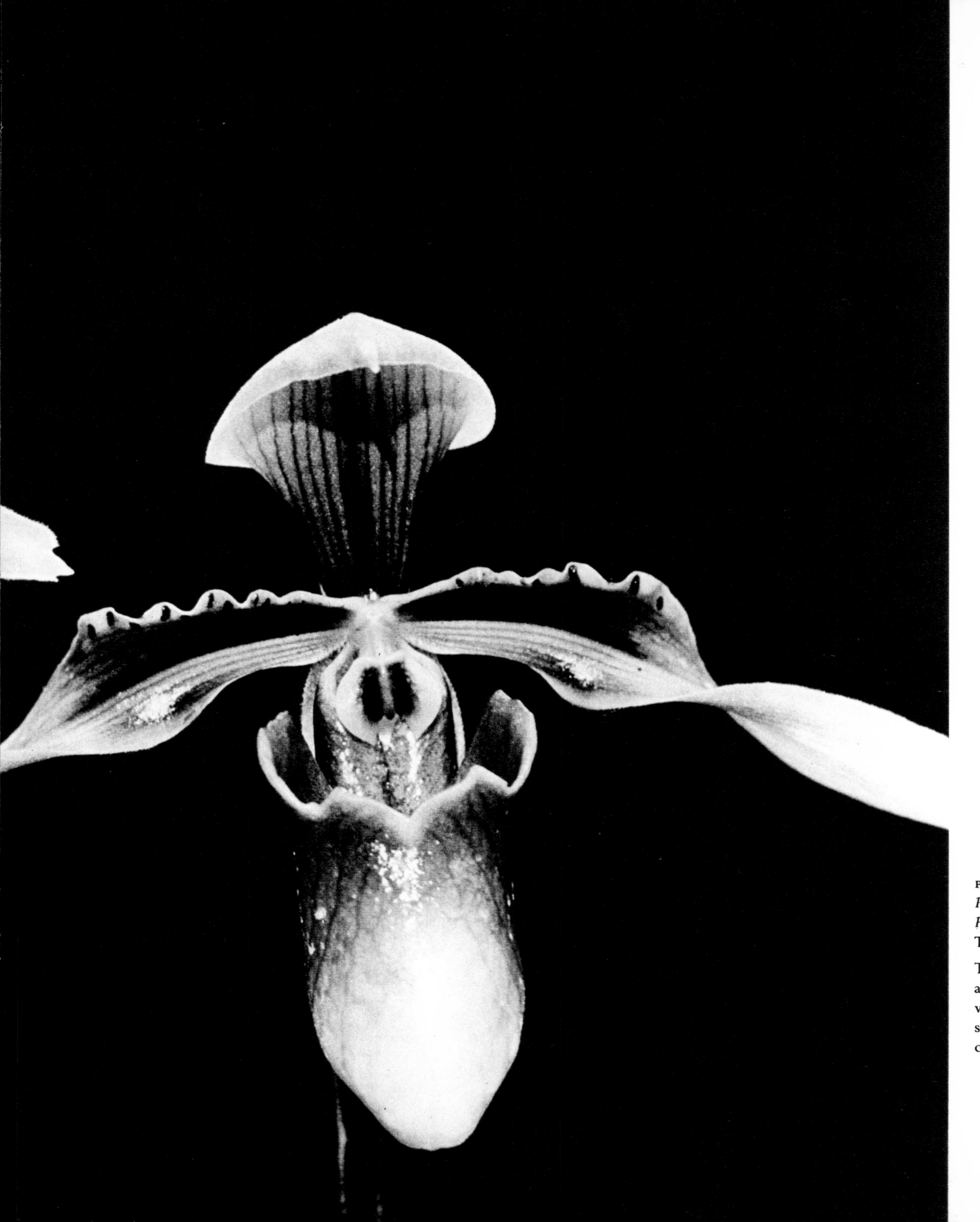

PLATE 19
Paphiopedilum
P. wolterianum (sublaeve)
Thailand

The slender scapes of this orchid bear a single flower, dark green flushed with purple. The lip is greenish-yellow shaded with purple. (Photograph courtesy of Hermann Pigors.)

PLATE 20
Paphiopedilum
P. spicerianum
Assam

This green, purple, and white orchid is ultradramatic in both markings and shape. The genus is widespread over a huge region that extends from China and the Himalayas throughout Southeast Asia and Indonesia to New Guinea. (Photograph courtesy of Joyce R. Wilson.)

PLATE 21
Paphiopedilum
P. sukhakulii
Thailand

Rediscovered recently, this is a stunning lady's-slipper orchid with exquisite form and markings. The color contrast is remarkable—pale green, mauve, white. (Photograph courtesy of Joyce R. Wilson.)

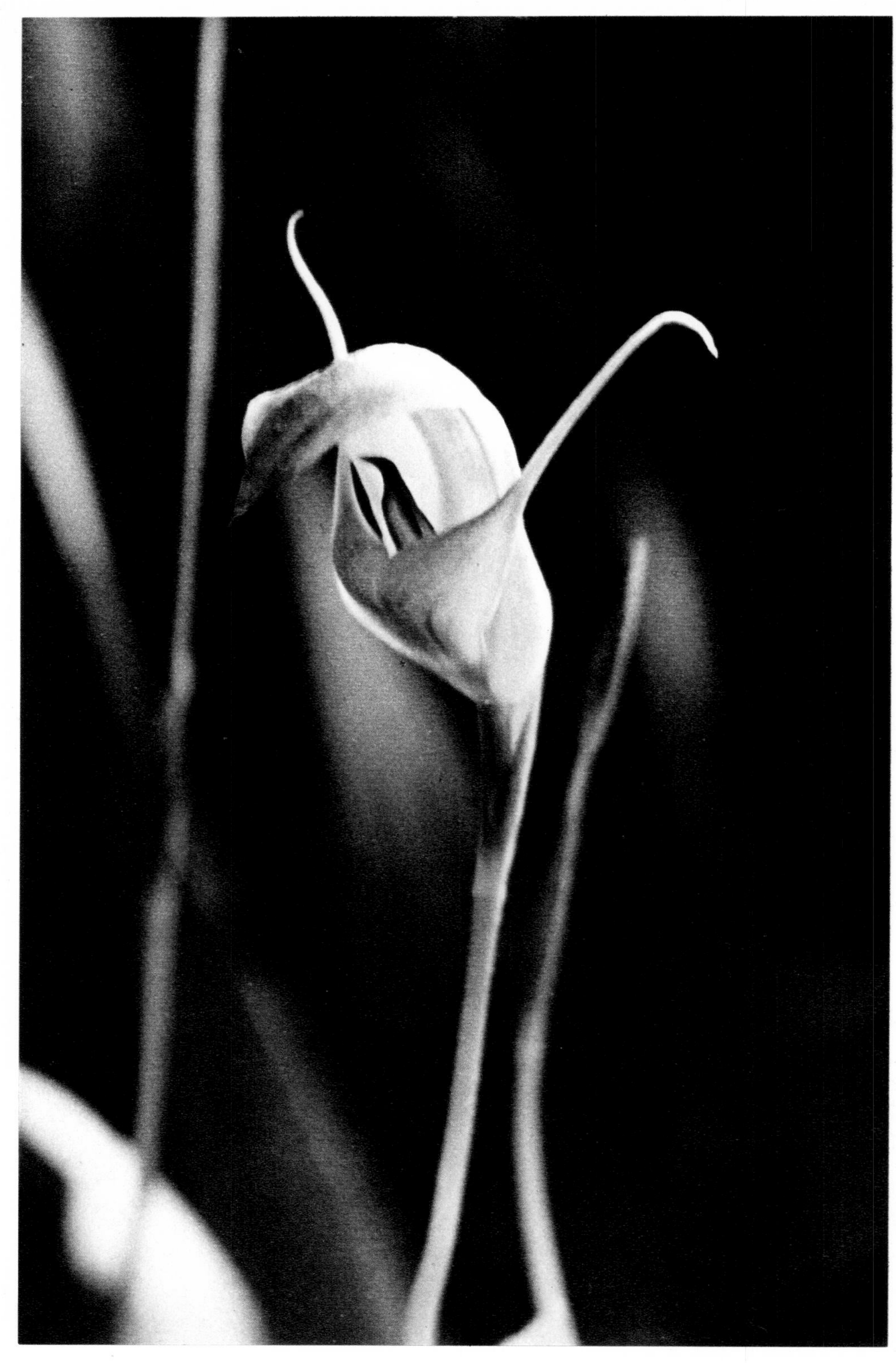

PLATE 22
Pterostylis
P. baptistii
Australia from Queensland to East Victoria

Primarily a terrestrial orchid, this species is still quite infrequent in collections outside its native habitat, despite the fact that the "greenhood" as it is known in Australia, is an exceptionally interesting plant. Photographed at the University of California Botanical Gardens. (Photograph courtesy of Andrew R. Addikison.)

PLATE 23
Stenoglottis
S. longifolia
Natal

A rosette of apple-green leaves bears an erect spike of tiny purple fringed flowers—a beauty! A genus consisting of three known species, it has no known hybrids and its genetic affinities have not been deduced. (Photograph courtesy of Joyce R. Wilson.)

PLATE 24
Calopogon
C. pulchellus
North America

With its pale yellow tufted lip and gracefully upturned petals, this orchid is strikingly distinctive in form. The genus comprises four species of hardy, terrestrial orchids that are mostly native to the southeastern United States, with one species found also in eastern Canada. (Photograph courtesy of Hermann Pigors.)

PLATE 25
Macodes
M. petola
Sumatra to the Philippines

This leaf orchid has velvety green leaves with golden veins. The genus consists of about seven species of rare and extremely handsome terrestrial orchids in the Malaysian region, especially in Indonesia. The blossoms are insignificant. (Photograph courtesy of Hermann Pigors.)

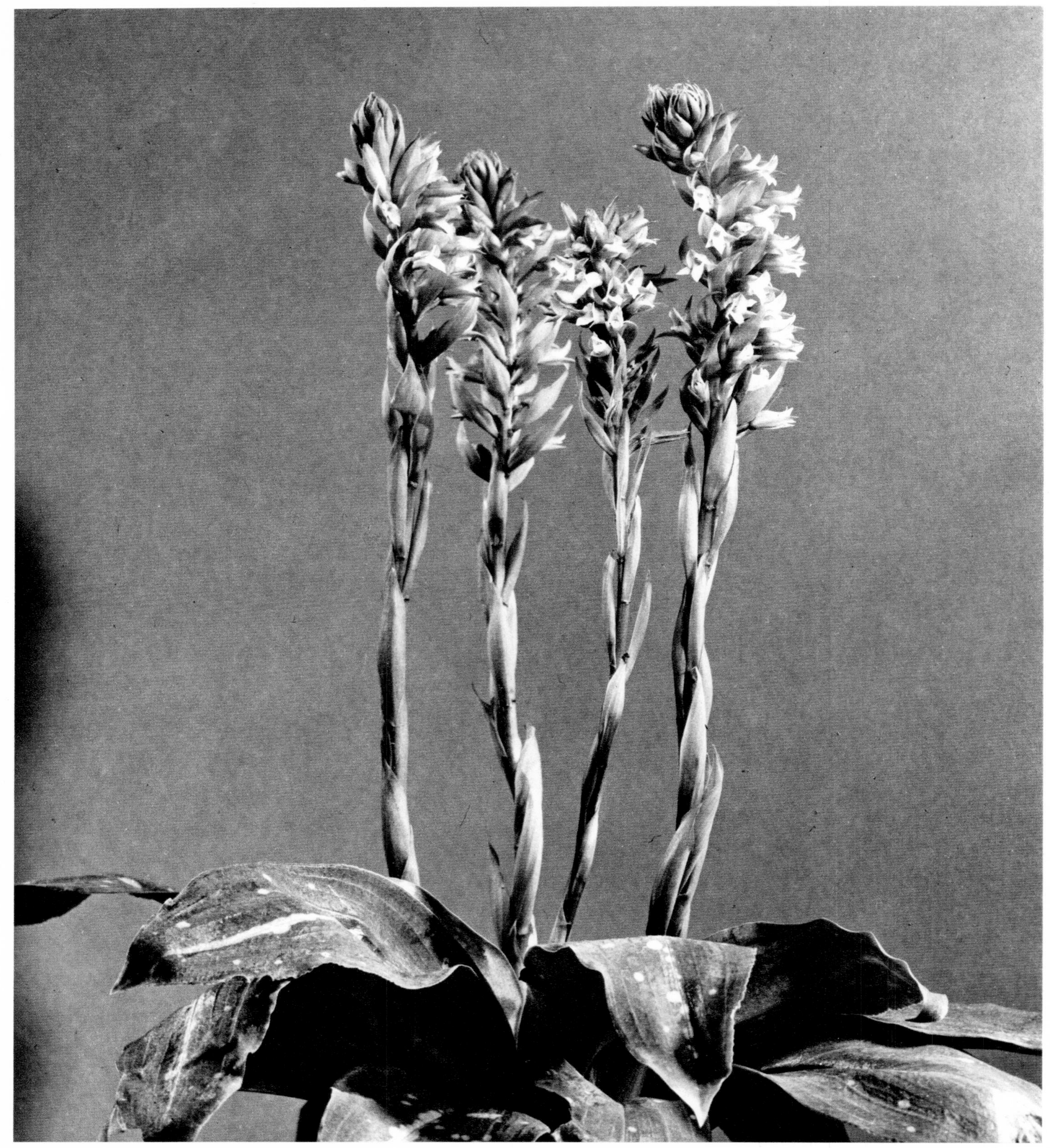

PLATE 26
Spiranthes (*Stenorrhynchus*)
S. speciosa
Cuba, Jamaica, Puerto Rico, Guatemala, south to Colombia and Venezuela

Large spikes of closely packed tiny red-and-white flowers make this spiranthes look more like a garden plant than an orchid. These primarily terrestrial orchids constitute a group that is among the most exasperatingly complex in the entire family; almost every authority on the Orchidaceae exercises his own particular opinion concerning taxonomy in this aggregation. See plate 27. (Photograph courtesy of Joyce R. Wilson.)

PLATE 27
Spiranthes (*Stenorrhynchus*)
S. speciosa
Cuba, Jamaica, Puerto Rico, Guatemala, south to Colombia and Venezuela

With rosettes of handsome dark-green leaves, this select form of the species has small flaming red flowers on long stalks. The plant grows, blooms, and then rests for a few months before it repeats its cycle. See plate 26. (Photograph courtesy of Joyce R. Wilson.)

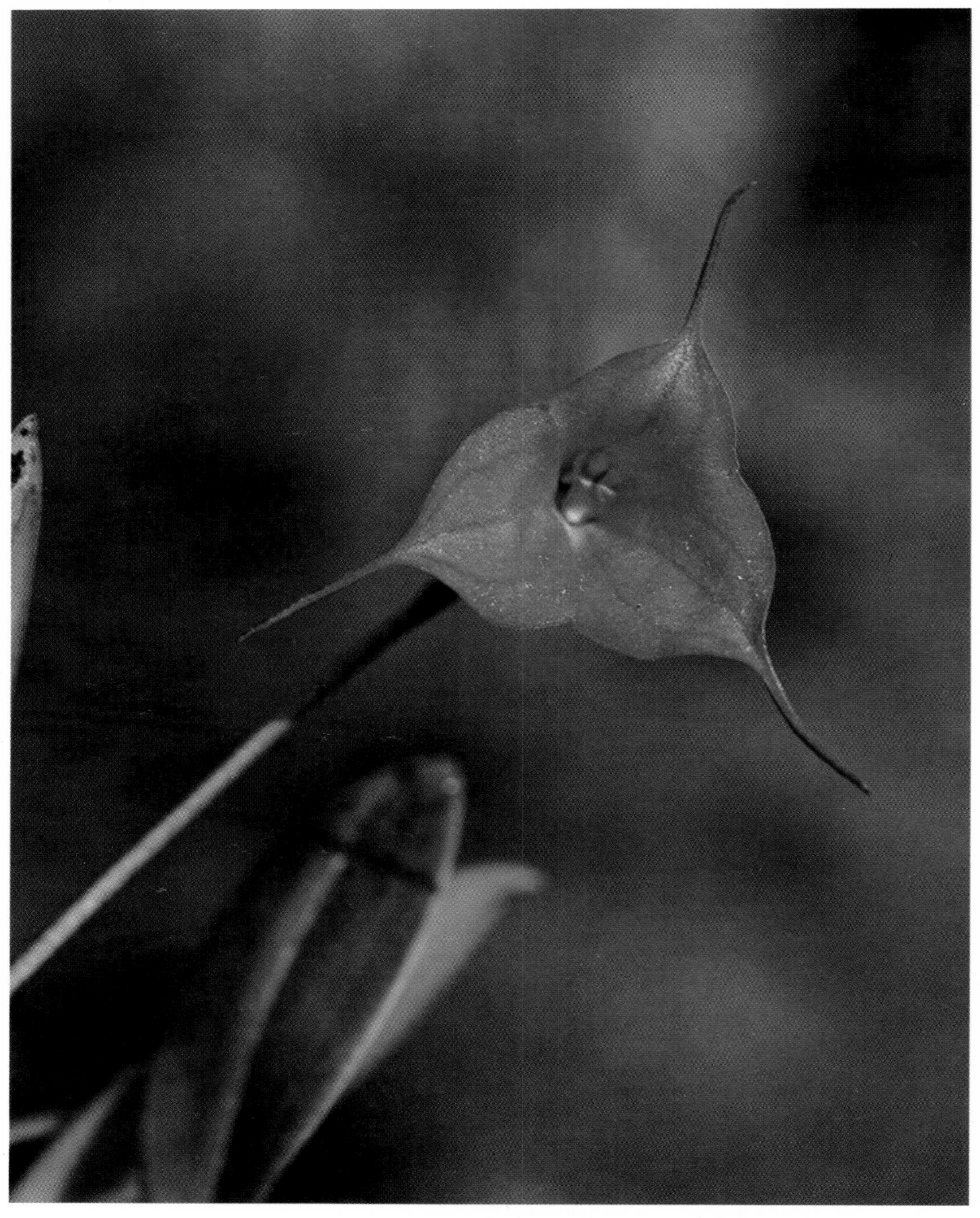

PLATE 28
Masdevallia
M. amabilis
Northern Peru

This breathtaking orchid has dramatic flowers. The plant is small, to 6 inches tall, with a wiry stem bearing a solitary flower, which is about 1 inch across, including the spurs. (Photograph courtesy of Joyce R. Wilson.)

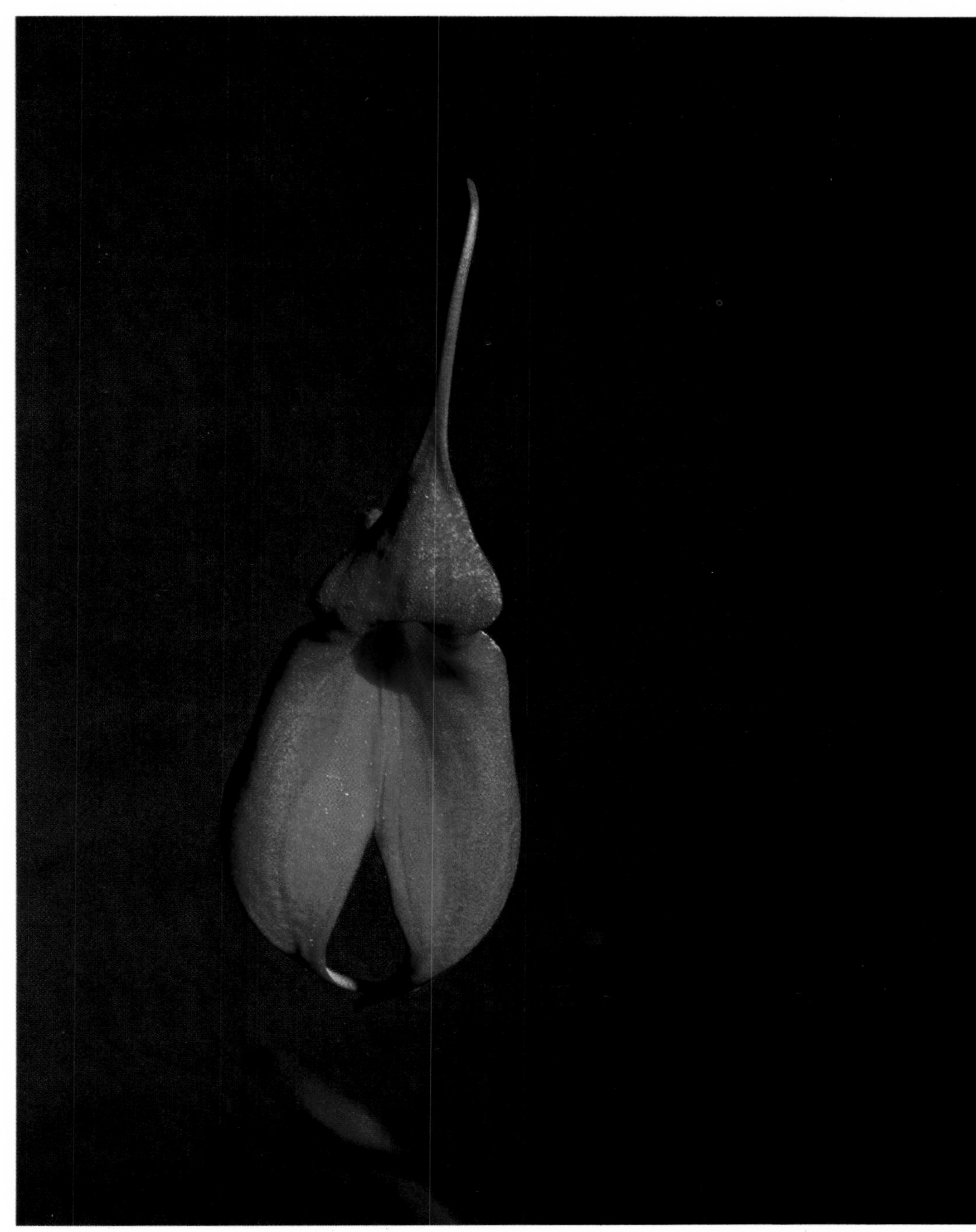

PLATE 29
Masdevallia
M. veitchiana
Peru

From the high country of Peru (11,000–13,000 feet) comes this orchid, looking hardly like an orchid but rather like a colorful kite. The plant was discovered by R. W. Pearce on the Andes and introduced in 1867. The leaves are only 5 to 6 inches long; the flowers, only 3 inches long, but they are borne on 20-inch stems. (Photograph courtesy of Joyce R. Wilson.)

PLATE 30
Masdevallia
M. infracta
Brazil

Discovered in the early 1800s by the French traveler and naturalist Michel Descourtilz, it was found growing on the wooded mountains which separate Rio de Janeiro from the Campos. Gathered by G. Gardner on the Organ Mountains in 1837, it was sent by him to Messrs. Loddiges in England. (Photograph courtesy of Andrew R. Addkison.)

PLATE 31
Pleurothallis
P. apothesa
The Andes from Bolivia to Mexico

This is a curiously textured and shaped orchid with 1-inch flowers. It is found as high as 10,000 to 12,500 feet toward the southern limit of the mountain range; species are also found on the mountains of Brazil and in the West Indies. (Photograph courtesy of Joyce R. Wilson.)

PLATE 32
Coelogyne
C. corrugata
India

Clusters of 1- to 2-inch white flowers characterize this fine species. First gathered by Dr. Robert Wight about the year 1845 on the Neilgherry Hills in southern India, it was first cultivated in England in the Royal Botanic Gardens at Kew in 1863. Though a difficult orchid to bring into bloom, it is much favored by hobbyists. (Photograph courtesy of Guy Burgess.)

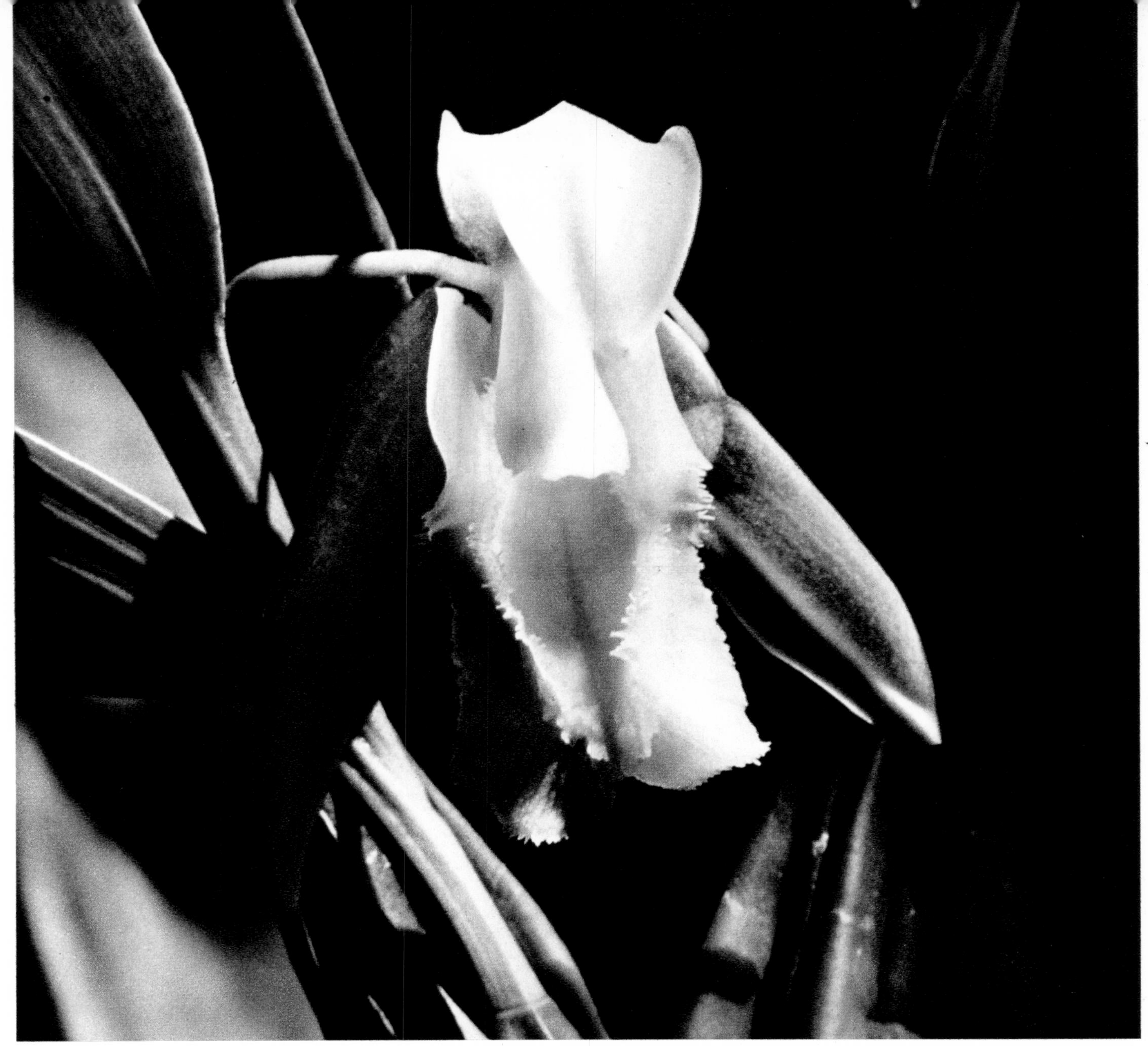

PLATE 33
Coelogyne
C. speciosa var. *alba*
Sumatra, Java

First discovered by the Dutch botanist Karel Lodewijk Blume in the early 1800s, this orchid was found on the Salak Mountains in Java, at an elevation of 3,000 to 5,000 feet. It was first introduced into European gardens in 1846. (Photograph courtesy of Andrew R. Addkison.)

PLATE 34
Coelogyne
C. cristata
The Himalayas at high elevations, 4,500 to 7,500 feet

Discovered by Dr. Nathaniel Wallich in 1824, this species was introduced by John Gibson in 1837. There is no record of its having flowered in England until the spring of 1841, when a flowering occurred in the collection of George Barker of Springfield, who received a Knighton Medal that year at a meeting of the Royal Horticultural Society. (Photograph courtesy of Andrew R. Addkison.)

PLATE 35
Coelogyne
C. pandurata
Borneo

This is the legendary black orchid, but it is not black, and there are no legends about it except those found in Hollywood movies. The stained lip is actually a deep blackish-green, not a true black. The plant bears magnificent flowers that capture the eye of even the nongardener. First discovered in 1852 by Sir Hugh Low, it flowered in Conrad Loddiges' nursery in 1853. (Photograph courtesy of Joyce R. Wilson.)

PLATE 36
Dendrochilum (Platyclinis)
D. filiforme
Borneo, Sumatra, Philippines

With many fragrant yellow flowers on pendent racemes, this species is considered by many authorities to be the best in the genus. Though especially abundant on the islands cited above, the species is distributed over a huge area extending from Burma to New Guinea. In many locations this orchid is known to grow only in a single valley or on one particular mountain, giving evidence of extreme endemism in the genus. (Photograph courtesy of Guy Burgess.)

ATE 37
ptotes
bicolor
azil, Paraguay

miniature with 2-inch white-and-agenta blooms, this species is an pecially fine one. First introduced om the Organ Mountains by Mrs. rnold Harrison of Liverpool 1831 or 332, it was sent afterward by G. ardner from the same region to the 'oburn Abbey Collection, in England, here it flowered for the first time in ebruary, 1839. (Photograph courtesy Andrew R. Addkison.)

PLATE 38
Epidendrum
E. mariae
Mexico, moderate high elevations

Though a small plant, to 12 inches high, it bears handsome large flowers of white and apple green. An amenable orchid that is truly lovely. (Photograph courtesy of Joyce R. Wilson.)

PLATE 40 ▶
Epidendrum
E. (*nanodes*) *medusae*
Ecuador

A most extraordinary plant in bloom, with 1-inch flat-faced chocolate-brown flowers, *E. medusae* is a native of the higher Andes of western South America. It has not become established as an import because it is quite difficult to cultivate. Controlled and cool growing conditions are necessary. (Photograph courtesy of Joyce R. Wilson.)

PLATE 39
Epidendrum (*syn. Encyclia*)
E. megolantha
Brazil

This fine species has 1-inch flowers, several to a stem. The color is beige-rose lined with purple. (Photograph courtesy of Guy Burgess.)

PLATE 41
Epidendrum
E. atropurpureum
Central and South America

First discovered by F. H. A. von Humboldt and Aimé J. A. Bonpland in Venezuela about 1836, this is an orchid that is distributed over an especially wide range. The flowers are possibly the largest in the genus, about 2½ inches; they are chocolate-brown and pale yellow-green. (Photograph courtesy of Joyce R. Wilson.)

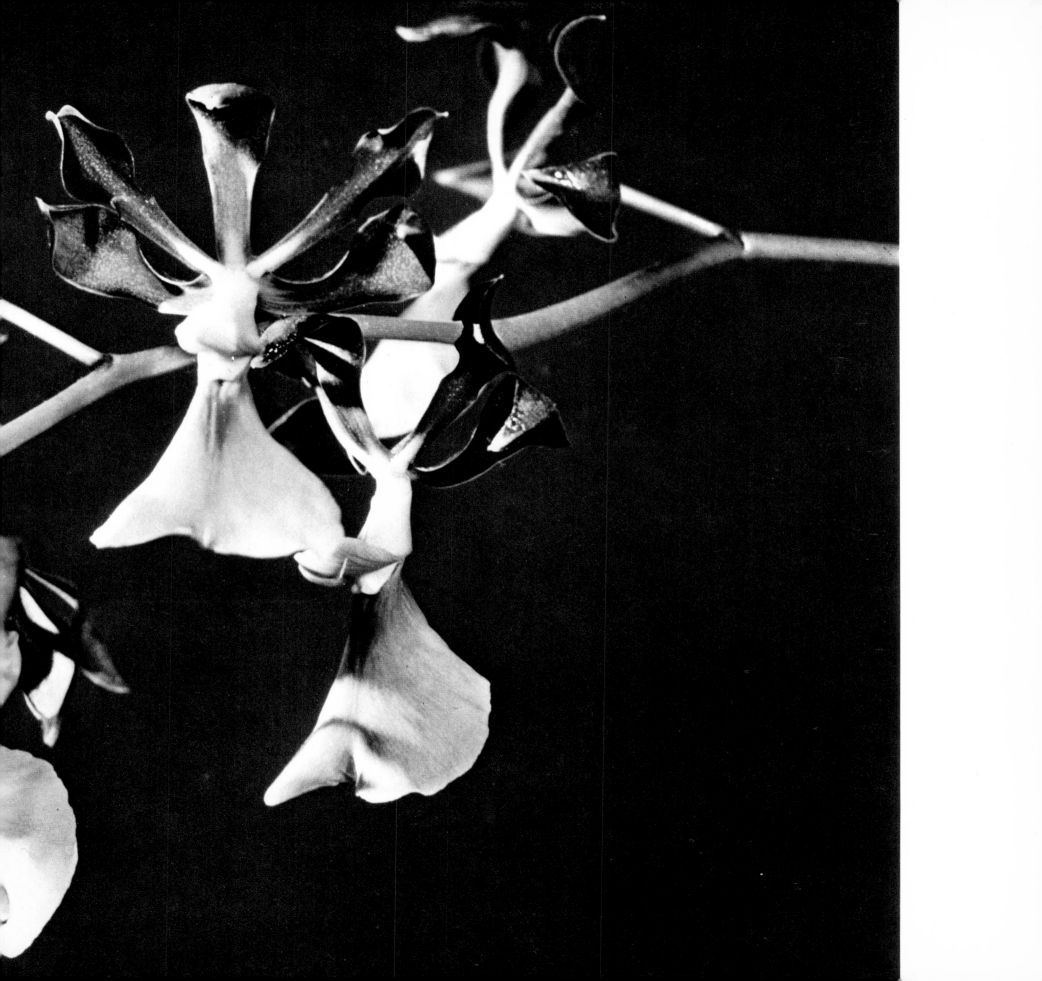

PLATE 42
Epidendrum
E. stamfordianum
Mexico to Panama, Colombia, Venezuela

This handsome species produces long arching stems with ½-inch yellowish-green blooms. Discovered by G. Ure Skinner in Guatemala in 1837, it was sent to James Bateman, in whose collection at Knypersley, England, it flowered in the spring of the following year. (Photograph courtesy of Guy Burgess.)

PLATE 43
Epidendrum
E. stamfordianum
Mexico to Panama, Colombia, Venezuela

A close-up of the flower. See plate 42 for description. (Photograph courtesy of Joyce R. Wilson.)

PLATE 44 ▶
Epidendrum
E. lindleyanum
Mexico, Central America

The fragile elegance of its form and the rose-purple color of its flower make this orchid a true aristocrat. The number of star-shaped flowers varies from three to ten per plant. Especially striking is the lip, white with a deep purple mark at the tip. The species name is in honor of the famous Dr. John Lindley of the Royal Horticultural Society. (Photograph courtesy of Joyce R. Wilson.)

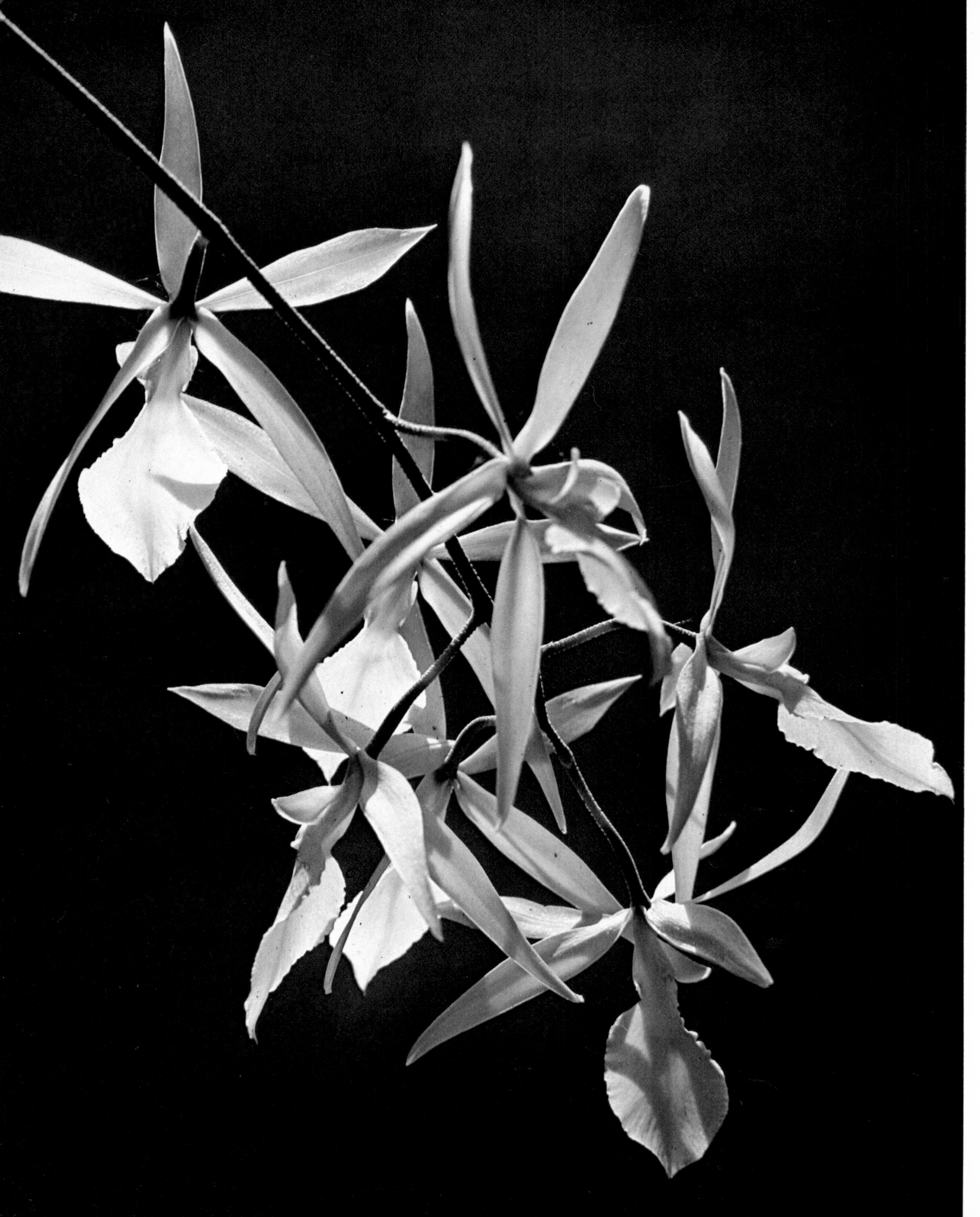

PLATE 45
Epidendrum
E. nemorale
Mexico

With egg-shaped pseudobulbs and stems growing to about 20 inches tall, this epidendrum was first imported by Conrad Loddiges from Mexico about 1840. It is a tree-dweller often seen in the regions around Oaxaca. The flowers are about 5 inches across, scented, and remain in color for six weeks on the plant. (Photograph courtesy of Andrew R. Addkison.)

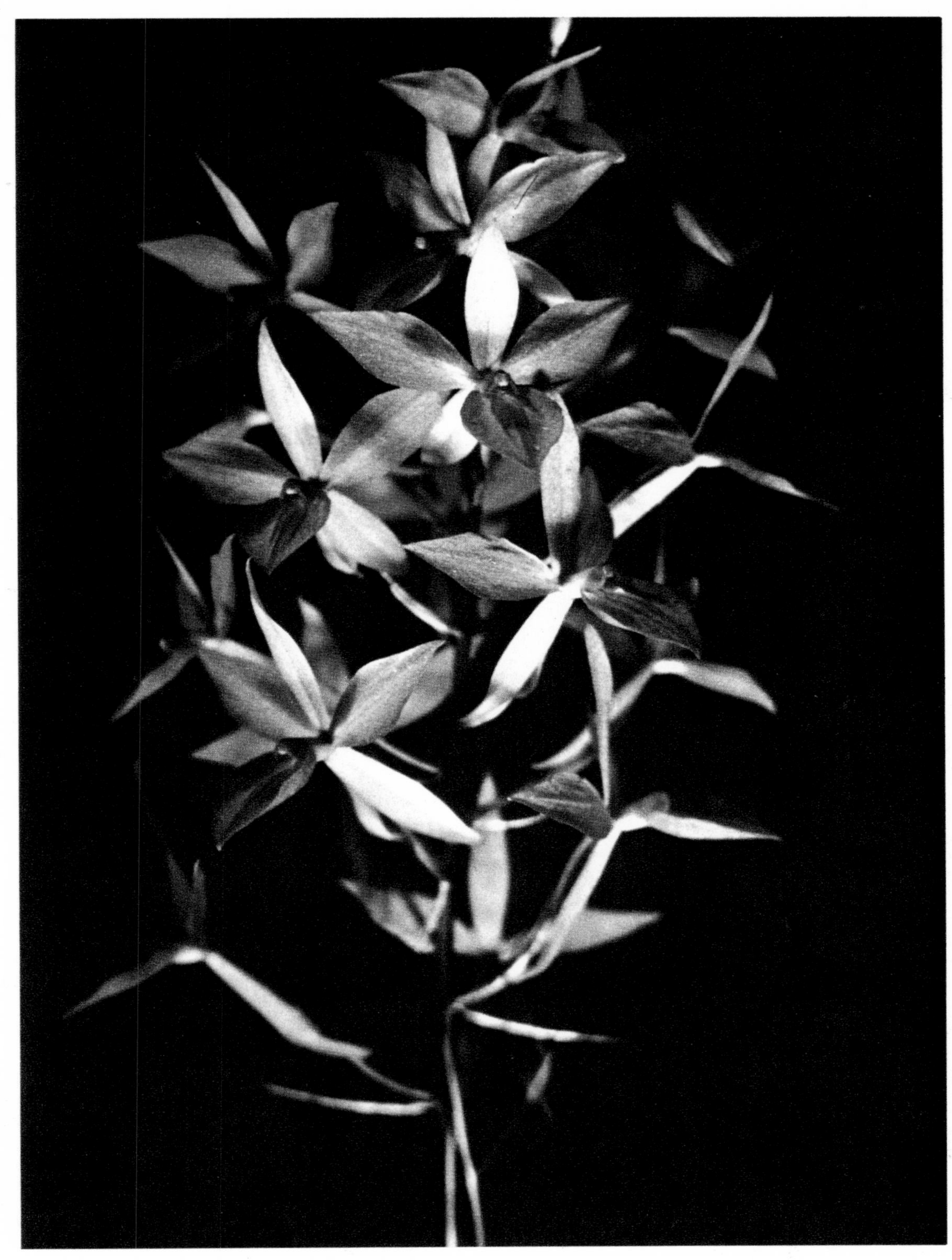

PLATE 46
Barkeria (Epidendrum)
B. skinneri
Mexico, Guatemala

These plants are deciduous, losing their leaves during their season of rest. The flowers are a striking magenta. The species is now often included in the genus *Epidendrum*. (Photograph courtesy of Andrew R. Addkison.)

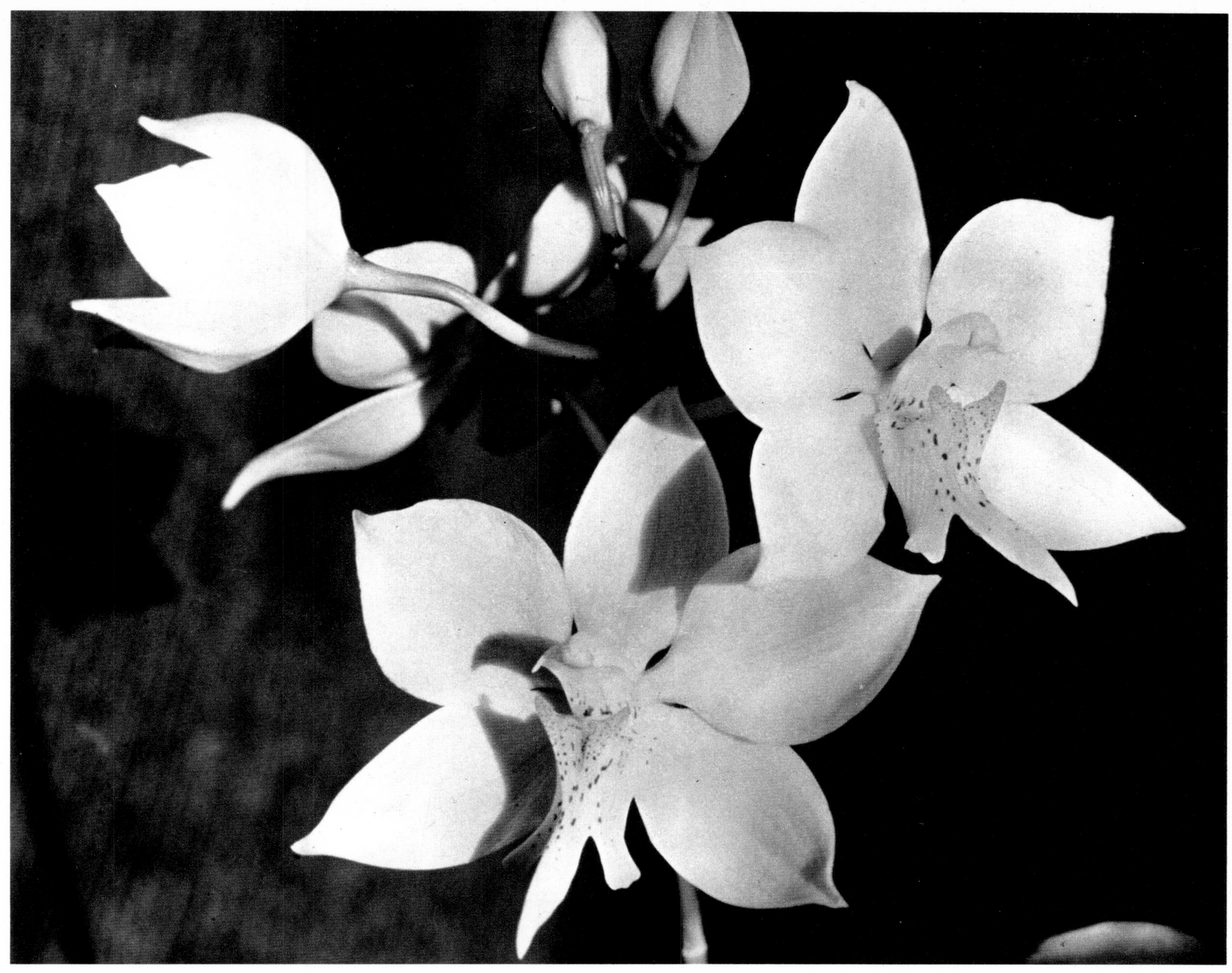

PLATE 48
Diacrium (Caularthron)
D. bicornutum
Venezuela, Trinidad, Tobago, Guyana, Brazil

A fine dwarf orchid with handsome white 1½–2½-inch flowers and 5-inch leaves, it was first introduced from Trinidad in 1833. Because of its pure white color, it is known sometimes as the virgin orchid. Plants in the wild often grow near fire-ant nests, so collecting them is hazardous. (Photograph courtesy of Andrew R. Addkison.)

◀ PLATE 47
Barkeria (Epidendrum)
B. skinneri
Mexico, Guatemala

A close-up of the flower. See plate 46 for description. (Photograph courtesy of Joyce R. Wilson.)

PLATE 49
Diacattleya
D. Chastity (hybrid)

This popular, inexpensive floriferous orchid is highly desirable because of its blush-pink color. It is a cross between *Cattleya granulosa* and *Diacrium bicornutum*. (Photograph courtesy of Joyce R. Wilson.)

PLATE 50
Cattleya
C. forbesii
Brazil

Introduced by the Royal Horticultural Society of London in 1823 through their collector John Forbes, this orchid is quite common on low trees and rocks near the sea in the neighborhood of Rio de Janeiro. It has large 5-inch flowers; their color is variable in hue but is usually olive green or yellowish-green. (Photograph courtesy of Andrew R. Addkison.)

PLATE 51 ▶
Cattleya
C. Frasquita (hybrid)

A hybrid made originally in 1900, it is a cross between the species *C. bic* and *C. velutina*. The plant grows to inches tall, and the handsome flowe are easily brought into bloom. (Photograph courtesy of Joyce R. Wilson.)

PLATE 52
Cattleya
C. intermedia var. *aquinii*
Brazil

This rather rare natural variety of orchid has petals splashed with deep lavender. It is always consistent in form, and the petals imitate the lip. (Photograph courtesy of Hermann Pigors.)

PLATE 53
Cattleya
C. skinneri
Guatemala

This floriferous cattleya is a most amenable plant. It can be grown in shade or sun under various weather conditions. Discovered in Guatemala in 1836, it has been popular ever since. Truly a bouquet of beauty. (Photograph courtesy of Guy Burgess.)

PLATE 54
Cattleya
C. luteola
Brazil, Amazon Basin, Peru

This small plant, with 2-inch yellow flowers, is a delightful addition to a collection. The genus *Cattleya* was founded by Dr. John Lindley upon *C. labiata* and dedicated to William Cattley of Barnet, England, a liberal patron of horticulture in the early 1800s. (Photograph courtesy of Guy Burgess.)

PLATE 55
Cattleya
C. Princess Bells (hybrid)

An exceptionally fine orchid, it is a cross between C. Bob Betts and C. Empress Bells. The stud, C. Bob Betts, is one of the finest white-flowered orchids in existence. (Photograph courtesy of Guy Burgess.)

PLATE 56
Cattleya
C. velutina
Brazil

Introduced into cultivation about 1872, this species first flowered in England under J. Broome in Didsbury, Manchester. The plant is similar to *C. bicolor,* and it was once known as *C. fragrans*. The plant is tall, growing to 60 inches, and has very fragrant flowers. (Photograph courtesy of Joyce R. Wilson.)

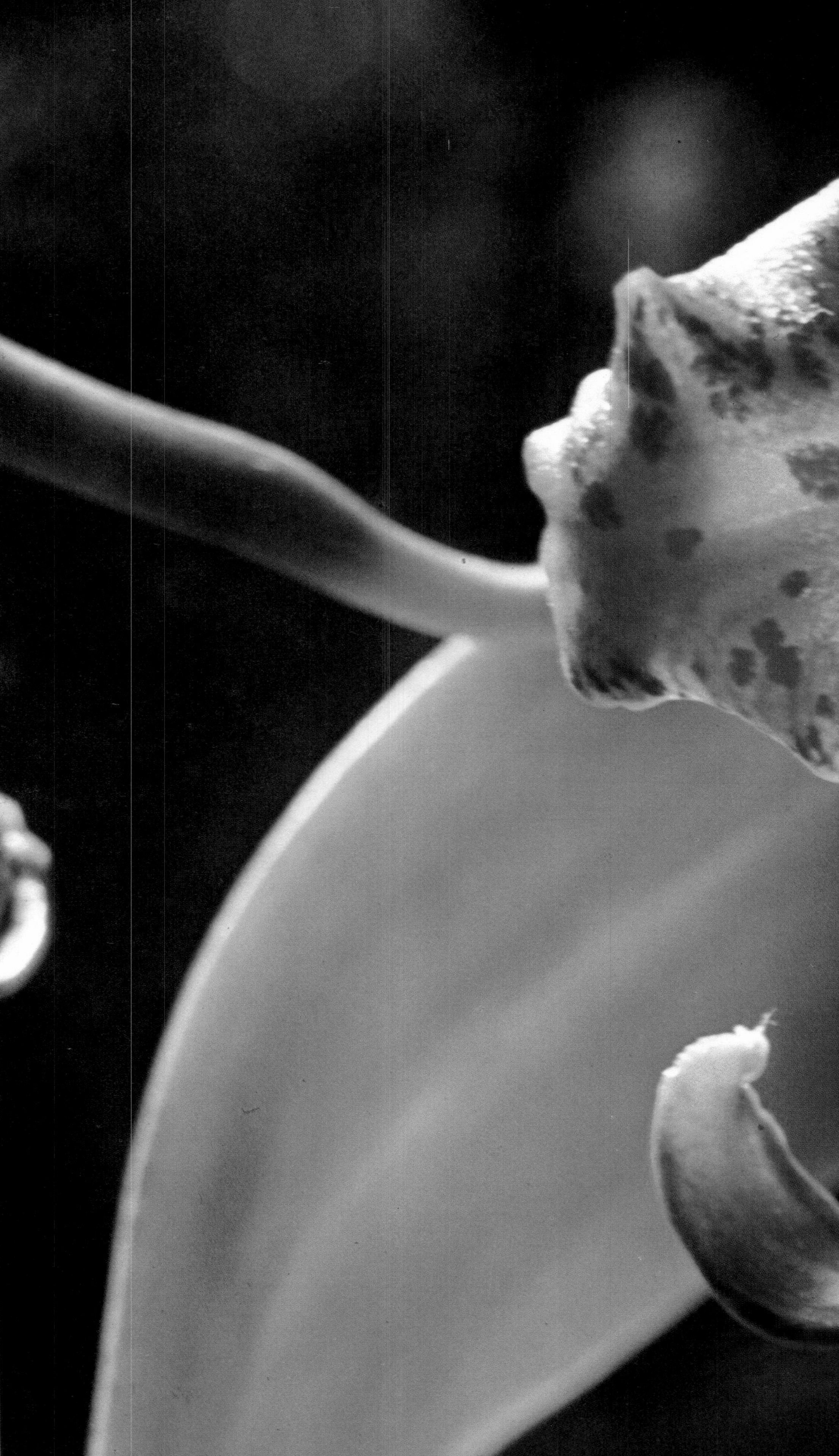

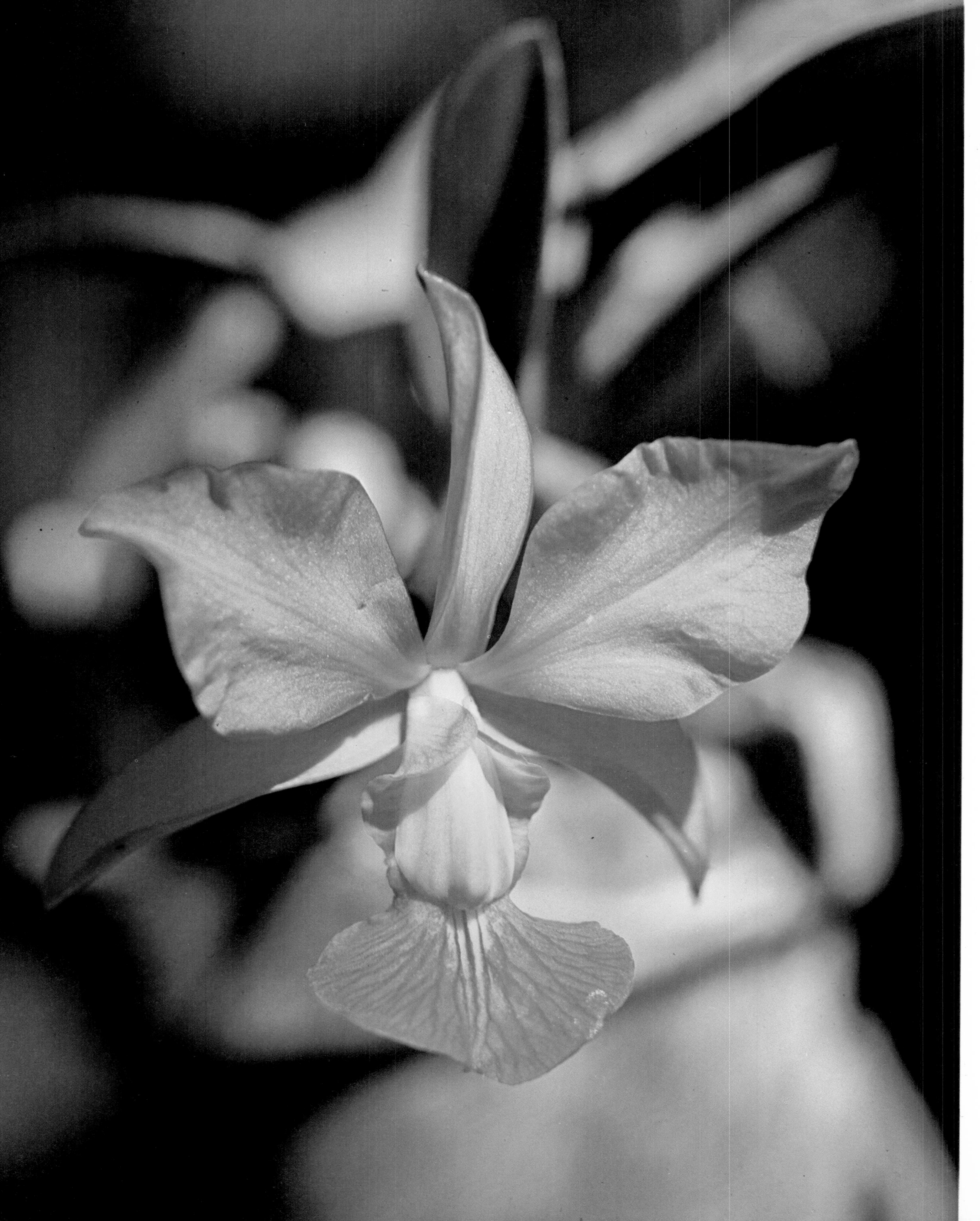

PLATE 57
Cattleya
C. walkeriana
Brazil

Collected in 1939–40 and named after Edward Walker, this orchid is a rather small plant, growing only up to 12 inches tall but bearing large solitary flowers. (Photograph courtesy of Joyce R. Wilson.)

PLATE 58
Laelia
L. flava
Brazil

Introduced into English collections in 1839, this lovely epiphytic orchid has small, elegant golden-yellow flowers. (Photograph courtesy of Hermann Pigors.)

◀ PLATE 59
Laelia
L. acuminata var. *rosea*
Guatemala

This compact-growing small plant bears 1-inch pale rose-colored flowers that last only a few days. Variety *rosea* is distinguished by its purple markings. (Photograph courtesy of Joyce R. Wilson.)

PLATE 60
Laelia
L. cinnabarina
Brazil

See plate 62 for description. (Photograph courtesy of Joyce R. Wilson.)

PLATE 62
Laelia
L. cinnabarina
Brazil

This species was introduced into England by Messrs. Young, nurserymen, in 1836. It is a medium-size plant, to 24 inches tall. A favorite with hobbyists, it is spectacular in flower, easy to cultivate, and is a dependable bloomer. Pictured here is a select form of the species. (Photograph courtesy of Guy Burgess.)

PLATE 61
Laelia
L. purpurata
Brazil

This fine species is distinguished by handsome large flowers veined with amethyst purple. It was first discovered in 1847 in southern Brazil. (Photograph courtesy of Hermann Pigors.)

◀ PLATE 63
Laelia
L. grandis
Brazil

This outstanding species has 5-inch flowers on a 12-inch plant. It first became known in European gardens in 1849, when sent to M. Pinel, who had found it in Bahia, Brazil. (Photograph courtesy of Joyce R. Wilson.)

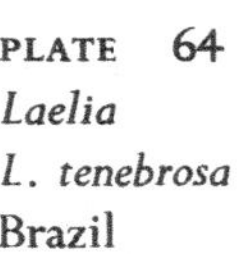

PLATE 64
Laelia
L. tenebrosa
Brazil

A close-up of the flower. See plate 65 for description. (Photograph courtesy of Joyce R. Wilson.)

PLATE 65
Laelia
L. tenebrosa
Brazil

This plant is 30 inches tall, with 7-inch flowers. A magnificent sight in bloom, it can tolerate a variety of temperatures from 55° to 80° F. (Photograph courtesy of Joyce R. Wilson.)

PLATE 66
Laelia
L. superbiens
Mexico, Guatemala

Discovered by G. Ure Skinner in 1838–39 in Honduras and introduced into England in 1844, *L. superbiens* is an unusual plant. It has large pseudobulbs and bears a 4-foot flower spike crowned with clusters of blooms. The plant is a sun-lover and not easy to bring into bloom. (Photograph courtesy of Guy Burgess.)

PLATE 67
Laeliocattleya
Lc. Copperglen (hybrid)

This stunning garnet-and-gold orchid is known for its excellent form. It is a cross between Lc. Gatton Glory and Lc. Lee Langford. (Photograph courtesy of Joyce R. Wilson.)

PLATE 68
Laeliocattleya
Lc. Lydia Hubbell (hybrid)

This is a classically showy orchid—flamboyantly colored and opulent in form. It is a cross between C. Nellie Roberts and Lc. Pacific Sun. (Photograph courtesy of Joyce R. Wilson.)

PLATE 69
Sophrolaeliocattleya
Slc. Trizac (hybrid)

This orchid is one of the most popular and ostentatious florist offerings. An exciting color combination of magentas and red-orange, it is a cross between Slc. Anzac and *C. trianaei*. This photograph was taken in the greenhouse of Klaus Abegg, Colorado Springs, Colo. (Photograph courtesy of Guy Burgess.)

PLATE 70 ▶
Schomburgkia (Laelia)
S. tibicinis
Mexico to Costa Rica

Large, to 40 inches high, this species has tall spikes of lilac flowers streaked with purple. Discovered by G. Ure Skinner in Honduras, it first flowered in England about 1840. (Photograph courtesy of Andrew R. Addkison.)

◀ PLATE 71
Brassolaeliocattleya
Blc. Puregold (hybrid)

The intense sun-gold petals of this gorgeous orchid are made still more dramatic by the blood-red markings on its lip. It is a cross between Blc. Golden Llewellyn and Lc. Pacific Sun. (Photograph courtesy of Joyce R. Wilson.)

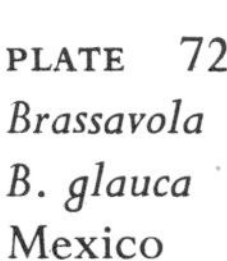

PLATE 72
Brassavola
B. glauca
Mexico

Waxy white 5-inch flowers tinged with green characterize this orchid. It is difficult to bring into bloom. The genus, as now delimited, extends from Mexico and Jamaica to Brazil, Bolivia, and Peru. (Photograph courtesy of Joyce R. Wilson.)

PLATE 73
Brassavola
B. digbyana
Honduras

Because of its beautiful fringed lip, this orchid is used extensively for hybridization. The blossom is unusually large for an orchid, measuring 6 to 7 inches. The scent is exquisite and powerful. Though a difficult plant to coax into bloom, the effort required produces results that are well worth the trouble. Today, this species is hard to find in its native habitat because of its desirability to collectors and hybridists. (Photograph courtesy of Lymon Emerson.)

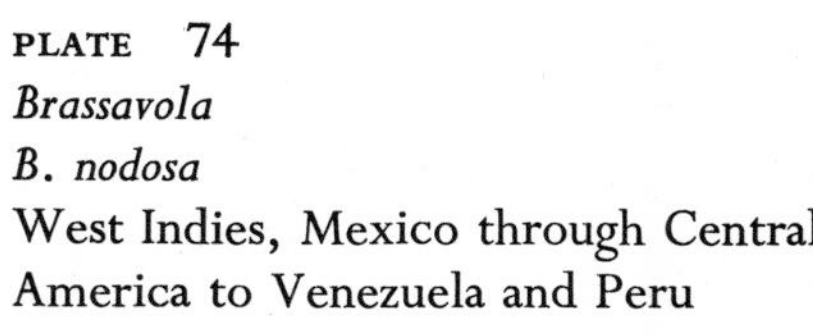

PLATE 74
Brassavola
B. nodosa
West Indies, Mexico through Central America to Venezuela and Peru

Known as lady-of-the-night, this orchid (in the foreground) is sweetly scented and small in stature. It practically grows by itself. In the background are blossoms of *Dendrobium phalaenopsis,* standard form. (Photograph courtesy of Guy Burgess.)

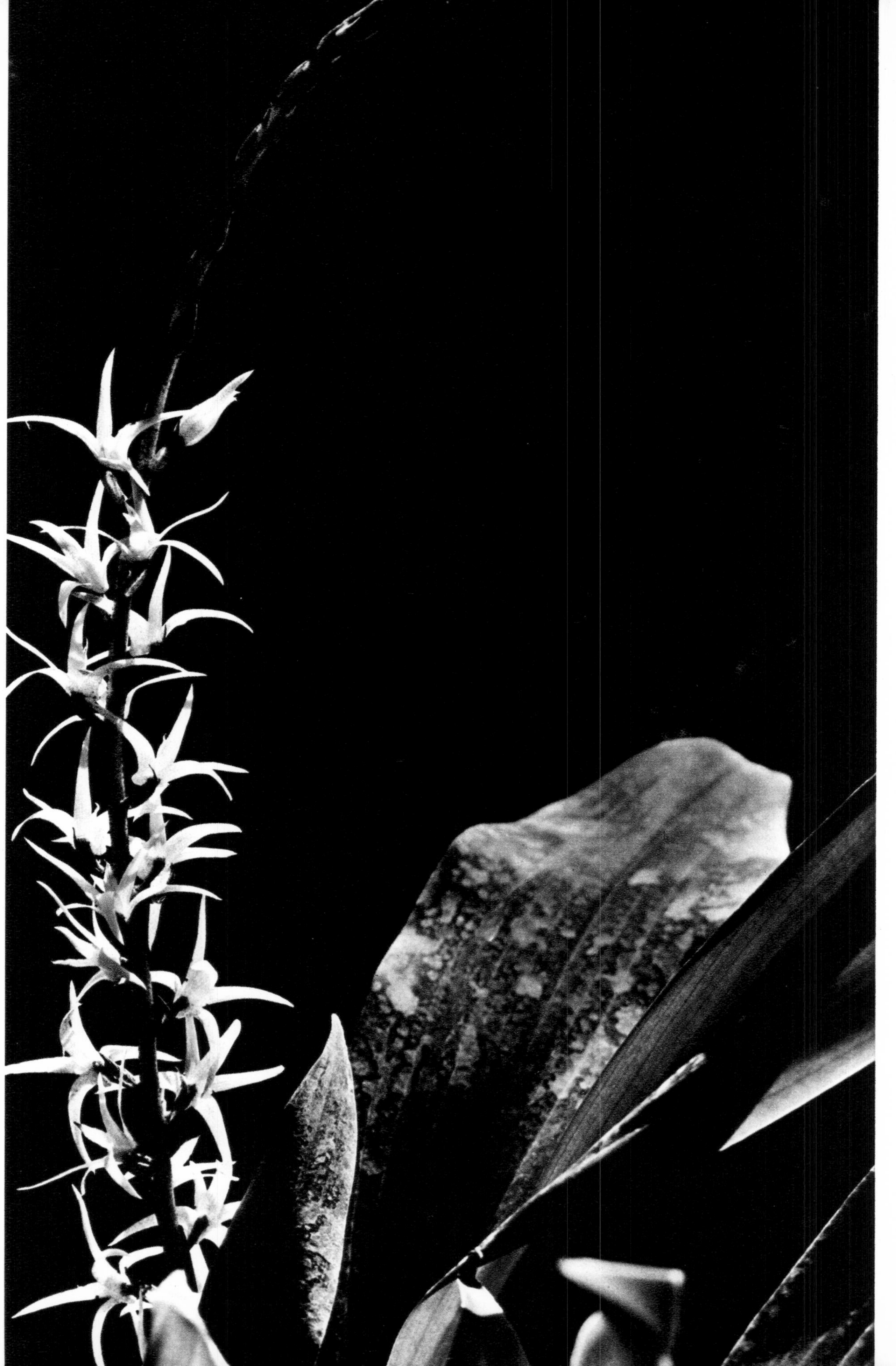

PLATE 75
Eria
E. stellata
Java

The genus *Eria* is one of the larger orchidaceous aggregations, but it is infrequently seen today despite the large number of showy and handsome flowers that it offers. The range of the genus extends from China, the Himalayas, Ceylon, and India throughout an immense region to Samoa and the Fiji Islands. Many are found in Indonesia and New Guinea. (Photograph courtesy of Joyce R. Wilson.)

CONTINUED FROM PAGE 24

ior man and the scent of the blooms to the joys of friendship. (The word *lan* quite possibly referred to other flowers as well.) More properly, orchids were cited as *lan hua*. In a book by Matsuoka, printed in 1772 (rewritten in Chinese and quite possibly taken from the original Japanese book titled *Igansai-ranpin,* printed in 1728), six orchids were cited: *Cymbidium ensifolium, Angraecum falcatum, Cymbidium virescens, Dendrobium moniliforme, Sarcochilus japonicus,* and *Bletia hyacinthina*. Fragrance is indeed a great attribute of these plants, for I have grown five of the six, and a single flowering plant perfumes an entire garden room.

References to orchids in earlier books appeared as far back as A.D. 290–370, but these books treated orchids more in the botanical than the aesthetic sense. In the Northern Sung period (960–1279) there were special monographs on orchids, and the Chinese painters of the Yüan dynasty (1279–1368) were well known for their depiction of the plants.

Several orchids, including dendrobium and vanda, were mentioned by early Chinese writers, but the cymbidium was the most popular. These orchids were especially revered by Chinese painters for their grassy, graceful foliage, the tapered leaves and sculptural flowers being ideally suited to the calligraphic art of

This exquisite Chinese work (ink on paper) by Hsü Wei (1520–93) shows twelve flowers accompanied by poems. The grassy foliage is a stylized representation of cymbidium leaves.
(Photograph courtesy of Freer Gallery of Art.)

ink and brush. The painting of cymbidiums was very like the beautiful calligraphy of the Chinese; short strokes of the brush were used, simplicity was the style, and mood the ultimate goal. These are certainly not botanical drawings in the true sense of the word, rather, they are lovely, eye-pleasing pictures. There was no counterpart to them in European wood-block illustrations of herbals, where botanical accuracy and horticultural importance were stressed.

The most famous group of Chinese orchid paintings is contained in the treatise *Mustard Seed Garden Painting Manual* (*Chieh Tzu Huan Chuan*), by Wang An-Chien and his three brothers. In this work the grassy foliage of the cymbidium is depicted in short, deft strokes in black and white, like a silhouette (a form called ink orchids).

Orchids were known and admired in China and Japan long before they were appreciated in Europe, and knowledge of them remained in the Far East. There was no exchange of plant information with the rest of the world. The Japanese found Christianity an evil, and they were intensely afraid of invasion by foreign powers. (When Western maps became available, the Japanese realized their country was small in comparison to the rest of the world, where many powers were engaged

The grassy leaves and delicate flowers of cymbidiums are beautifully represented in this seventeenth-century hand scroll (ink on paper) by Sheng-Yu. (Photograph courtesy of the Art Institute of Chicago.)

Handsome cymbidiums grace this hand scroll (ink and color on paper) by Tsai Ching-yi of the Hsi period (1662–1722). It is titled *Flowers and Insects*. (Photograph courtesy of the Art Institute of Chicago.)

Timeless beauty of form and decoration characterize this stoneware jar (c.1650) of the Korean Yi dynasty. The representation of orchids here has a startlingly Abstract Expressionist quality. (Photograph courtesy of the Art Institute of Chicago.)

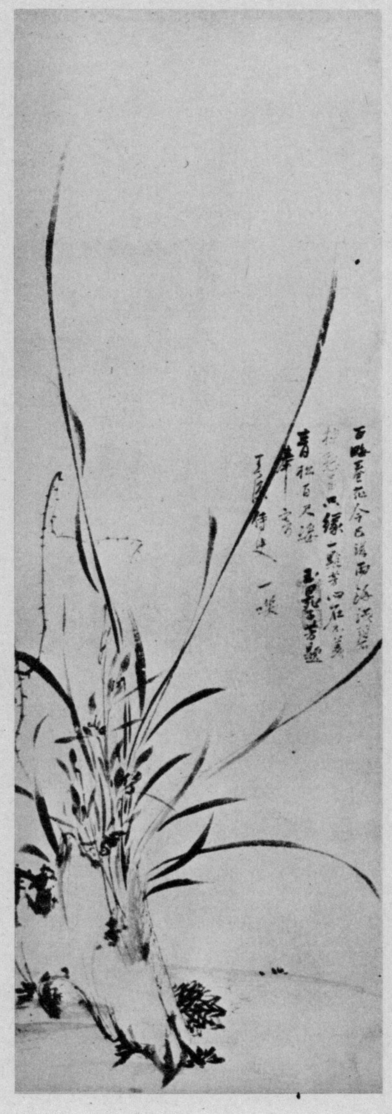

These graceful cymbidiums, painted by Gyokuen Bompo (1344–c.1420), are found in volume 11 of *Genshoku Nihon no Bijutsu,* which is housed in Rokuo-in Temple, Kyoto. (Photograph courtesy of the University of California, East Asian Library.)

in wars of conquest.) In 1639, all foreigners were restricted to a man-made island called Deshima, in Nagasaki harbor, and a year later the only foreigners allowed were certain members of the Dutch East India Company. Communication with European countries ceased, and only Asian ships were permitted to trade in Japanese ports.

How Orchids Came to Europe

Systematic evidence of orchids in Oriental cultures appeared as early as the Sung dynasty (960–1279), but orchids did not begin to create interest in Europe until about 1750. The first European reference to Oriental orchids appeared in 1712 in *Amoenitatum exoticarum,* by Englebert Kaempfer, a German physician attached to the Dutch East India Trading Company. The first non-European tropical orchid, *Bletia verecunda,* flowered in England in 1733. It had been sent to a well-known collector, Peter Collinson, from New Providence Island in the Bahamas. The plant showed signs of life despite a voyage of several months. It was acquired by Sir Charles Wagner, and it flowered the next summer with clusters of small but bright magenta blooms. Because certain orchids could obviously survive in Europe (if conditions similar to their native habitat were provided), and because the West Indies (particularly Jamaica) were easily accessible to Europeans, naval officers started bringing more orchids home, either as botanical specimens or as gifts for their ladies. In 1760 *Epidendrum rigidum* was introduced, and in 1765 some vanilla species followed. Reports from the naval officers said that the plants grew to amazing heights, with their thick vines and aerial roots strangling branches and smothering trees. People therefore quickly tagged orchids as parasites—plants that have to prey on something in order to survive. This misconception about orchids was so persistent that in 1815 *The Botanical Register* confirmed it. (Actually, orchids are epiphytes, living *in* trees but not taking their nourishment from them.)

The first European to collect Asiatic orchids was Dr. John Fothergill. In 1778 he returned from China with *Phaius grandifolius* and *Cymbidium ensifolium*. He gave the phaius to his niece, and the plant produced an abundance of large, pinkish-blue flowers on tall spikes.

In August, 1768, the H.M.S. *Endeavour,* under the auspices of the Royal Society, planned an expedition to the South Seas for plant exploration with James Cook as commander and Joseph Banks as director. The first collection of plants was made at Tierra del Fuego in South America. In 1780 another expedition went to Australia and other places and brought back orchids.

Later Banks consulted with the king about the possibility of bringing breadfruit from the Pacific Islands to the West Indies as a commercial crop. Banks was given permission and organized the journey. William Bligh was appointed to transport the trees and command the H.M.S. *Bounty*. The undertaking was a failure because of the well-known mutiny. However, in 1793, Captain Bligh was sent again on the H.M.S. *Providence*. This time he was successful, and from the South Pacific he brought back fifteen orchids including *Oncidium altissimum, Oncidium carthaginense, Lycaste barringtoniae, Epidendrum ciliare,* and others. Although all were different orchids, they were then classified as epidendrums.

Work progressed on orchids in other countries—Belgium, Germany, and France—but England led the way. John Lindley (1799–1865) started modern orchidology as we know it today. (Lindley, a professor of botany and Secretary of the Royal Horticultural Society also edited the basic English horticultural journal, *The Gardener's*

This illustration of the handsome *Cattleya loddigesii* is from John Lindley's *Monographia Digitalium* (1821). It was discovered in Brazil in 1815. (Photograph courtesy of the University of California.)

Chronicle, a periodical still published today.) In 1830 Lindley suggested growing orchids in damp, humid conditions; unfortunately, he based his suggestion on information pertaining to certain orchids in a restricted geographical location. The public at the time interpreted this to mean that all orchids should be grown in this way; the results were grave—thousands of plants perished. In Lindley's defense it must be stated that by 1835, with keener insight and more research on orchids in their native lands, he had determined that orchids grew at various altitudes and under a variety of conditions. He knew that the plants required different cultural environments. But the pattern was already set, and people continued to grow orchids in stagnant conditions. (Some orchids are, in fact, bog plants.)

Lindley wrote several books on general plant classification, but it was his work on orchids, primarily *The Genera and Species of Orchidaceous Plants* (1830–40), that brought him fame. Between 1852 and 1859 he produced *Folia Orchidacea;* though never completed it is a classic in botany.

Other notable men who contributed to orchidology were George Bentham, Sir Joseph Banks, Sir Joseph Dalton Hooker, Sir Joseph Paxton (gardener to the

These representations are from Sir Joseph Hooker's *A Century of Orchidaceous Plants* (1851). It was selected from an issue of *Curtis's Botanical Magazine*. (Photograph by George M. Cushing; courtesy of the Massachusetts Horticultural Society.)

Duke of Devonshire), and B. S. Williams. Conrad Loddiges, James Veitch, and numerous others were also prominent in this time of "Orchidomania."

Though there was little correct information about growing orchids at the time, there were several periodicals that carried orchid data. *Curtis's Botanical Magazine* was started by William Curtis in 1787, *The Botanical Register* in 1815. *The Gardener's Chronicle* and Paxton's *Magazine of Botany* were other sources for orchid news. It was quite evident that the orchid was "the plant of the times" because so much was written about it in so many periodicals.

In 1862, during the latter part of Lindley's career, the great naturalist Charles Darwin published *On the Various Contrivances by Which British and Foreign Orchids Are Fertilised by Insects*. The main part of the book discussed the morphology of the orchid flower, and it long remained a valuable reference work on plant-insect relations.

After Lindley's death Heinrich Gustav Reichenbach (1824–89) became the leading orchid authority in Germany; he identified and sketched species from all over the world. In other countries many notable persons were contributing to orcihdology with various books and papers.

Orchids in England

Orchid collecting in England began with the flowering of the first imported specimen in 1733, as mentioned. Cultivation of exotic orchids for sale and in private collections began a little before 1800. In 1787 *Epidendrum cochleatum* bloomed in what is now the Royal Botanic Gardens at Kew, near London, and by 1794 there were fifteen different epiphytic (air plant) orchids in that collection, mostly of West Indian origin.

England in the early 1800s was a gardening nation, as it still is, and plants were most important in the English way of life. Orchids were unlike any flowers that had ever been seen. When a new plant bloomed, it was an exciting news item reported in periodicals and newspapers and by word of mouth. Orchids were considered oddities; it was said that they bloomed without soil and devoured insects in order to produce striking flowers. Bewilderment about how to grow orchids was justified, for no one knew what conditions they needed to flourish. Because they were known to come from tropical and humid lands, they were put in airless glass cases containing half-rotted tree stumps and branches. They

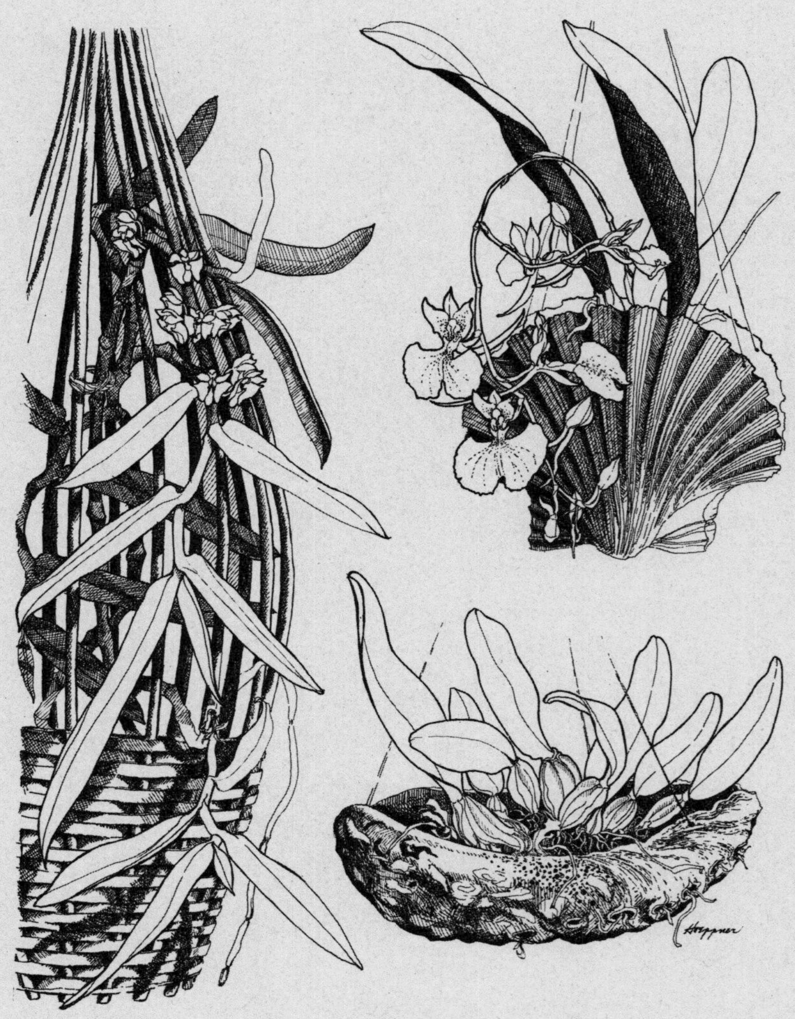

Early Orchid Containers

were treated more as performing animals than as plants. Yet the curiosity persisted, interest accelerated, and more orchids were imported.

In 1815 Conrad Loddiges, a gardener and editor of a botanical journal, started to raise orchids successfully by unorthodox methods. He placed the plants in well-ventilated areas and watered them frequently; he kept them under glass but treated them as ordinary garden plants rather than oddities. They thrived. Other growers, too, started to experiment, some putting orchids in wooden or raffia containers and in sea shells. They gave orchids more ventilation and more light, and the plants responded.

Loddiges, after this first success with orchids, asked William Roxburgh, the director of the Botanic Gardens in Calcutta, India, for plants and received species of vanda, aerides, and dendrobium. He began cultivating orchids for sale, and his work furnished considerable knowledge about how to grow the plants.

The first South American orchid to arrive in the Old World was *Oncidium bifolium,* which came from Montevideo. A traveler who brought back a plant said that it hung in his ship cabin and flowered without soil during the long journey. Although he was ridiculed by some for telling an outlandish tale, others accepted his story.

This illustration of a typical English glasshouse of about 1850 appeared in *Cranston's Patent Buildings as Applied to Horticulture*. (Photograph by George M. Cushing; courtesy of the Massachusetts Horticultural Society.)

And indeed in 1818 *The Botanical Register* confirmed his report, stating that some Asian orchids did bloom without soil.

In 1813 Fairbairn, a well-known gardener, was already having success with aerides and vanda species by growing them in suspended baskets and dunking them in water several times a day. By 1830 a more sensible treatment of orchids had started in England.

"Orchidomania" set in as the plants became fashionable. Social gatherings and parties were centered around the blossoming of an orchid; a craze gripped England that had no rival, not even the seventeenth-century "tulipomania" that caused financial chaos in the Near East and the Netherlands.

The orchid became popular both for its beauty and for the definite challenge of coaxing it to produce such beauty. Around 1840 collectors were sent in droves to all parts of the globe to find orchids to satisfy the public demand. The auction sales at Stevens Rooms, King Street, Covent Garden, and at other establishments were fraught with the excitement of a racetrack, and orchids were sold for sums incredible at the time. One cattleya sold for $600!

The clamor for and about orchids was heard also in Belgium, France, and Germany: at an international exhibition in Brussels, fifteen different cattleyas were shown, and Belgian firms joined English companies in the sale of orchids.

Collecting Orchids

The orchid craze that started in England in 1840 and reached its peak in 1850 was the result of several influences. The desire for the flowers was not generated as it is now, primarily by their beauty. To the Victorian these plants were curiosities. The attraction of the bizarre and exotic was symptomatic of the times, but the practical contribution of one man, Nathaniel Ward, furthered the role of orchids as favorites of the era. Between 1830 and 1834 Ward perfected a closed glass-and-wooden case for shipping plants from foreign lands. The cases were not foolproof, but in them many orchids, rather than only a few, reached their destination. (Today, such glass containers are still called Wardian cases.)

As more plants came to England and more suitable ways of growing them were found, more people wanted them. In 1845 the repeal of Britain's glass tax and the general acceleration of industry made greenhouses or smaller glasshouses possible for many people. Furthermore, coal to heat the greenhouses was cheap, as was the labor to maintain them. As these "crystal palaces" appeared, so did unprecedented demands for plants to fill them, mainly orchids, for these were the gardeners' pet protégés in a world of great private gardens. By 1850 the English collectors started penetrating Central and South America, areas where exotic orchids grew in profusion. James Veitch, a nurseryman, sent William Lobb to South America to collect orchids. But perhaps the best-known collector of Central and South American orchids was Benedict Roezl, a Czech, who introduced many orchids from regions extending from Bolivia to the Atlantic and Brazil. No one knows whether he was luckier, more intelligent, or merely sturdier than his fellow collectors in surviving steaming forests and rugged terrain, but he furnished England with prodigious numbers of orchids.

Importation reached its peak in the 1850s, but four-fifths of the imported orchids died in transit, and no wonder. The penetration of jungles filled with insects and natives was only the first obstacle in getting the plants back to England: they then had to be packed into crates and transported by pack animals or by native bearers to a riverbank to await shipment, and often a boat did not arrive for weeks. Once on board they were stored in damp, warm holds lacking the two prime req-

In a South American rain forest, a young boy collects orchids growing high on a tree. (Photograph by Charles Marden Fitch; courtesy of the American Orchid Society.)

A man collects orchids growing on a tree on the island of Great Comoro, in the Mozambique Channel. (Photograph by R. I. M. Campbell; courtesy of the American Orchid Society.)

uisites of orchids, light and air. After a three- or four-month journey thousands of plants were found dead on arrival. But because they were rare, the demand for orchids soared and the supply was never enough.

During the mid-nineteenth century, orchid collectors also ventured into India, Africa, Java, Borneo, Indonesia, and New Guinea. Stories of their struggles drifted back to England and became magnified. One popular story of the time concerned a lost orchid, a cattleya that had died in an English collection and had to be replaced. But no one knew where it had originally grown! Such tales were common, and for forty or fifty years a species might be impossible to collect until a clue to its place of origin was found, often in some writings. A map showing a location for orchids had the value of a treasure map; collectors, in their zeal to look out for themselves, frequently removed all traces of a stand of plants in its native habitat, or even forged maps to throw off rival collectors. A few plant hunters became very wealthy men, but many never returned to England with their treasures.

Stories of native tribes using orchids as religious and sex symbols were spread by collectors to glamorize the flower—the more unusual the stories, the more desirable the orchids became. Several orchids were actually used by native tribes in their ceremonies. The natives were dependent on their crops for food, and if by chance a brilliant mass of orchids bloomed about harvest time the natives viewed this as an omen: the orchids heralded a fertile harvest, and men could not survive without one.

During World War I many fine orchid collections in Europe were destroyed or perished because of lack of fuel to heat the greenhouses. But in the United States such losses did not occur, and the popularity of orchids increased. Since the early 1900s private collections in the tradition of the English had been building, and orchids as corsage flowers were starting to compete with roses.

By 1930 the importation of orchids to England almost ceased because English firms no longer had collectors in all parts of the world. Nurseries were established in several tropical countries. In America and Europe great strides were being made in orchid hybridization, and plants were being cultivated on a large scale.

This painting, titled *Orchids and Humming Birds* (c. 1865), is by Martin J. Heade (1819–1904). It shows the full glory of orchid flowers. (Photograph courtesy of the Museum of Fine Arts, Boston; collection M. and M. Karolik.)

The Orchid Family

In the Orchidaceae we find one of the largest number of flowering plants known to man, with thirty thousand wild species and thirty thousand or more registered hybrids. (This figure of course fluctuates, as new hybrids are registered with the American Orchid Society and with societies in England and Europe.) Species—orchids untouched by man—grow wild in nature. Occasionally, natural hybrids are produced, but most hybrids are the work of man—the plants bearing the best (or certain desirable) characteristics are mated with other plants bearing other particularly desirable characteristics. For instance, a plant with large but poorly colored flowers might be mated with one which has small but beautifully colored blossoms in order to produce a plant bearing large *and* beautifully colored flowers.

Botanically, orchids belong to the system of flowering plants called monocotyledons. They bear a single seed leaf, or cotyledon, on germination; additional leaves are then produced from the center of the stem, passing outward. True bark is absent, and leaves generally have parallel veins, and the parts of the flowers (petals, etc.) in threes or in multiples of three. Dicotyledons, on the other hand, are distinguished by the production of two or more seed leaves on germination; the formation of young wood on the outer part of the stem; leaves generally with netted veins; and flowers with sepals, petals, and stamens in fours or fives or a multiple of those numbers.

Although iris, lilies, and amaryllis would also be identified by the above classifications, orchids have made such great advances in flower structure that the family appears unique among plants. With their intricate structure and ingenious methods of propagation, they function at the highest level of efficiency.

Mimicry and Sex in Orchids

In most flowers it is easy to see the sexual organs—stamen and pistil, anther and stigma—but in orchids the anther and stigma are contained in one body, the column.

The flower of an orchid, which we love for its color and form, serves as a landing pad for insects which pollinate it. Charles Darwin understood the function of the orchid's sexual apparatus and described it in the treatise previously mentioned—*On the Various Contrivances by Which British and Foreign Orchids Are Fertilised by Insects.* His gentle Victorian readers might not have believed that the beauty of a flower was used for such vulgar processes, but so it was and is.

Like other flowers, orchids have sepals and petals, three of each. One petal, usually much larger than the others, is called the labellum or lip.

The labellum, often the most conspicuous part of the flower, assumes an infinite variety of forms. It may be lobed, divided, or spurred; it may be slipper-shaped as in paphiopedilums, or trumpet-shaped as in other genera; it may have various appendages; it may be twisted or curved into complicated structures that recall old legends of the orchid's magical powers. The structure of the labellum, or lip, varies considerably from species to species in each genus, but its function is always the same—to assist in the fertilization of the flower.

The complex lips are really simple mechanical devices. Some, as in *Calopogon pulchellus* (see plate 24), are baited with imitation stamens, apparently loaded with pollen to attract insects. Others, as in *Coryanthes maculatus* (see plate 130), are bucket-shaped with a small quantity of water in them. Petals and sepals grasp the pollinator and drop him into the bucket; he emerges from the flower through tunnel-like structures and is loaded with pollen. In such ways the future of the orchids is secured.

The labellum may also form a lid hinged with a claw-like appendage. When the flower opens, the labellum turns around and falls back, covering the column and enclosing the insect. The device remains closed while the insect is inside, but if movement ceases, the lid soon opens again. The insect is freed, and the flower awaits its next pollinator.

Bulbophyllum barbigerum has a lip with layers of very fine hairs. At the end of the lip a delicate set of long purple threads waves in the slightest breeze, the constant motion attracting the pollinator. Many species within the genus *Pterostylis* have sensitive labellums: when touched by the weight of even the smallest insect, the labellum springs up to the column and imprisons the pollinator, dumping him into an intoxicating liquid. As he drunkenly staggers to make his escape, the insect carries off pollen.

Many orchids seem to mimic insects deliberately so that they can lure insect pollinators and thus ensure reproduction. The bee orchid, *Trichoceros parviflorus* (see plate 189), is a fine example. The male bee, thinking he sees a female, is attracted to the flower and is snared.

The highly sophisticated shapes and forms of the flowers serve to trap the pollinator once it is lured to the plant; scents and colors are other entrapments orchids use to ensure themselves a continued place in nature.

Many cypripediums lure their victims, usually flies, with a somewhat fetid odor. Others, in the genus *Cryp-*

tostylis, are more subtle; their scent simulates the odor of the female insect. Coryanthes orchids drug their pollinators and then push them down an oiled chute into the flower, where they are drenched in pollen. When they recover, they crawl out to complete their role in nature.

By these deceptions orchids ensure their survival, and the appearance, smell, or shape of the labellum is matched to their selective system of pollinators. Often the flowers can be pollinated only by a specific member of a single variety of insect belonging to a single species. Such selectivity assures the plant of its continuation as a distinct species and reduces the changes of hybridization by crossbreeding.

Flowers of the Four Seasons

Orchids have been called flowers of the four seasons because some plants bloom in spring and summer and others in fall and winter. Generally, they bloom once a year and are quite dependable. Flowers are produced in a rainbow of colors, with perhaps yellow and brown predominating, as in many oncidiums and odontoglossums. Apple green appears frequently; ironically, lavender, the color of the popular cattleya, is not very common, nor is true pink. Scarlet, orange, blue, and virtually all other color combinations are found, except for true black, which does not exist. The so-called black orchid, *Coelogyne pandurata* (see plate 35), has a very dark green-purple lip. Colors may also be in pastel shades, delicate and gay, or they may be vibrant and bold, as in many of the hybrid paphiopedilums.

There is a remarkable range in the size of flowers and the texture. Some bulbophyllums and platyclinis species bear blooms less than 1/32 inch in diameter, but certain species of sobralia flaunt flowers the size of dinner plates. Some flowers have such transparent texture that you can almost see through them. Others, like ascocentrums, have sepals and petals that appear crystalline in sunlight, and many paphiopedilums have a waxy texture.

Just as the flowers themselves are diversified, so is the method of bearing blooms. Many species have a solitary bloom on a short stem; others have hundreds of flowers on long sprays. Flowers may come from the base of the plant (as in the lycastes) or may appear on stems borne from the leaf axils (such as the angraecums and vandas). The stems may be pendent, reaching 6 or 7 feet long in

Dendrobium superbum, or they may be stiffly erect, to 9 or 10 feet high in *Schomburgkia tibicinis*. Some trichopilias bear flowers that hug the pot rim, and acinetas and stanhopeas produce flowers on vertical stems 3 or 4 feet long. (These plants should be in open baskets; in pots, the flower spike will often break the clay bottom to bloom!) Many cirrhopetalums and bulbophyllums bear flowers in a cluster of twenty or thirty tiny blossoms, a spherical bouquet that is an incredible sight.

Eighty percent of orchids are intensely fragrant. *Lycaste aromatica* has a scent of cinnamon; the odor of musk is easily recognizable in *Dendrobium moschatum,* while *Maxillaria atropurpurea* has a delicious scent of violet. *Dendrobium superbum* smells like rhubarb, and *Oncidium ornithorhynchum* is reminiscent of new-mown hay. Many angraecum and aerides flowers have a heavy fragrance much like gardenias, and *Brassavola nodosa* is so intensely scented that one flower perfumes a room. Mexican stanhopeas have medicinal (but not unpleasant) scents of menthol or camphor, most noticeable in the morning or early evening.

Most orchid flowers stay fresh far longer than roses or carnations. Cymbidiums are vibrant on the plant for two months; cattleyas last for a month. Many species of oncidium, cut and placed in a vase of water, last more than four weeks, and lycaste flowers are colorful on the plant for six weeks. A few orchids are short-lived: stanhopeas last a few days, and sobralias fade in three days.

Common Names of Orchids

Common orchid names are often associated with animals and insects (for example, the butterfly orchid, the moth orchid, the bee or spider orchid, the cow-horn orchid, and the foxtail orchid) because the shape of the flower resembles a particular insect or characteristic part of an animal. Orchid names may also have religious connotations: *Peristeria elata* is the Holy Ghost orchid; in Guatemala, *Lycaste skinneri* var. *virginalis* is the white nun and *Epidendrum radicans* the crucifix orchid because of the shape of the flowers. The Mexican *Schomburgkia* (*Laelia*) *superbiens* is known as St. Joseph's staff and *Oncidium tigrinum* is the "flower of the dead" because it blooms on All Souls' Day and is used to decorate graves. Perhaps the loveliest name belongs to *Phalaenopsis amabilis,* known in Java as the moon orchid because its blooms last longer than a moon, a month or more.

CONTINUED ON PAGE 197

PLATE 76

Dendrobium

D. chrysotoxum

South China and the Himalayas to Burma, Thailand, and Laos

This plant is medium-sized and bears a pendent scape composed of 1-inch bright yellow flowers. As a genus it was monographed in 1910 by Fritz Kraenzlin, but his work was at best fragmentary, and many species have since been added. (Photograph courtesy of Joyce R. Wilson.)

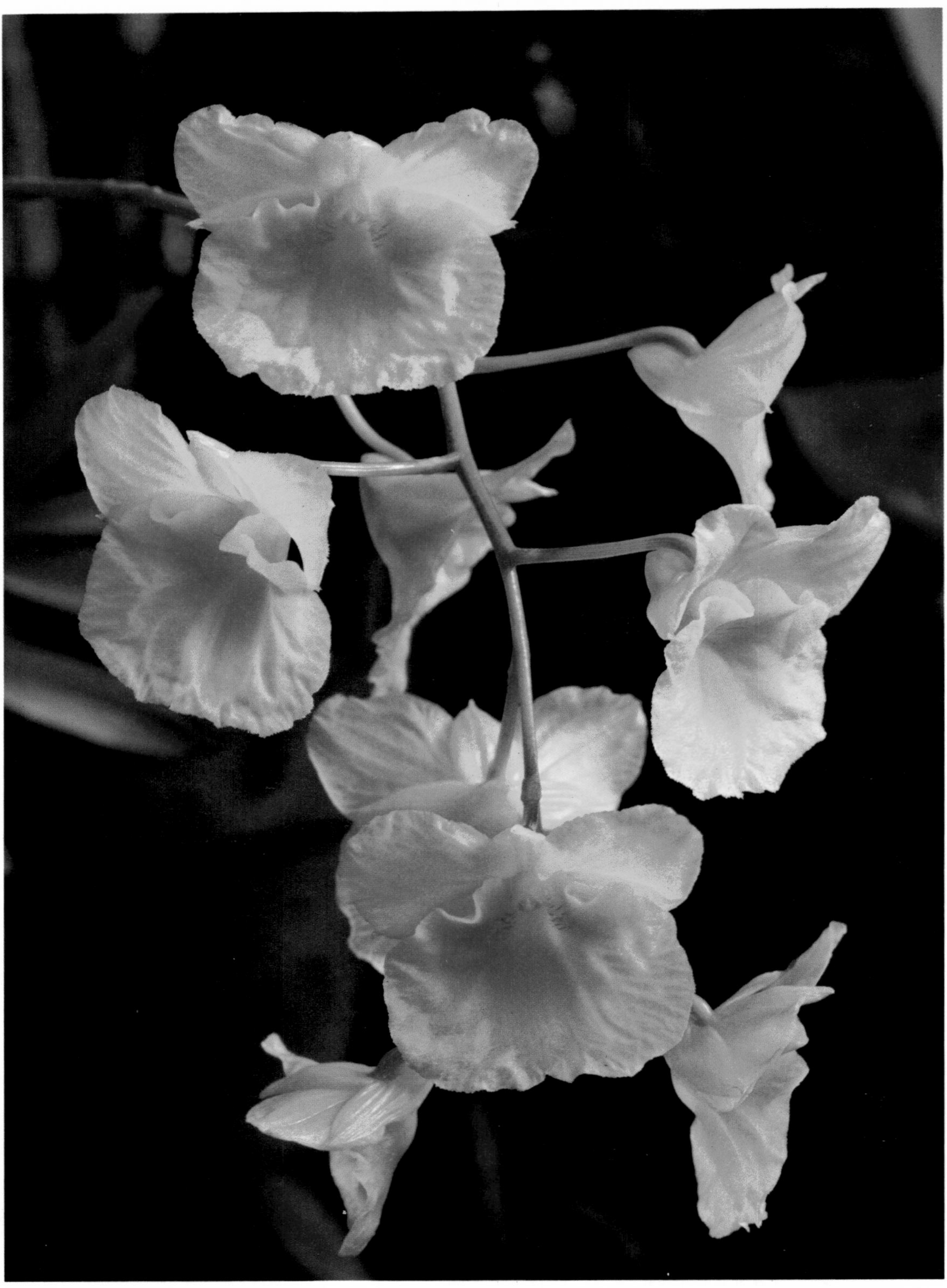

PLATE 77
Dendrobium
D. aggregatum var. *majus*
The Himalayas to Burma, India

This plant, small and compact, produces dozens of flowers on pendent scapes. Though a somewhat difficult variety to grow, it is well worth the effort. An orchid of great charm. (Photograph courtesy of Guy Burgess.)

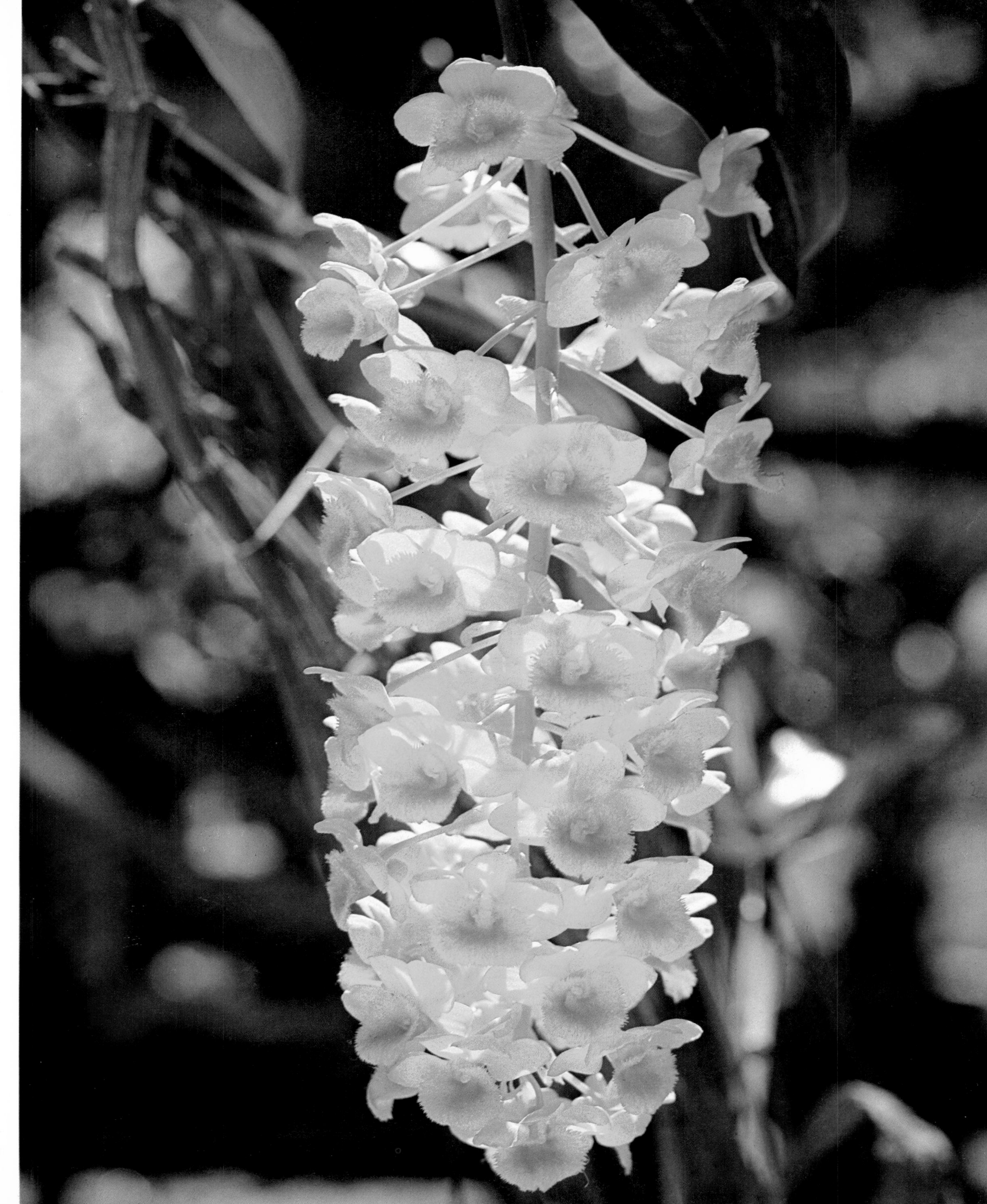

PLATE 78
Dendrobium
D. densiflorum
The Himalayas to Burma

Discovered by Dr. Nathaniel Wallich in the early nineteenth century, this species flowered for the first time in England in Messrs. Loddiges' nursery in 1830. The plant produces scapes from nodes along branches; the inflorescence resembles a large bunch of grapes with as many as thirty flowers per scape. (Photograph courtesy of Joyce R. Wilson.)

PLATE 79
Dendrobium
D. dalhousieanum
Burma

This large plant grows to 6 feet tall and bears 5-inch flowers of beige and maroon. It was introduced into England in 1837 by John Gibson, who obtained it from the Calcutta Botanic Gardens. (Photograph courtesy of Andrew R. Addkison.)

PLATE 80
Dendrobium
D. devonianum
China and the Himalayas to Burma, Thailand, and Vietnam

The flowers of this fragrant orchid are creamy white, tinged with pink. The petals are tipped purplish-magenta, and the lip is white, purple-bordered, and blotched orange at the base. A spectacular plant, it was first grown successfully in the nineteenth century by Sir Joseph Paxton. (Photograph courtesy of Andrew R. Addkison.)

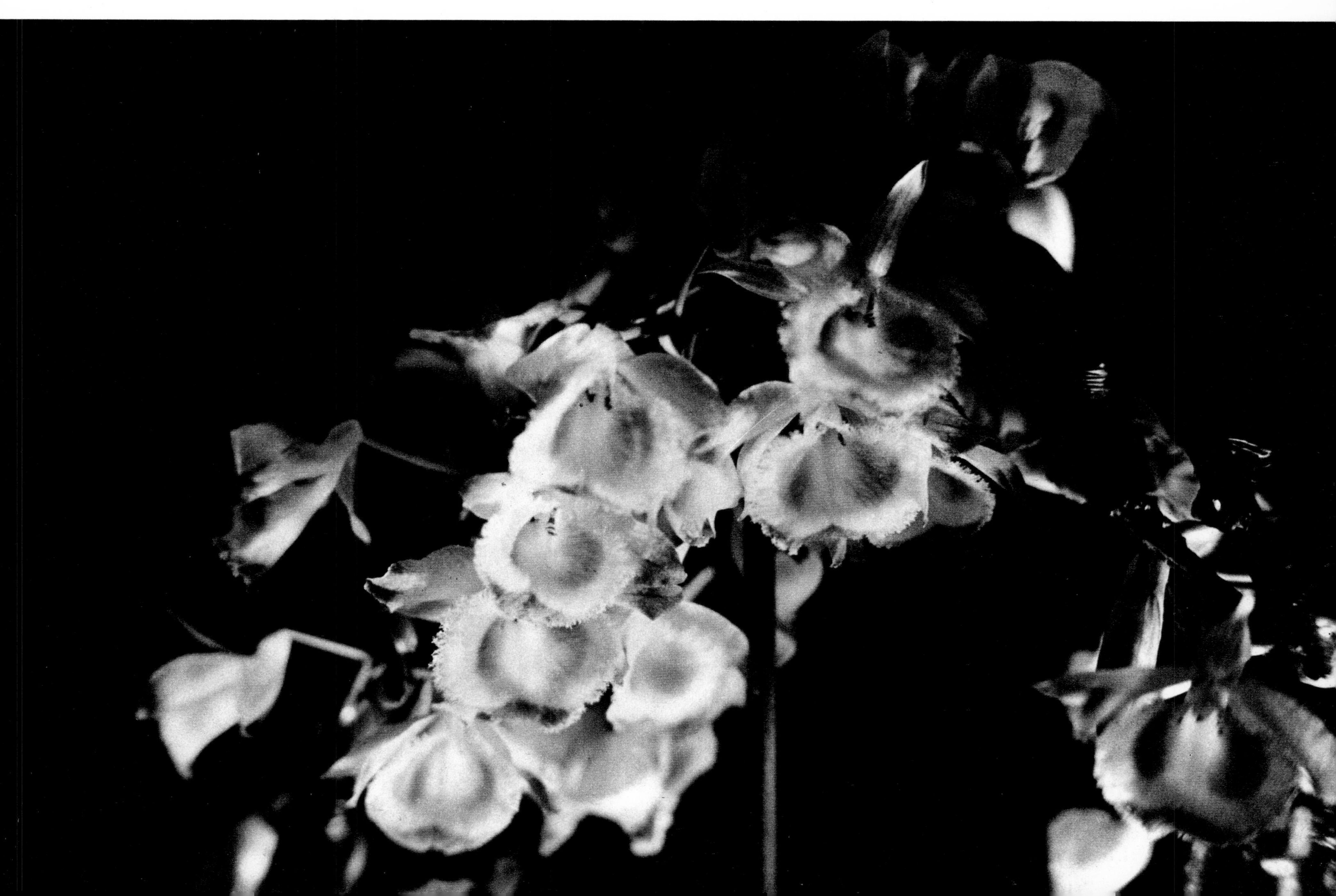

PLATE 81
Dendrobium
D. phalaenopsis
Ceylon

Originally procured from northern Australia and New Guinea, this singularly beautiful orchid has arching stems of many flowers. The color varies from deep purple to pinkish-white. See plate 88. (Photograph courtesy of Hermann Pigors.)

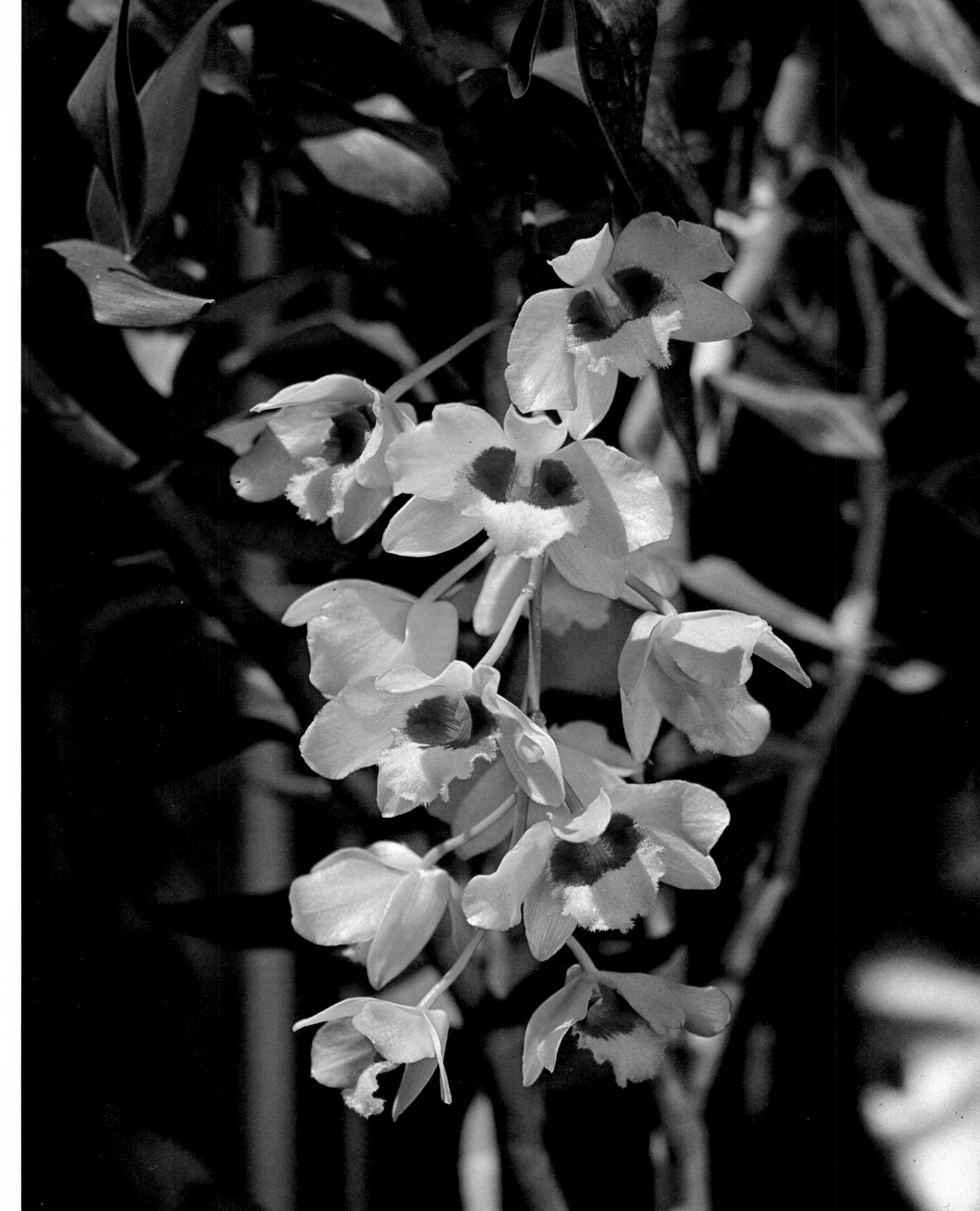

PLATE 82
Dendrobium
D. Gatton Sunray (hybrid)

This fine dendrobium, a cross between *Dendrobium dahlhousieanum* var. *luteum* and *D. Illustre,* was obtained in 1919 and registered then. It is a floriferous hybrid with hundreds of flowers to a mature plant. (Photograph courtesy of Joyce R. Wilson.)

ATE 83
ndrobium
phalaenopsis: hybrid

is dark-purple-flowering hybrid of *ndrobium phalaenopsis* parentage is ssibly of Hawaiian origin. It is riferous, bearing a profusion of wers. (Photograph courtesy of Guy rgess.)

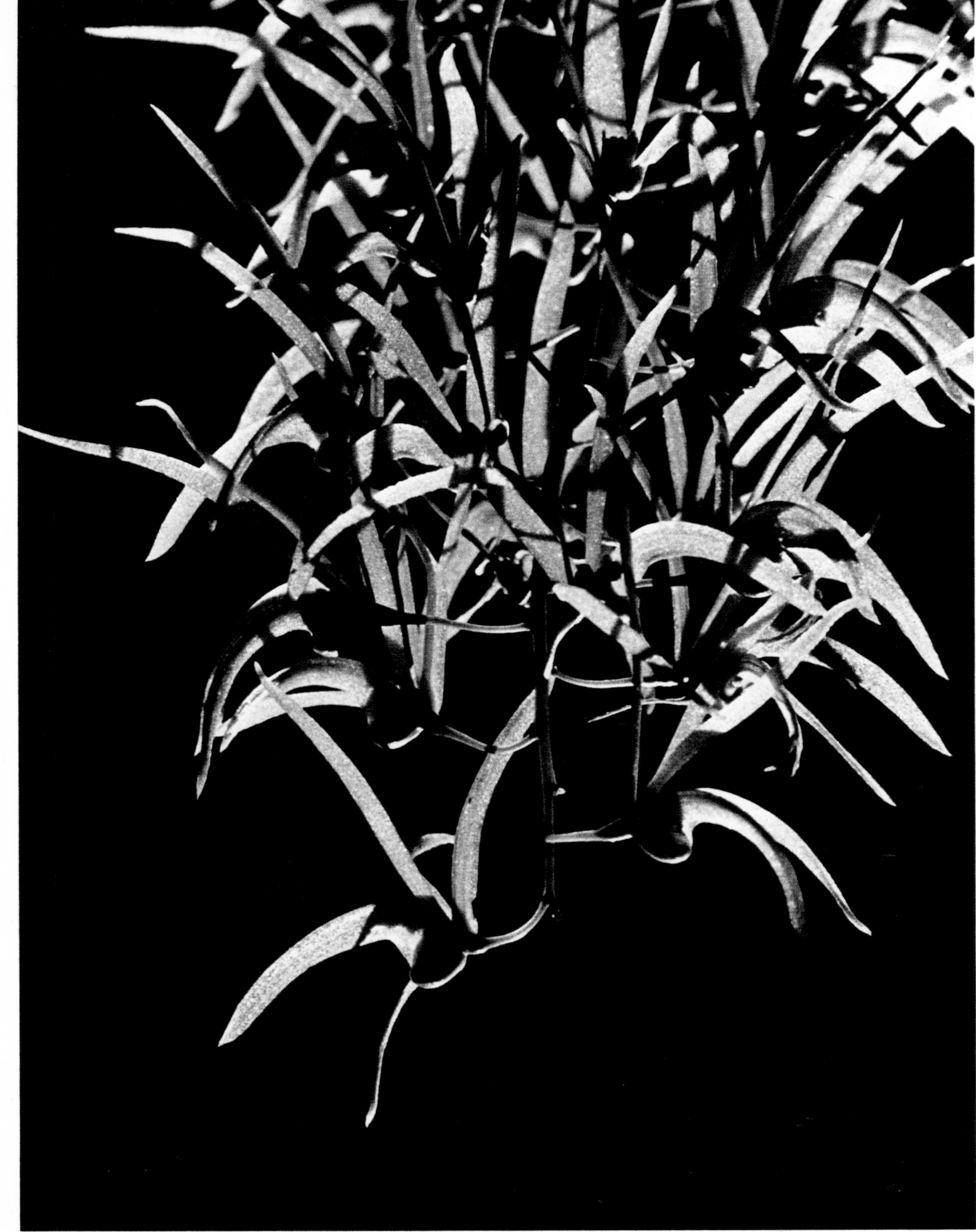

PLATE 84 ▶
Dendrobium
D. linguiforme
Australia, New South Wales, Queensland

A miniature, this orchid has 1-inch succulent leaves and ½-inch fragrant white flowers with narrow sepals and petals. It is shown here greatly magnified. (Photograph courtesy of Joyce R. Wilson.)

PLATE 85
Dendrobium
D. moschatum
The Himalayas to Burma, Thailand to Laos

The genus name refers to the epiphytic habit, meaning "living on a tree." Some dendrobiums are deciduous, but this one is evergreen and can grow to 6 feet high. The blooms are musk-scented. (Photograph courtesy of Joyce R. Wilson.)

PLATE 86
Dendrobium
D. nobile
South China, the Himalayas, Thailand, Laos, Vietnam, Formosa

One of the deciduous dendrobiums, this species was supposedly depicted in Chinese drawings. The first live plant in England was brought from China by John Reeves, who purchased it in the market at Macao about 1837. The flowers form on upper nodes of generally leafless cane pseudobulbs. Many horticultural variants have been produced. (Photograph courtesy of Joyce R. Wilson.)

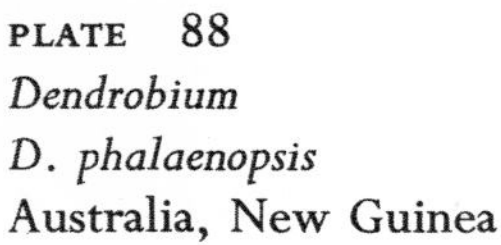

PLATE 87
Dendrobium
D. New Guinea (hybrid)

This very floriferous orchid bears masses of whitish-yellow flowers marked with red. An amenable plant, it grows well in a moderately warm temperature. It is a cross between *D. macrophyllum* and *D. atroviolaceum*. (Photograph courtesy of Joyce R. Wilson.)

PLATE 88
Dendrobium
D. phalaenopsis
Australia, New Guinea

This is one of the few orchids that bloom on old pseudobulbs year after year. It has large flowers, to 4 inches across, varying from white to rosy-mauve or rich purple. The plant has cane growth to 5 feet. Similar in appearance to *D. bigibbum*, and sometimes listed as a variety of this species, it is a popular plant with hobbyists. Many fine hybrids have been developed. See plate 81. (Photograph courtesy of Guy Burgess.)

PLATE 89
Dendrobium
D. superbum
Philippines

A deciduous orchid, it was first discovered by Hugh Cuming in Manila about 1836 and flowered in England in 1839, at Messrs. Loddiges' nursery in Hackney. The plant bears pendent leafless scapes, sometimes 4 feet long, with large scented blooms. An outstanding species. (Photograph courtesy of Joyce R. Wilson.)

PLATE 90
Dendrobium
D. superbum var. *dearei*
Philippines

This orchid is the white form of *D. superbum*. See plate 89 for description. (Photograph courtesy of Joyce R. Wilson.)

PLATE 91
Dendrobium
D. pierardii
India, China, the Himalayas to Burma, Thailand

With cane-type growth to 5 feet, this deciduous plant has pink flowers produced on leafless stems. First sent to the Royal Botanic Gardens at Kew by Dr. William Roxburgh in the early part of the nineteenth century, it flowered in the Liverpool Botanic Garden in 1821. (Photograph courtesy of Andrew R. Addkison.)

PLATE 92 ▶
Dendrobium
D. schuetzei
Philippines

This dwarf orchid has beautiful 2-inch white blooms. As a genus it was monographed in 1910 by Fritz Kraenzlin. *D. schuetzei* is known for its lasting quality—the blooms stay fresh for two months. (Photograph courtesy of Joyce R. Wilson.)

PLATE 94 ▶

Ansellia

A. africana

Tropical and South Africa

This orchid, with its flamboyant markings, is native to a large area of tropical Africa. Represented is a select form in which the brown markings are deeper and richer than in the standard species. It was photographed in the garden of Klaus Abegg, Colorado Springs, Colo. (Photograph courtesy of Guy Burgess.)

PLATE 93

Dendrobium

D. victoriae-reginae

Philippines

With cane growth, this species bears magnificent 1-inch blue-violet flowers. It is highly prized and rather rare. (Photograph courtesy of Guy Burgess.)

LATE 95
nsellia
. *gigantea* var. *nilotica*
ropical and South Africa

he genus name is from John Ansell,
gardener who, on expedition, found
n epiphyte growing on an oil palm
ee. Later, the dried specimen was
nt to England to Dr. John Lindley,
ho named the genus for the
iscoverer. The plant had dramatic
right yellow blooms with dark brown
ots. (Photograph courtesy of Joyce
. Wilson.)

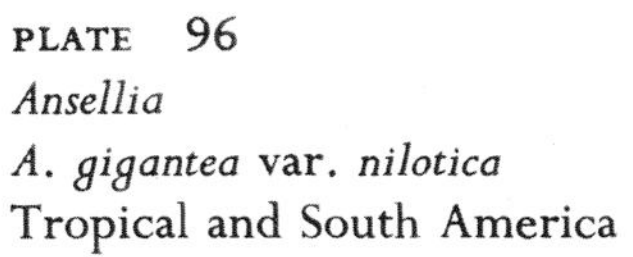

PLATE 96
Ansellia
A. gigantea var. *nilotica*
Tropical and South America

A close-up of the flower. See plate 95 for description. (Photograph courtesy of Joyce R. Wilson.)

PLATE 97
Galeandra
G. devoniana
Colombia, British Guiana

This very handsome species has grassy leaves and grows to about 50 inches tall. First described by M. R. Schomburgk about 1838, it was sent to Dr. John Lindley. The species is named after the Duke of Devonshire, at that time one of the successful cultivators of orchids. *G. devoniana* can be grown as a terrestrial or as an epiphyte. (Photograph courtesy of Joyce R. Wilson.)

PLATE 98 ▶
Calanthe
C. Bryan (hybrid)

One of the fine calanthe hybrids, this deciduous beauty bears white flowers, which are usually marked with magenta. It blooms at Christmastime or shortly afterward. A cross between *C. vestita* and *C. williamsii,* it was obtained by Clive Cookson in 1894. One of the first successful orchid crosses. (Photograph courtesy of Joyce R. Wilson.)

PLATE 99
Calanthe
C. William Murray (hybrid)

Though it bears a different name, this orchid is the same as C. Bryan. See plate 98 for description. (Photograph courtesy of Joyce R. Wilson.)

PLATE 100
Phaius
P. tankervilliae (grandifolius)

Brought from China about 1778 by Dr. John Fothergill, this was one of the earliest tropical orchids in British collections. A terrestrial plant, it produces erect spikes bearing many flowers. (Photograph courtesy of Guy Burgess.)

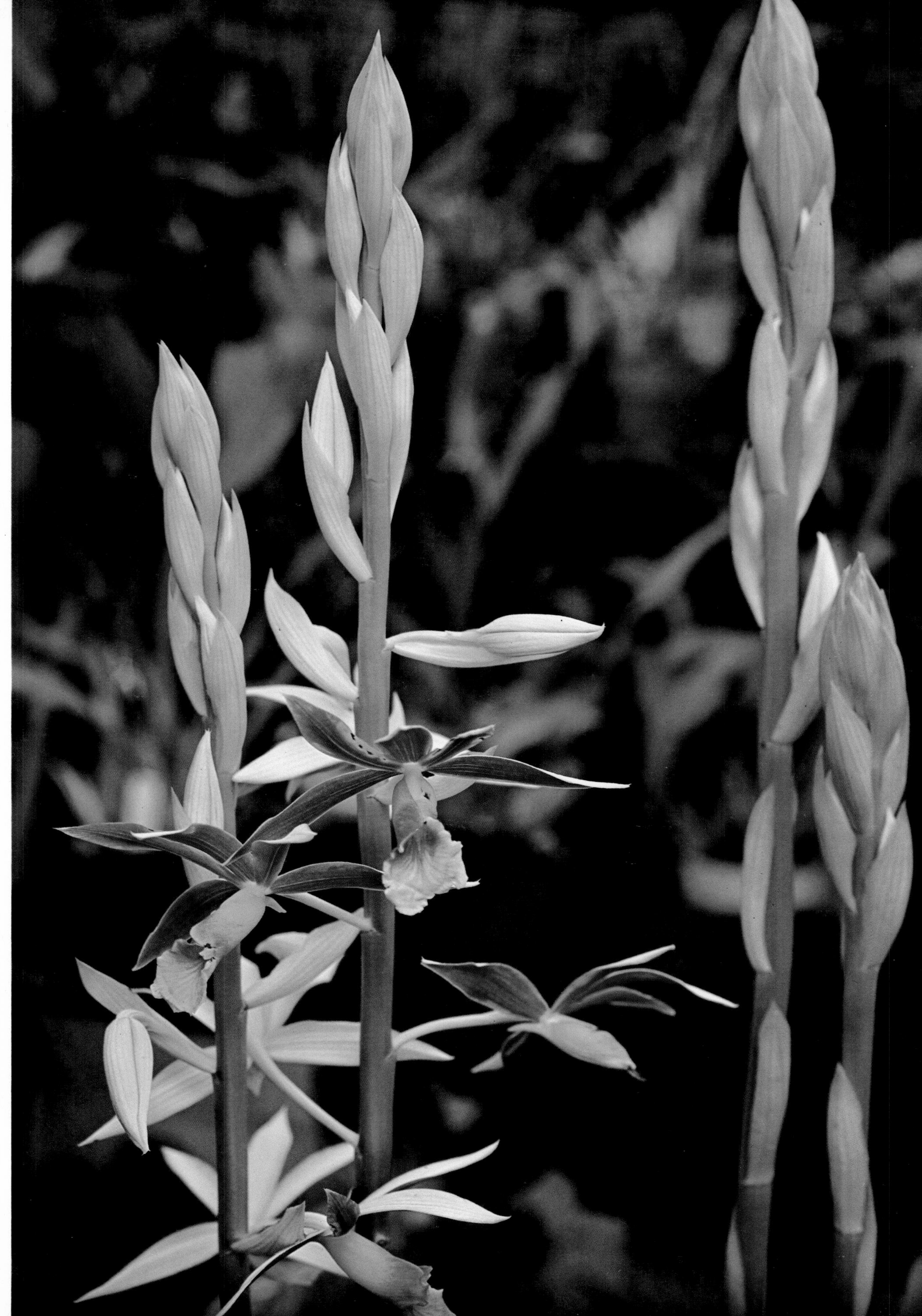

PLATE 101
Phaius
P. Gravesii (hybrid)

A cross obtained by N. C. Cookson between *P. grandifolius* and *P. wallichii,* it flowered first in the collection of H. Graves of Orange, N. J., and was dedicated to him. (Photograph courtesy of Guy Burgess.)

PLATE 103
Acanthophippium (Acanthephippium)
A. mantinianum (montanus)
Philippines

With fragrant tulip-shaped flowers (2 inches across), this is a rare terrestrial orchid that is easy to grow. The author's blooms yearly in his garden room. (Photographed courtesy of Joyce R. Wilson.)

PLATE 102
Phaius
P. maculatus
Northern India, Japan

Big, to 40 inches tall, and showy, this robust species was first introduced about 1882. The foliage (not shown here) is atypical among orchids; it is of rather thin texture and decorated with yellow spots. (Photograph courtesy of Joyce R. Wilson.)

PLATE 104
Bletia
B. purpurea
Florida, West Indies, Mexico, Central America, northern South America

The genus *Bletia* was founded by the Spanish botanists Hipólito Ruiz Lopez and José Antonio Pavon on *B. catenulata,* a Peruvian species allied to *B. sherrattiana,* very rarely seen in cultivation, and dedicated by them to their countryman Don Luis Blet, an herbalist and apothecary. Growing from a cormlike root, this plant is often confused with *B. verecunda*. It produces handsome magenta flowers, small but desirable. (Photograph courtesy of Joyce R. Wilson.)

PLATE 105 ▶
Bletia
B. purpurea
Florida, West Indies, Mexico, Central America, northern South America

A close-up of the flower. See plate 104 for description. (Photograph courtesy of Hermann Pigors.)

PLATE 106
Chysis
C. laevis
Mexico to Costa Rica

This species has long pendent canes with paper-thin green leaves. The flowers, 1 to 2 inches across, are a striking brown. It was introduced from Mexico by G. Barker, in whose collection at Springfield, near Birmingham, England, it flowered for the first time in 1840. (Photograph courtesy of Joyce R. Wilson.)

PLATE 107
Eulophidium
E. pulchrum
Africa, Madagascar

A small plant up to 12 inches high, with pseudobulbs, it bears a solitary leaf and has an erect spike of small but attractive flowers. The plant is rarely seen in cultivation. (Photograph courtesy of Joyce R. Wilson.)

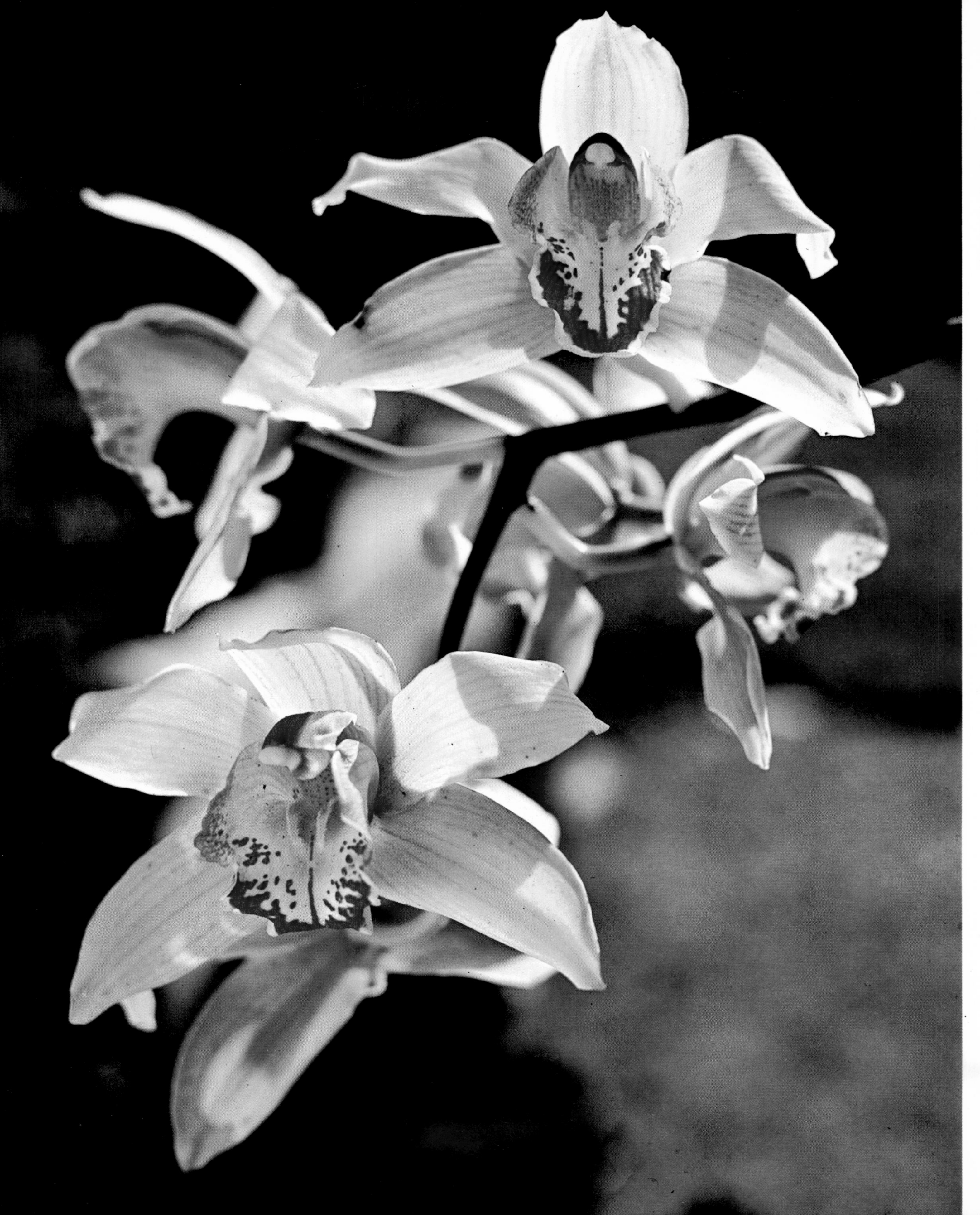

PLATE 108
Cymbidium
C. Alexette (hybrid)

The dainty refinement of this exquisite orchid is a perfect counterpart of its name. It is a cross between C. Alexanderi and C. Janette. (Photograph courtesy of Joyce R. Wilson.)

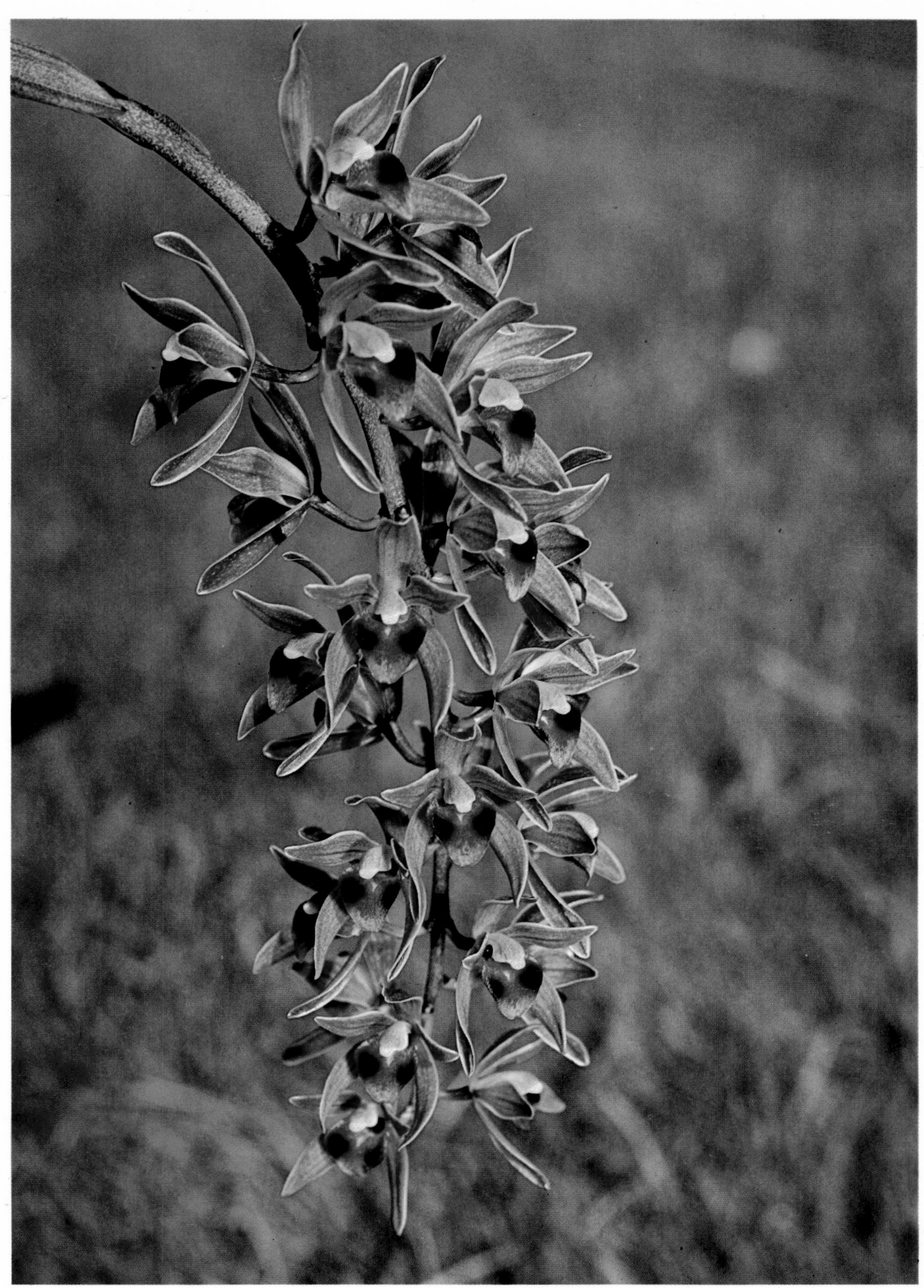

PLATE 109
Cymbidium
C. devonianum
India

This orchid was introduced to England about 1837, finally flowering there in 1843. It remained a rare plant until 1865. The species is variable in color and is one of the few cymbidium species still cultivated. (Photograph courtesy of Joyce R. Wilson.)

PLATE 110
Cymbidium
C. Atlantis Cameo (hybrid)

Cymbidiums, so popular in California, are terrestrial orchids. Most are large plants and bear hundreds of flowers. This one is a cross between C. Alexanderi and *C. erythrostylum*. (Photograph courtesy of Joyce R. Wilson.)

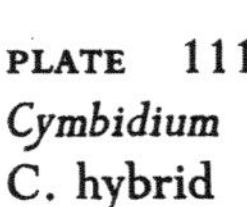

PLATE 111
Cymbidium
C. hybrid

The flowers of cymbidiums are noted for their exquisite form and color. This holds true for this hybrid of unknown parentage. The blooms of this plant are pinkish-white and have centers marked with a dark pink—a particularly handsome combination. (Photograph courtesy of Joyce R. Wilson.)

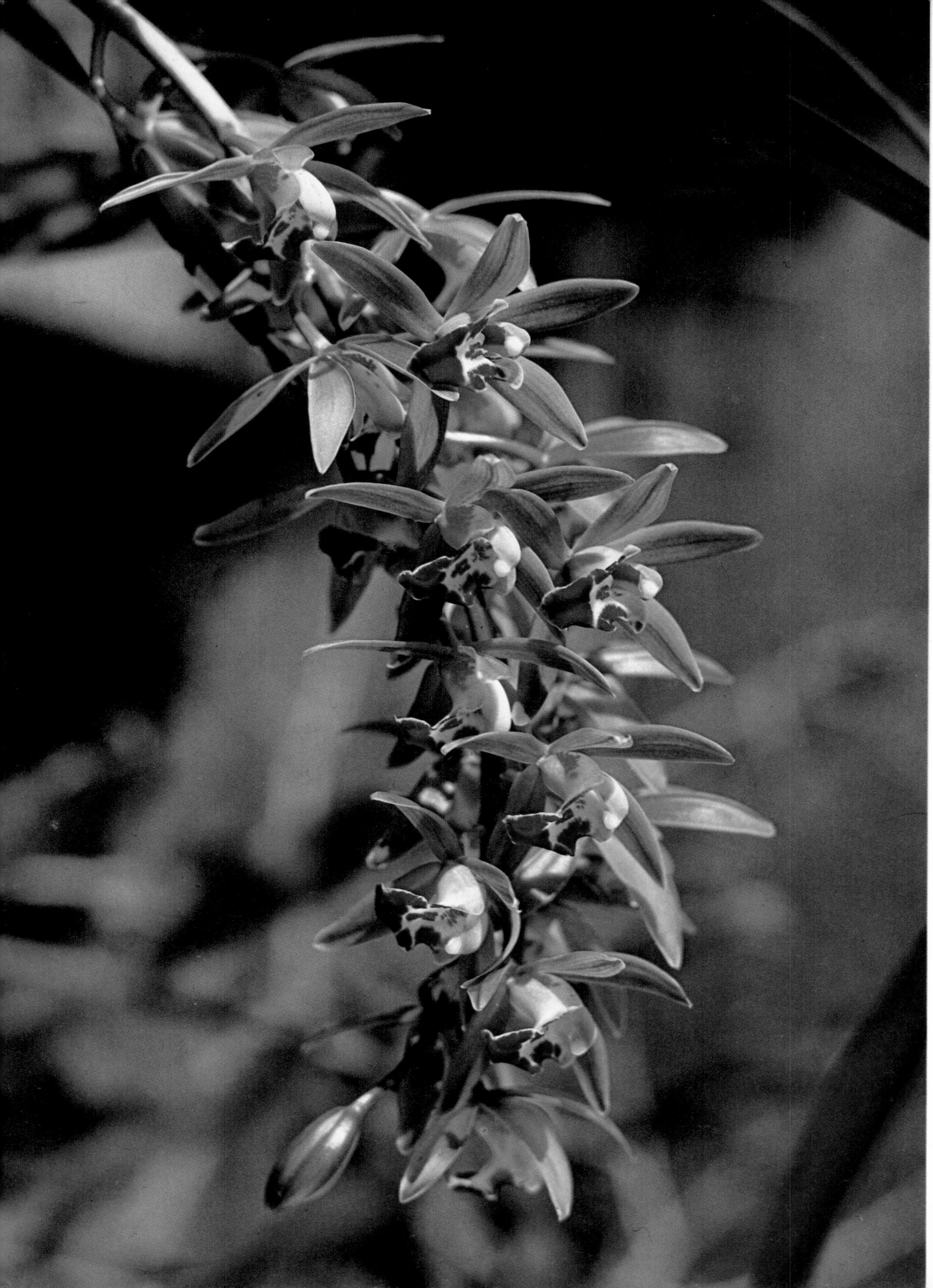

PLATE 112
Cymbidium
C. Orchid Conference (hybrid)

This highly distinctive product of man's orchid-breeding ingenuity truly lives up to its name. A luxuriant row of tightly clustered flowers adorns the gracefully arching scape. Orchid Conference is a cross between C. Sola and *C. pumilum*. (Photograph courtesy of Joyce R. Wilson.)

PLATE 113 ▶
Cymbidium
C. Tapestry 'Red Glory' (hybrid)

Large flowers with dramatic red markings characterize this fine cymbidium. In every respect, 'Red Glory' is a most desirable orchid. It is a cross between C. Khyber Pass and C. Voodoo. (Photograph courtesy of Joyce R. Wilson.)

PLATE 114
Cymbidium
C. Oriental Legend (hybrid)

This second-generation miniature orchid bears medium-size flowers that are peach to pink in color. Its many dramatic markings make it especially interesting. It is a cross between *C. pumilum* and C. Babylon. (Photograph courtesy of Hermann Pigors.)

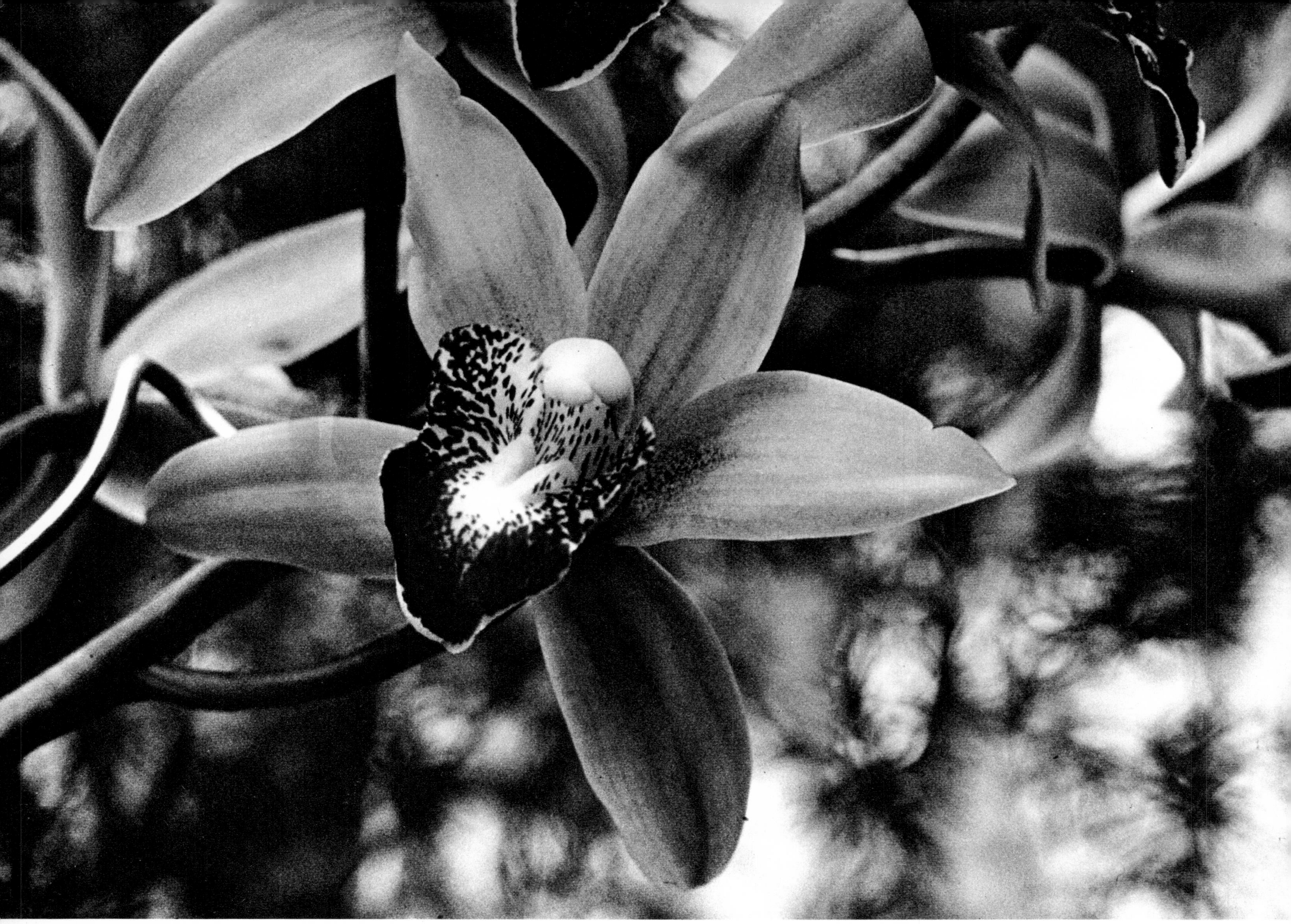

PLATE 115
Cymbidium
C. Peter Pan 'Greensleeves' HCC/AOS (hybrid)

An early flowering miniature, this cymbidium bears small green flowers in profusion. It is pleasantly scented and sometimes blooms twice a year. One of the finest of recent cymbidium hybrids. (Photograph courtesy of Hermann Pigors.)

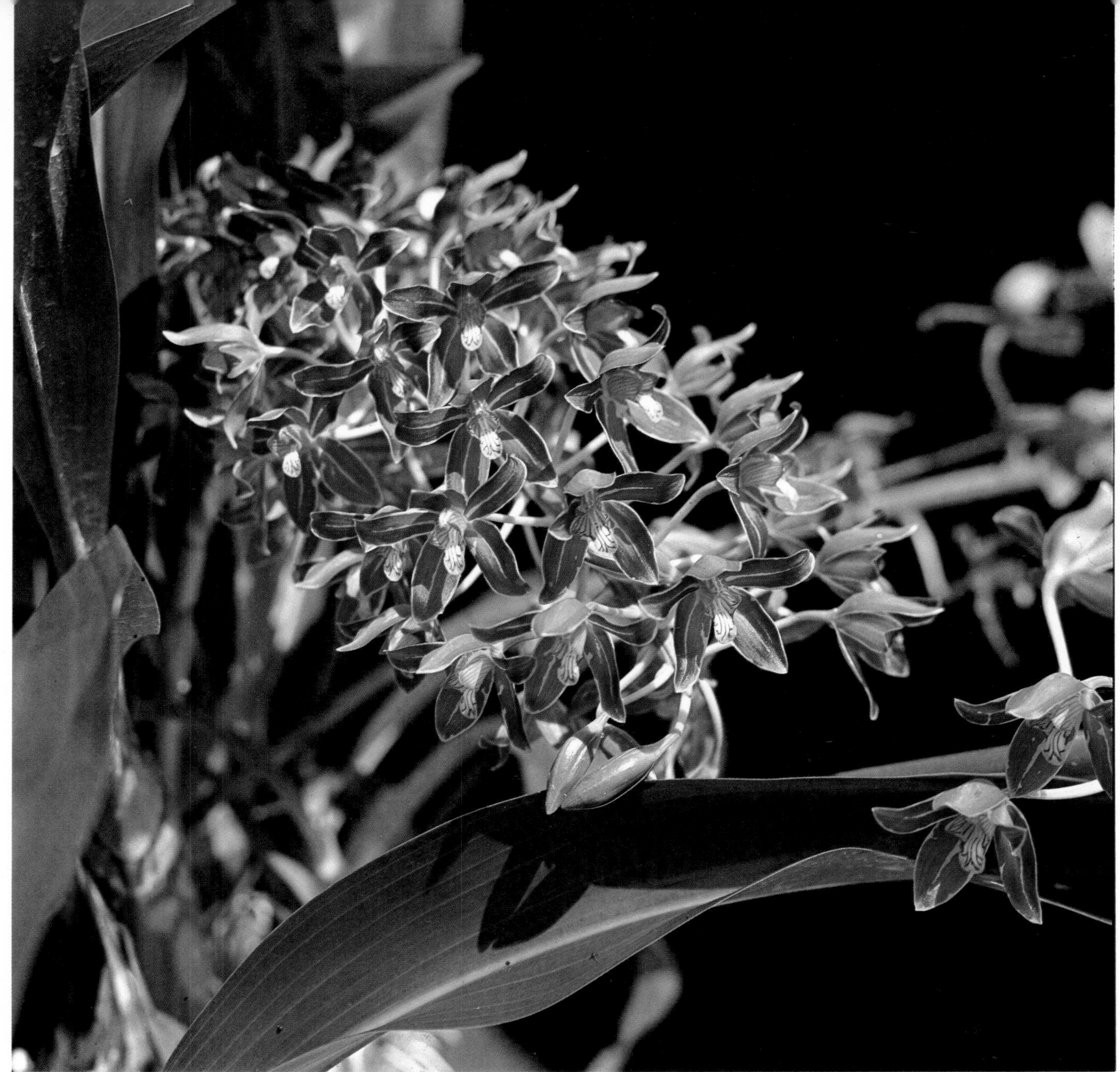

PLATE 116
Grammatophyllum
G. scriptum
Borneo, Philippines, New Guinea, Solomon Islands, Moluccas

Some species of this genus attain a remarkable height of 20 or 30 feet. The generic name, meaning "a mark of character and a leaf," alludes to the markings on the flowers. The author's plant had more than 200 flowers, which stayed fresh over six weeks. *G. scriptum* is sometimes called the letter plant. (Photograph courtesy of Joyce R. Wilson.)

TE 117
rmodes
colossus
sta Rica, Panama

s deciduous orchid bears blooms, iable in hue, on leafless stems. It s introduced by Jósef Warscewicz ut 1850 from the mountains of ntral America at an elevation of 00 to 7,000 feet. (Photograph rtesy of Andrew R. Addkison.)

TE 118
nodes
ineata
temala

eciduous plant with ½-inch brown- ed blooms, it belongs to a genus ome twenty species that extends Mexico throughout Central and h America to Brazil. (Photograph tesy of Andrew R. Addkison.)

PLATE 119
Catasetum
C. cliftonii
Central America

The genus includes some of the most unusual and handsome of all orchidaceous plants. A considerable number have found favor with collectors today. This particular species varies greatly in color and form. (Photograph courtesy of Andrew R. Addkison.)

PLATE 120
Catasetum
C. pileatum (bungerothii)
Venezuela, Colombia, Ecuador

This is an orchid of unusual beauty with unique flower form. The plant itself is small, about 10 inches tall, with flowers sometimes to 7 inches across. Intensely fragrant, it is Venezuela's favorite flower. (Photograph courtesy of Joyce R. Wilson.)

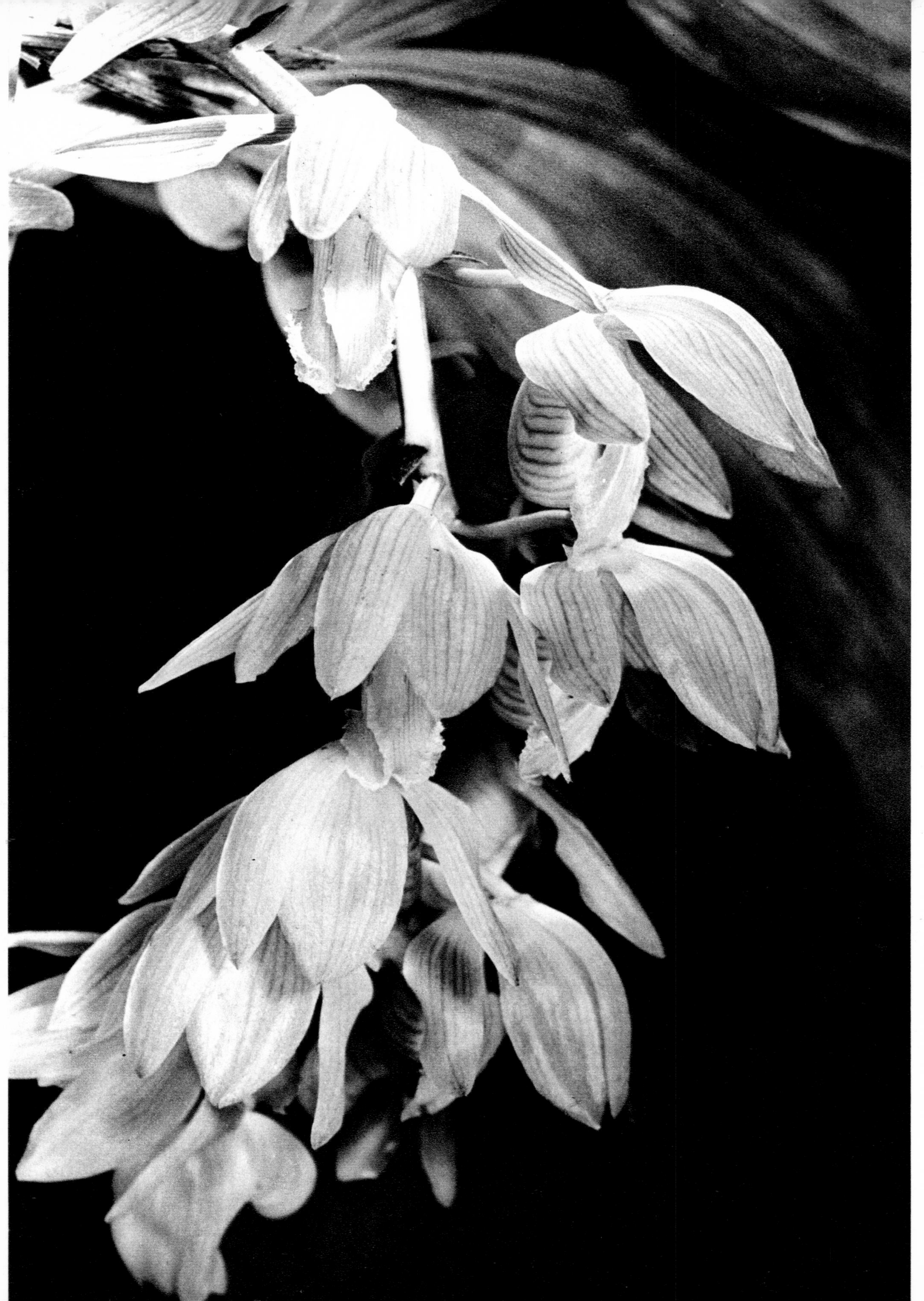

PLATE 122 ▶
Cycnoches
C. egertonianum
Mexico, Guatemala, Colombia, P
Brazil

This orchid has unusual flowers o long pendent scapes. Female flow are shown here. Male flowers, sm in size, are green and dark red. T earliest notice of this species in cultivation occurs in *The Botanical Register* of 1843. (Photograph cou of Hermann Pigors.)

PLATE 121
Catasetum
C. russellianum
Mexico, Guatemala, El Salvador, Honduras, Nicaragua, Panama

Pendent spikes of 2-inch green-striped flowers make this a superlative species; it is generally deciduous. A genus of truly remarkable orchids, it has flowers that are often large, with a hawthorn-like scent. (Photograph courtesy of Hermann Pigors.)

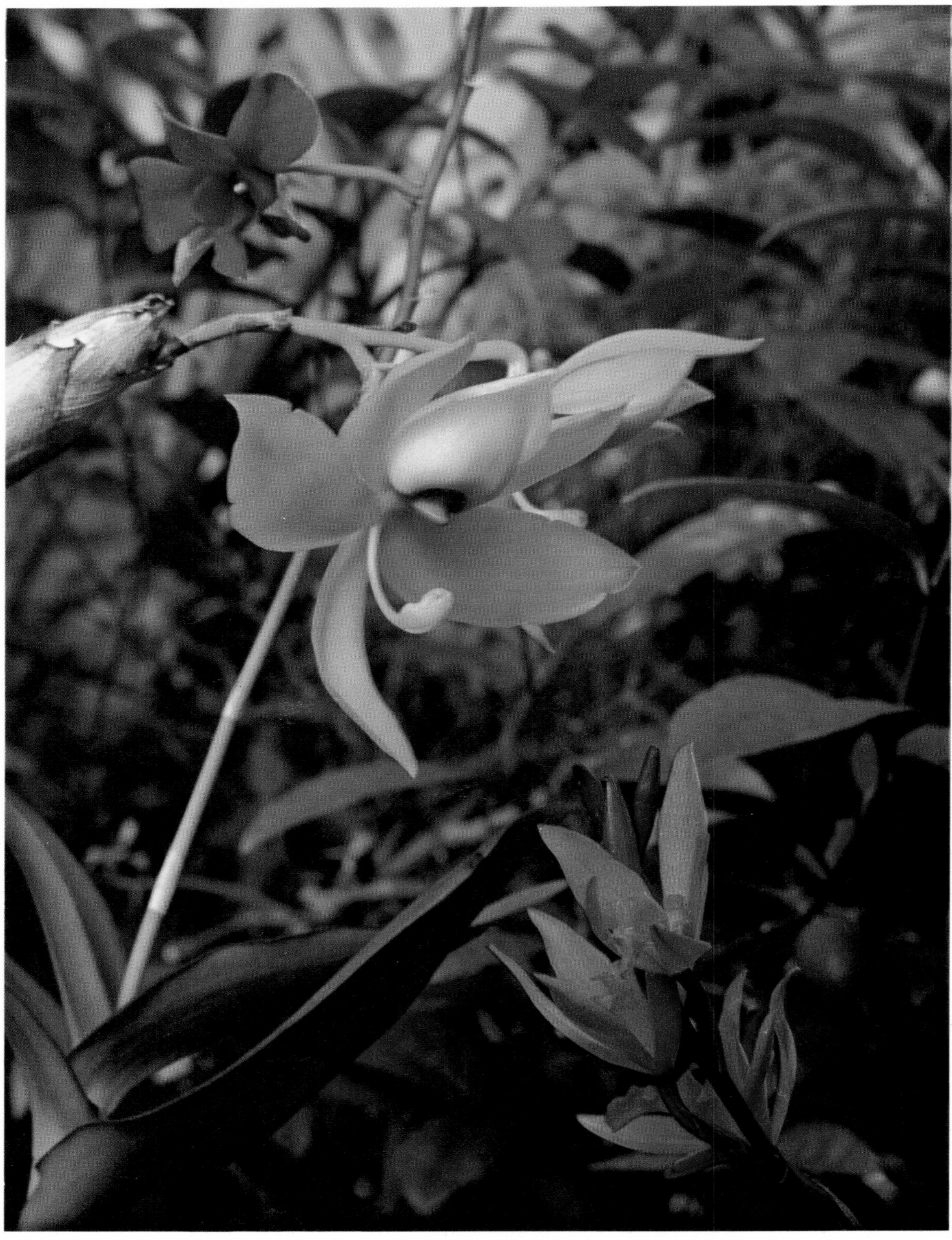

PLATE 123
Cycnoches
C. ventricosum var. *chlorochilum* (center)
Panama, Colombia, Venezuela

Discovered by Karl Moritz in Venezuela in 1838, this species was sent to the Berlin Museum. It flowered in England for the first time about the same year. Because of the shape of the flower, it is popularly known as the swan orchid. The red orchid (top) is a *Dendrobium phalaenopsis* hybrid. The orange orchid (bottom) is a *Laelia cinnabarina*. The marked differences among orchids are made apparent by seeing the three included in this photograph. Note the lip of the cycnoches; usually the species grows with the lip at the bottom of the flower—the reverse is the case here. (Photograph courtesy of Guy Burgess.)

PLATE 124
Acineta
A. humboldtii
Colombia, Venezuela

A rare plant, it is difficult to bring into bloom under cultivation but well worth the extra time and effort. The flower spike grows straight down from the base of the pseudobulb, and, in this case, it broke its clay pot to bloom. The species is alleged to have been discovered by the great traveler F. H. A. von Humboldt in Ecuador, but the first living plant seen in England came from Venezuela and flowered in 1842. To compound the problem of its origin further, the author's plant was imported from Colombia. (Photograph courtesy of Joyce R. Wilson.)

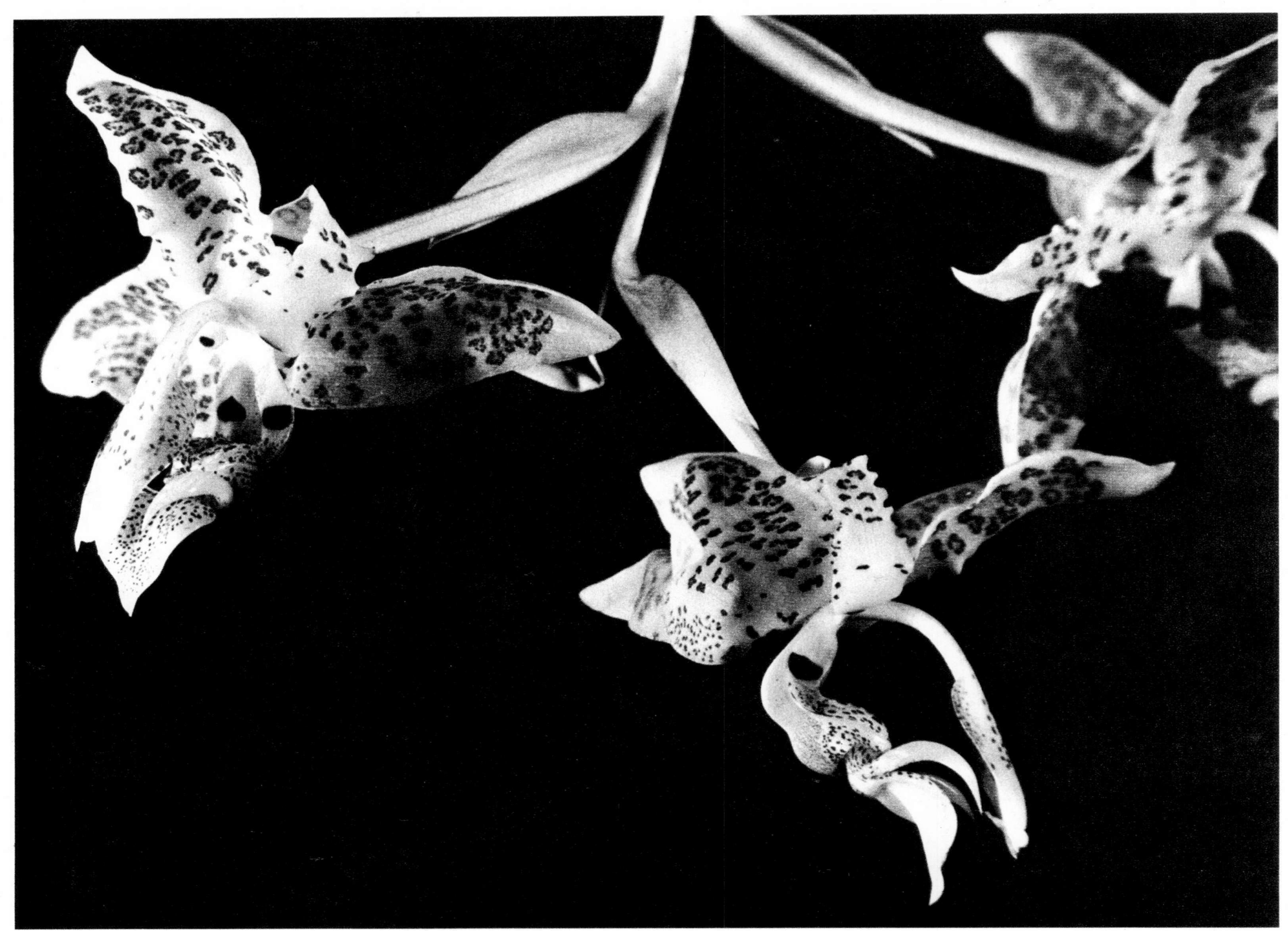

PLATE 125
Stanhopea
S. oculata
Mexico, Honduras, Costa Rica, Panama

This plant has large fragrant flowers, to 6 inches across, borne on pendent scapes. Usually yellow in color, it is a popular summer orchid. (Photograph courtesy of Andrew R. Addkison.)

PLATE 126 ▶
Stanhopea
S. wardii
Mexico to Panama, and possibly South America

This is the best known of the stanhopeas. It was originally introduced to England from La Guayra (the port of Caracas) by Messrs. Loddiges in 1828 through their correspondent Capt. Frank Kingdon-Ward, after whom it was named. (Photograph courtesy of Guy Burgess.)

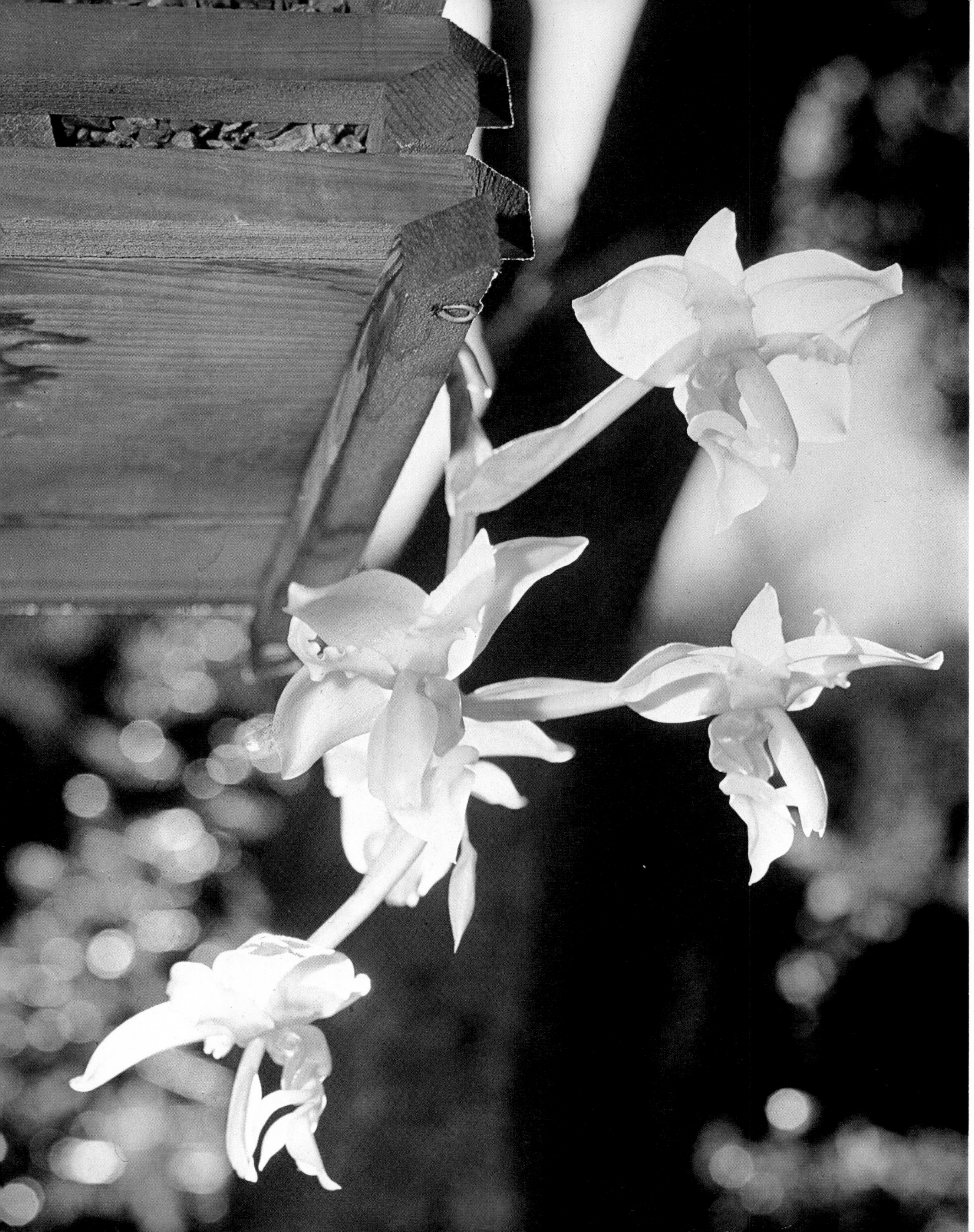

PLATE 127
Stanhopea
S. eburnea
Brazil, Trinidad, Venezuela

This species was first cultivated by Conrad Loddiges in 1824. The first stanhopea introduced in British collections, it flowered in James Bateman's collection at Knypersley in 1832. Although given in many sources as from Brazil, the plants shown here are from Trinidad and Venezuela. (Photograph courtesy of Joyce R. Wilson.)

PLATE 128
Gongora
G. scaphephorus
Peru, Ecuador

Originally described as from Ecuador, this rare orchid is more often found in Peru. The species name, *scaphephorus,* combines two Greek words and means "carrying a crib." The plant bears flowers on long pendent stems, sometimes 24 inches long. Unlike most orchids, this one blooms several times a year. (Photograph courtesy of Joyce R. Wilson.)

PLATE 129
Gongora
G. armeniaca
Nicaragua, Costa Rica, Panama

The genus ranges from Mexico to Peru and Brazil and includes some of the most extraordinary American orchids, such as this colorful yellow-and-red species. Gongoras are usually found growing on trees. (Photograph courtesy of Andrew R. Addkison.)

PLATE 130
Coryanthes
C. maculatus
Panama, Colombia, Venezuela, the Guianas, Brazil

This species has incredible flowers, some 7 inches across, of intricate structure. First found in British Guiana by a Mr. Ankers, it flowered for the first time in England in the Liverpool Botanic Garden in June 1831. (Photograph courtesy of Andrew R. Addkison.)

PLATE 131
Xylobium
X. squalens
Brazil

This orchid, not often seen in cultivation, offers ornamental foliage and small but lovely beige-white flowers. Even without flowers, it is a handsome green leafy plant. (Photograph courtesy of Joyce R. Wilson.)

PLATE 132 ▶
Stenocoryne
S. secundad
Brazil

A little-known genus, it has flowers that are unusual among orchids—bell-shaped and orange. (Photograph courtesy of Joyce R. Wilson.)

PLATE 133
Bifrenaria
B. harrisoniae var. *alba*
Brazil

Shown here is the rare white variety of the species. See plate 135 for description. (Photograph courtesy of Andrew R. Addkison.)

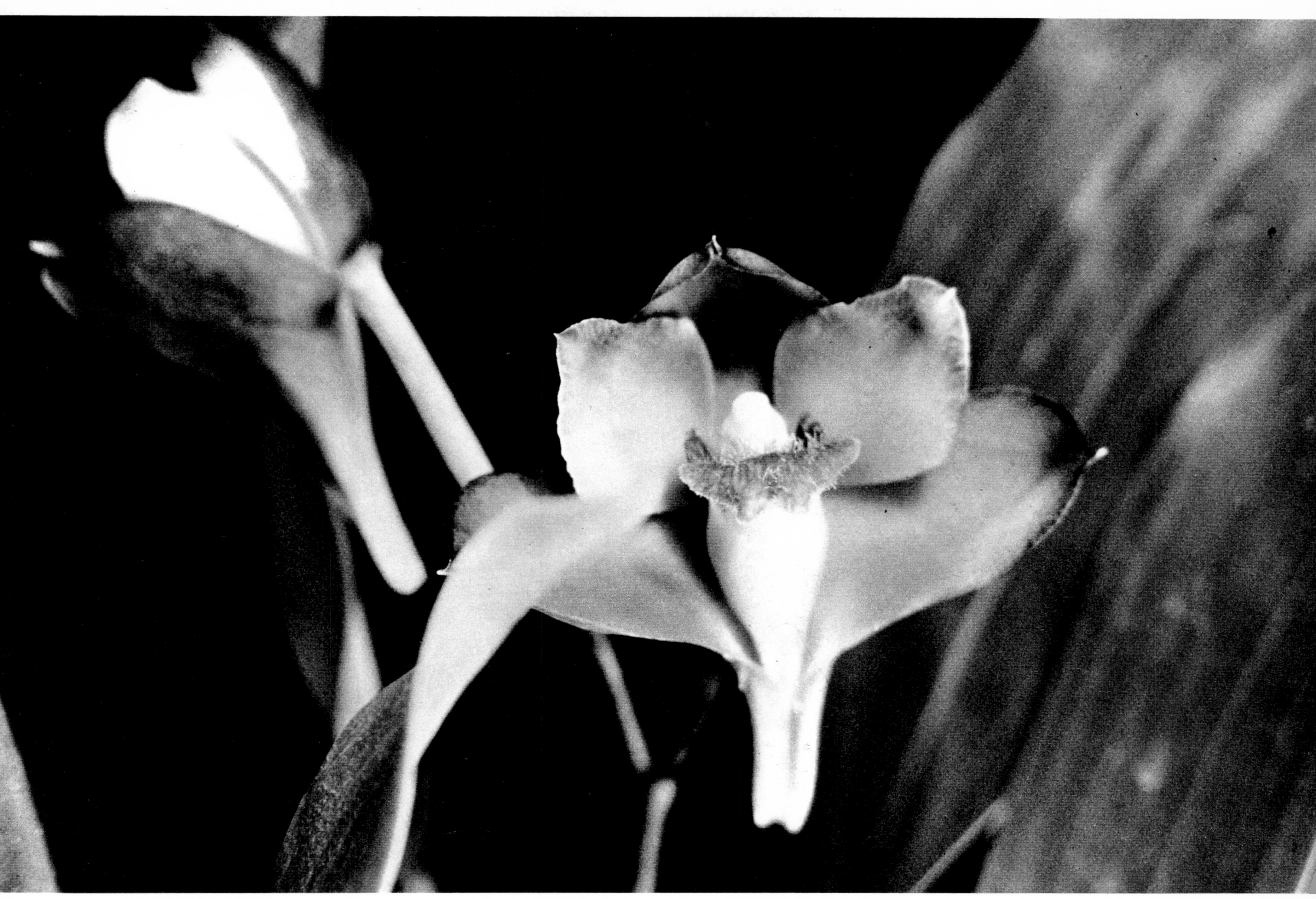

PLATE 134
Bifrenaria
B. tyrianthina
Brazil

In the wild, members of this genus are often found on trees and rock outcroppings. Blooms appear on short scapes and are reddish-purple—quite showy. (Photograph courtesy of Andrew R. Addkison.)

PLATE 135
Bifrenaria
B. harrisoniae
Brazil

This orchid was probably introduced into cultivation in 1821–22. The flowers, small or large, are variable in color and are produced singly, starting at the base of the pseudobulb. The plant rarely grows higher than 10 inches. (Photograph courtesy of Guy Burgess.)

PLATE 136
Lycaste
L. aromatica
Mexico, Guatemala, British Honduras, Honduras

The genus is named after one of the daughters of Priam, the last king of Troy. This species was first sent by Lord Napier from Mexico to the Edinburgh Botanic Garden before 1826. The plant bears 2-inch yellow flowers scented with cinnamon. (Photograph courtesy of Joyce R. Wilson.)

PLATE 137
Lycaste
L. fimbriata
Peru

See plate 138 for description. (Photograph courtesy of Hermann Pigors.)

PLATE 138
ycaste
.. fimbriata
Peru

panish botanists collected this plant n Peru about 1798. It was originally lassified in the genus *Maxillaria*. arge flowers are borne on short stems tarting at the base of a 30-inch plant. Photograph courtesy of Hermann igors.)

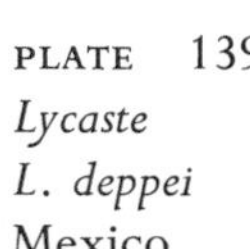

PLATE 139
Lycaste
L. deppei
Mexico

This plant grows to about 16 inches tall, and the flowers usually appear before, or when, the new growth starts and last for eight weeks on the plant. (Photograph courtesy of Joyce R. Wilson.)

PLATE 140
Lycaste
L. cruenta
Mexico, Guatemala, El Salvador, Costa Rica

This orchid produces a bounty of scented 2-inch yellow flowers. The leaves, to 16 inches long, are generally deciduous. Discovered in Guatemala by G. Ure Skinner about 1841, the species is one of the most generally cultivated of the lycastes. (Photograph courtesy of Guy Burgess.)

PLATE 141
Lycaste
L. macrophylla
Costa Rica, Panama, Colombia, Venezuela, Brazil, Peru, Bolivia

This is an amenable orchid with bold waxy flowers, to 4½ inches across. The petals are white, usually spotted with red-brown, and the sepals are a lovely olive green. (Photograph courtesy of Guy Burgess.)

PLATE 142
Lycaste
L. gigantea
Ecuador, Peru

As far as is known, this fine orchid first bloomed in England in 1845, although previous flowering in Belgium may have occurred. Once classed in the genus *Maxillaria,* this species produces 6-inch flowers on erect stems. The flowers in some ways resemble miniature lampshades of the Tiffany type. (Photograph courtesy of Joyce R. Wilson.)

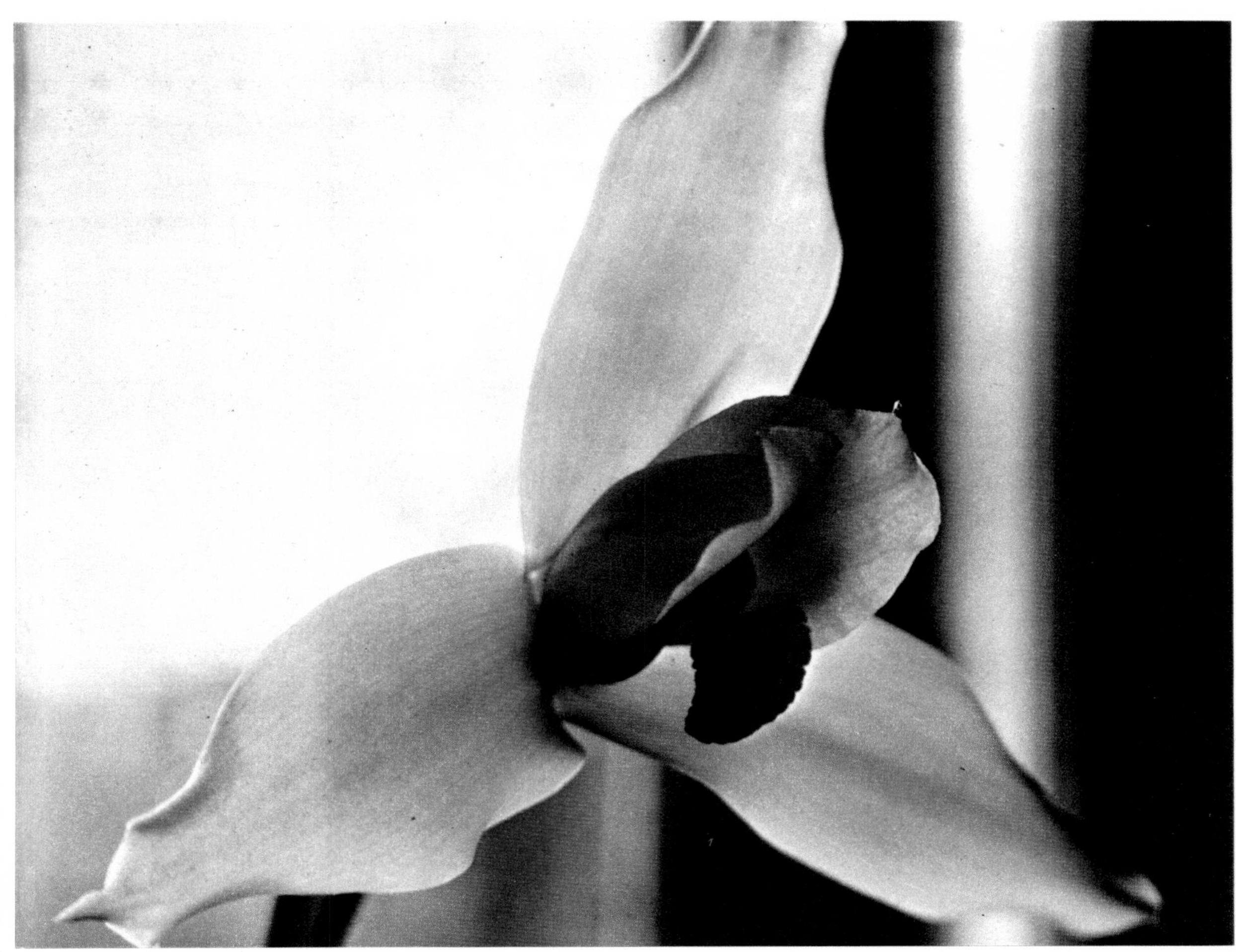

PLATE 143
Lycaste
L. skinneri
Guatemala

The national flower of Guatemala, this orchid bears pink and reddish flowers—the largest of any species in the genus. The range of the genus is from Cuba and Mexico to Peru and Brazil. A number of species are in cultivation today. (Photograph courtesy of Andrew R. Addkison.)

PLATE 144
Lycaste
L. skinneri (left)
L. dowiana (right)
Guatemala

See plate 143 for description of *L. skinneri*. *L. dowiana* has a 2-inch flower of pastel color. This is not an outstanding orchid, but it is often grown. (Photograph courtesy of Hermann Pigors.)

CONTINUED FROM PAGE 124

How Orchids Grow

Many orchids are air plants, or epiphytes. They may use a tree or bush as support (but derive no nourishment from it), or cling to barren rocks or cliffs (these are lithophytic orchids). Some orchids, mainly those native to the temperate zone, grow in the ground like ordinary herbaceous plants and take their nourishment from minerals and water in the soil and obtain their carbon supply from the air. They manufacture chlorophyll through the normal process of photosynthesis like other green plants. These orchids can be identified by a prominent growth of fine root hairs that are not present in the epiphytic or lithophytic groups.

A few orchids are saprophytes; that is, they exist on dead or decaying animal or vegetable matter in the ground or on rotting logs and do not manufacture chlorophyll. These plants are impossible to cultivate when taken from their native habitat.

A few orchids are semiaquatics and grow in water, and two rare Australian genera, *Cryptanthemis* and *Rhizanthella,* are subterranean, with only their tiny flowers appearing above the ground. There are also some leafless orchids such as those of the genera *Microcoelia,* found in Kenya, and *Polyrrhiza* in Florida, the West Indies, and Africa.

Although these are all distinct classes of orchids, the orchids themselves can, if necessary, sometimes adapt. A species that grows high in the trees may also thrive in the ground, and a terrestrial, if forced to, may take up life in the trees.

In the late nineteenth century Ernst Pfitzer proposed the first usable system of orchid classification, basing it upon the vegetative structures of the plants. Orchids that grew in one direction only were called monopodials; their stems lengthened indefinitely season after season and bore aerial roots. The flower was produced laterally from the leaf axils. The second vegetative class of orchids included the majority, and was called by Pfitzer the sympodials, plants in which the growth of the main axis or stem soon ceased, usually at the end of a growing season, and a lateral growth was produced in the next season. He further divided the sympodial orchids into two groups, and offered the third category of pseudomonopodial.

The Orchid Plant

Where present, the swollen base of the orchid stem, which may be ovoid and a few inches long or cylindrical or stemlike and several feet high, is called the pseudobulb. It is almost like an above-ground tuber, and it acts as a storehouse of water and nutrients for the plant in times of drought.

The rhizome is the primary stem from which comes the secondary stem; it may be either elongated and leafy, or abbreviated and thickened into a pseudobulb. The form of the rhizome varies from genus to genus and species to species, and pseudobulbs also vary considerably in appearance.

Most garden plants keep their roots in the ground, and some orchids such as cypripediums grow the same way. However, as mentioned, many orchids are epiphytes; to get light they start climbing trees by using their stout aerial roots, losing contact with the ground. Many species have thick aerial roots that will cling to wood or metal surfaces. The ropelike roots can, in time, engulf their support so firmly that to take the plant from rock, stone, or wood, you have to cut it loose with an axe.

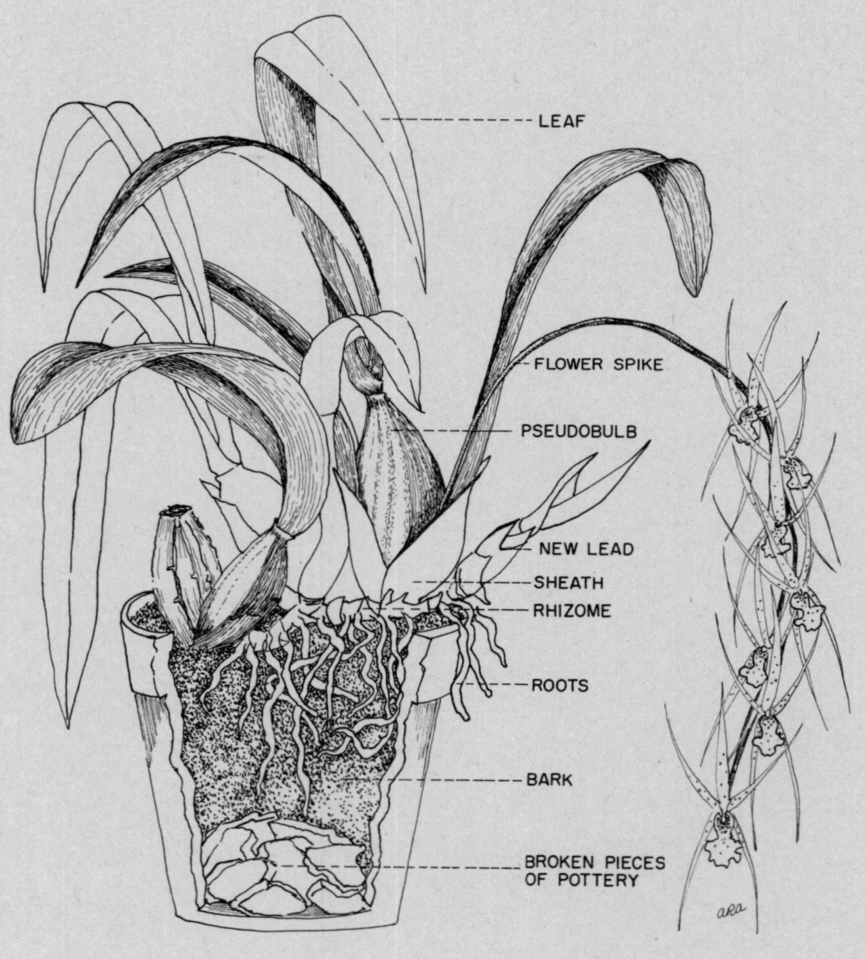

The Orchid Plant

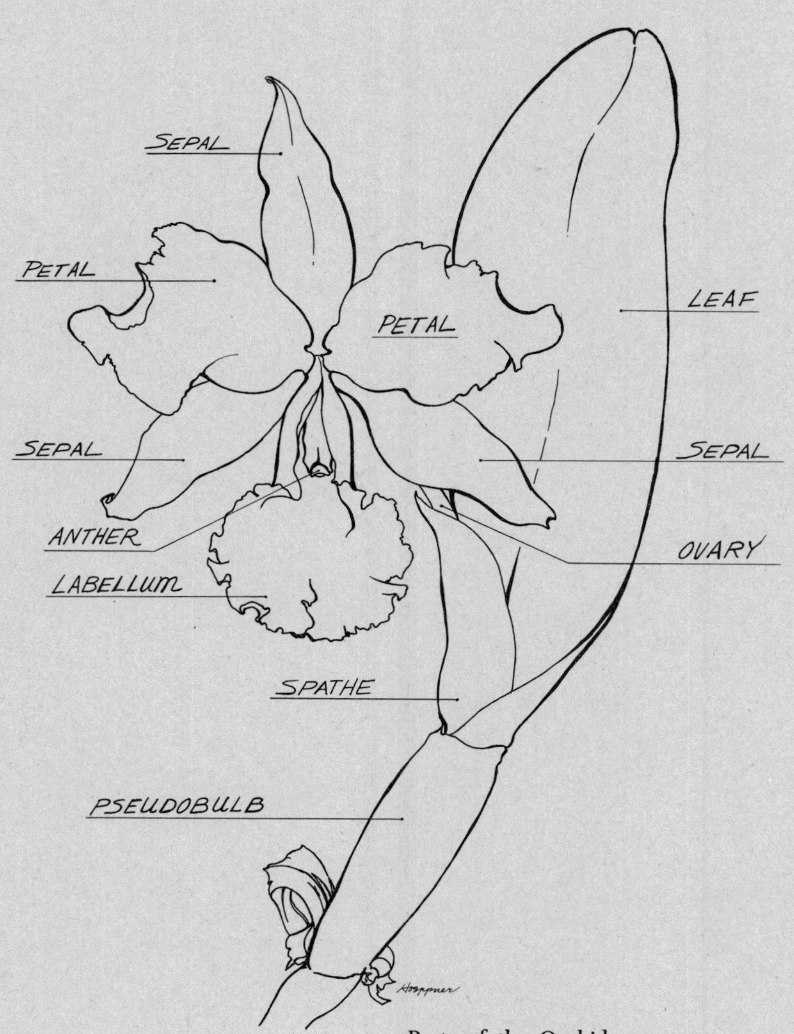

Parts of the Orchid

The diversity of orchid flowers is matched by the shape and color of the leaves. Some have foliage that hardly resembles leaves, such as *Brassavola nodosa* (see plate 74) and *Scuticaria hadwenii,* with pencil-like cylindrical leaves, or *Isabellia virginalis,* which has leaves as fine as tiny hairs. The common succulent gray-green leaf of cattleyas and laelias may be ovate, subcircular, oblong, or elliptical. Leaves may be deciduous, semideciduous, evergreen, or semievergreen, depending on the species.

There are also little-known but intensely beautiful orchids that are valued for their foliage rather than for their flowers. These are called jewel orchids, and many have leaves with bronze- or copper-colored netting: *Anoechtochilus roxburghii* is a deep velvety green; *Macodes petola* is generally olive green, with contrasting veining; and the haemarias are a deep maroon, almost a rich black, with bright veins. These orchids look like beautiful tapestries and are unmatched in the plant world.

Where Orchids Come From

Not all orchids grow in the steaming humid jungles. The majority are from the tropics and subtropics, but many kinds grow in temperate zones. Some members of the orchid family grow even in subarctic regions.

Calypso bulbosa, a bright magenta species, grows as far north as Finland. Lady's-slipper orchids are widespread in temperate North American zones, Alaska, and British Columbia, and orphys species are prevalent in Mediterranean areas.

In India the vast Himalayan mountain range is the home of many orchids—coelogynes, cymbidiums, and dendrobiums thrive at the various altitudes because the monsoon clouds from the Indian Ocean supply a tremendous amount of rain on the mountains' southern slopes. Orchids are well represented also in Burma, thanks to its clearly defined wet and dry seasons; the lovely *Vanda caerulea* grows at 6,000 feet in the Khasis Mountains of Assam.

The Philippines are rich in species, but perhaps New Guinea has more orchids than any other area, with approximately three thousand species. New Zealand and New Caledonia also have many orchids. The island of Madagascar off the coast of Africa produces dozens of angraecum and bulbophyllum species, for the warmth of the Indian Ocean and the extensive rainfall produce lush growth.

In Brazilian jungles, orchids are found growing on moisture-laden trees. (Photograph courtesy of Paul C. Hutchison.)

The west coast of South America is rich in orchids. Here orchids perch on the ends of tree branches. (Photograph courtesy of Paul C. Hutchison.)

From the vast grasslands of East Africa come species of habenaria, eulophia, and disa, rare orchids seldom seen in collections. In West Africa, aerangis and polystacha plants flourish; close to the equator, in Sierra Leone, Nigeria, Ghana, the Ivory Coast, and Liberia, there are also numerous orchids.

Brazil produces species of cattleyas, laelias, and oncidiums, which are popular for corsages and as cut flowers. From southern Brazil to the Amazon in the north, there are plants of bifrenaria, brassavola, cycnoches, epidendrum, and zygopetalum, to name a few. As altitude and climate change, so do the orchid species, with certain types growing in rain forests and others in the damp heat of the Rio Negro basin of the Amazon.

The west coast of South America is as rich in orchids as Brazil. The Andes mountains, like a great snake, run the length of the coast and influence the climate and therefore the vegetation. In the Andes of northern Peru, masdevallias grow at 12,000 feet in freezing night temperatures. In Colombia, in the Andes region, the cool rain forests at 6,000 to 8,000 feet have large stands of odontoglossums and miltonias. Coming down from the mountains to the forests of Colombia are cattleyas: *C. gigas, C. schroederiana,* and *C. trianaei.*

Venezuela is a land of contrasts, in weather as in customs. There are dry regions and rain forests, and in the northern mountains of the Cordillera grow oncidiums, cattleyas, and dozens of other genera; each area, dry, wet, or mountainous, has its own plants.

In Central America we find veritable treasure troves of orchids in Panama, Guatemala, Costa Rica, Nicaragua, and Honduras. In Guatemala and Mexico there are assorted types of orchids at different elevations; some species are located in the cool mountains, others in the warm lowlands. Mexico boasts hundreds of orchid genera: laelia, oncidium, rhyncostylis, epidendrum, and so forth. Oaxaca, where I have collected orchids, is especially rich in species.

To appreciate the incredible range of orchids throughout the world, the native country of each species is identified in the descriptions accompanying the photographs.

Orchids as Useful Plants

Most native Eastern orchids have tuberous roots filled with a nutritious, starchy substance with a sweet taste but somewhat unpleasant aroma. For many centuries in Turkey and Persia a starchy meal was obtained from the roots of certain species of orchis and eulophia and exported as *sahlep* (salep). After roasting, it was brewed into a tasty beverage (it was sold in London before coffee supplanted it, and is still used in the East as a hot drink in the winter). It was also an efficient demulcent agent in herbal remedies. Prepared from dried and ground tubers mixed with water, salep is today used in various bland gelatines and soups. The succulent leaves of some orchids were formerly used as vegetables in Malaysia and Indonesia.

Witches were supposed to have employed orchid tubers in magic potions; the fresh tubers to promote love, the withered ones to check passions. In seventeenth-century herbals, as mentioned, orchis was called satyria, from the legend that orchids were connected with satyrs. In classical mythology, Orchis, the son of a satyr and a nymph, was killed by the Bacchantes; through his father's prayers he was turned into the flower that bears his name.

Aside from mythical associations and herbal remedies, the large family Orchidaceae produces only one product of commercial importance—vanilla (*Vanilla planifolia*). The vanilla orchid is a tropical, climbing, vinelike plant with large, oval-shaped succulent leaves and large, tubular yellow flowers. The Aztecs of Mexico were using vanilla to flavor chocolate long before the discovery of America. Vanilla was brought to Europe about 1500, but little progress was made in its cultivation. Most of the plants did not flower under European conditions, and those that did failed to produce fruit.

Vanilla was first successfully cultivated in Europe in 1807. In the following decades the development of artificial pollination, along with successful propagation from cuttings, made possible the growing of vanilla as a commercial crop throughout the tropics. Great Britain, Belgium, and France grew vanilla in several of their colonial possessions.

At present, vanilla is grown commercially in many countries, with Madagascar producing about half the total world crop. Mexico ranks second in the amount produced. (Vanillin—artificial vanilla—was perfected in later years, and is now chiefly used in the baking trade as a substitute for the more costly true vanilla.) The plants themselves still remain difficult to grow. It is only recently that I have been successful with them, for they prefer a shady, moist, almost cool place. The mammoth yellow flowers have been well worth all my efforts.

The nutritive and healing properties of certain orchids have from time to time been employed throughout the world. Supposedly, natives in Madagascar make a scented restorative tea from the grassy leaves of *Jumellea fragrans*. Teas have also been made from the foliage or pseudobulbs of some species of renanthera and bletia. Roots of epipactis are used against arthritis in some regions and the flowers of gymnadenia as a preventative for dysentery. In Mexico, some laelias are used as fever cures, and *L. majalis* and *L. autumnalis* are used in cough medicines. For wounds and cuts, the mucilaginous juice (salep) of the terrestrial orchid *Eulophia arabica* is frequently used.

In Chile some spiranthes species are prepared as a diuretic, and it is said that the bulbs of *Bletia verecunda* of Jamaica are boiled and eaten as digestive aids.

North American Indians used various ferns for medicine and food as well as the roots of some lady's-slipper orchids. These were boiled with a sweet liquid, and the decoction taken as a cure for headaches.

The flexible stems of some dendrobiums are used in weaving and basketry in parts of the Philippines and

New Guinea, and intricate bracelets are made from the cane stems of other dendrobiums. In Brazil some natives use the mucilaginous sap of *Laelia autumnalis* as a glue in manufacturing musical instruments. In some sections of Central America the hollow pseudobulbs of schomburgkias are made into trumpets and horns.

Hybridization

In 1856 the first artificially produced orchid hybrid was perfected in England by John Dominy, head gardener for the Messrs. Veitch; he crossed *Calanthe masuca* with *Calanthe furcata* (the hybrid was named Calanthe Domnii). The early method of producing orchids from seed was called the symbiotic method; a host orchid or a specially prepared bed was used. The host plant was surrounded by a dressing of actively growing sphagnum, and seed was scattered over the compost and sprinkled with water. The special seed bed was prepared in clay pots and filled with sphagnum or chopped osmunda, and seed was sprinkled on top. The entire bed was then covered with glass.

In 1922 the American botanist Lewis Knudsen substituted suitable chemicals for sphagnum or osmunda. A sterilized medium (usually agar jelly) was produced from seaweed, with organic and inorganic nutrients added and adjusted to a suitable degree of acidity. This was called the asymbiotic method of growing orchids and was used for producing most plants until recently, when meristem culture was introduced.

Approximately a hundred years after the first artificial orchid hybrid was produced in England, the revolutionary method of growing plants by meristeming started in France. It is now widely used in America. This process is faster and easier than earlier methods, and it ensures a faithful reproduction of the parent plant.

Every living plant has within it the tiny buds of new growths, a formative plant tissue made up of small cells and called the meristem. In orchid propagation a new shoot is cut off the mother plant, and several layers of leaves and tissues are peeled off until the meristem is exposed. The growing tip is then cut out (it is about 1 millimeter in diameter) and placed in a flask of liquid nutrient solution. The flask is then placed on a rotating wheel or vibrator, and within three to four weeks the meristem shows growth; tissue starts to develop into massy balls. In another month these clumps of tissue are cut into twenty or thirty pieces; each one is again placed in a flask of nutrients, and within a month these, too, grow about one fourth in size. (They can again be cut and returned to the flask for further agitation. The pieces follow the same growth pattern and can be cut again and again.) When the agitation stops, the small clumps start growing into plantlets that are then potted in seedling beds. The resulting plants are called ''meri-clones.''

Orchids can also be reproduced by vegetative means —back bulbs or divisions—an easy and effective way for the home gardener to get more plants.

Today, most breeding work with orchids relies on the few that can be used as cut flowers—cattleyas, cymbidiums, paphiopedilums, and oncidiums. The parent is selected for its color, shape of lip, lasting quality, or scent, or for the ease with which it grows.

Organization and Names in the Orchid Family

The divisions of genus and species date back to Aristotle's time, but for the last two hundred years taxonomists have used these terms with some modifications. As in the case of plant nomenclature in general, the orchid family is organized into a number of genera, each genus having one or many related species in it. Thus, orchids have two names, a genus and a species name. *Laelia anceps* refers to one specific plant and denotes that this plant belongs to the genus *Laelia* and is distinguished by the species name *anceps*. However, even orchids of the same species may vary in color and size in which case a variety is recognized. Furthermore, even though *Laelia anceps* and *Laelia purpurata* are distinct species and may not look alike, they have enough characteristics in common to be in the same genus, which can consist of only two or three species or of several hundred.

Some of the best hybrids have been created by professional growers, but amateurs, too, have been successful in crossing orchids. Because of human curiosity and the desire to create something new, an infinite number of hybrids have appeared, and it soon became necessary to give a hybrid a name of its own rather than to call it by the name of a dozen ancestors. Thus, Cattleya Bow Bells × Cattleya Edithiae is called Cattleya Empress Bells. When an outstanding plant is introduced, a varietal name is added to the hybrid name and is set in single quotes, as in Cattleya Portia 'Mayflower.' Award-winning plants from the American Orchid Society (AOS) or the Royal Horticultural Society (RHS) are designated by initials after the name such as Cattleya Mount 'Vashon' A.M. (Award of Merit) or F.C.C. (First Class Certificate).

All named hybrids must be registered by definite procedures. This is now handled by the Royal Horticultural Society of England. When the society receives plant data and information from the grower, the official hybrid names are printed in the England journal *The Orchid Review*. A compilation of registered crosses that are approved is published every three years and is called *Sander's List of Orchid Hybrids*.

With the crossing of so many different plants, some code names and abbreviations have evolved for the majority of hybrids that are produced by man. Cattleya hybrids, for instance, involve numerous successive crosses within a large number of species, each capable of contributing an outstanding characteristic to the ultimate offspring. Crosses are frequently made between laelia and cattleya and are known as laeliocattleya and abbreviated as Lc. Because of its handsome fringed lip, brassavola is extensively used in crosses with cattleya: these crosses are called brassocattleya and abbreviated as Bc. Frequently, three plants—laelia, brassavola, cattleya—are used and known as trigeneric crosses called brassolaeliocattleya, a real tongue twister shortened to Blc. Potinara is the code word for crosses that involve brassavola, laelia, cattleya, and sophronitis. Dialaeliocattleya has no coined name or abbreviation, so one must struggle with its pronunciation.

Orchids as Cut Flowers

Today, as twenty years ago, the orchid is the corsage flower for special occasions. No flower is more beautiful for corsages than the orchid, and the public shows its admiration by purchasing millions of cut orchids annually for Mother's Day, anniversaries, and other festive occasions. Hybridization has produced mammoth blooms of incredible beauty that are hard to resist; though prices for corsages are still high, costs should decrease as meristem culture progresses.

Commercial flower growers, such as the Rod McLellan Company in California and Orchids by Hausermann in Illinois, who devoted their growing space to sweet peas in the 1920s and gardenias and roses in the 1940s, now consider orchids their primary crop. In addition to cut flowers, retail plant sales constitute 25 percent of their business. There are about a dozen suppliers who offer the cut-flower and plant-sales services in this

Brassosophrolaeliocattleya
Potinara 'Edwin Hausermann' (hybrid)

Probably one of the flashiest orchids ever bred, Potinara (as it is now officially known) is distinguished by overwhelming beauty of color and form. It is a quadrigeneric cross between Blc. Mem. Crispin Rosales and Slc. Kermit Hernlund. (Photograph courtesy of Guy Burgess.)

Coelogyne
C. lawrenceana
Vietnam

A fine epiphytic species, it has two-leaved oval pseudobulbs and large, waxy, fragrant flowers, 4 inches across, borne on an erect stalk. An orchid of true elegance and grace. (Photograph courtesy of Guy Burgess.)

country, and there are about two hundred mail-order companies that sell orchids to hobbyists and have no cut-flower operation. These companies have well-controlled crop-timing programs using shading, black cloth, or artificial lighting to produce flowers for the appropriate holidays of Easter, Mother's Day, and Christmas, and for the wedding months of June and July.

A typical orchid range such as Hausermann's has two hundred thousand producing plants under glass. Their annual marketable cut is estimated at five hundred thousand blooms. The Rod McLellan Company, with sixty-seven acres under glass, markets approximately one million cut flowers along with some one hundred thousand plants yearly.

Orchids are no longer just for the rich. The few private collections that once dominated the 1900s (the Rothschild in Europe, the Sherman in Boston) have been dispersed, given to public gardens, or sold to growers. In their place, thousands of more modest but superb collections of orchids have sprung up. However, a few private collections like the Du Pont orchids at Longwood Gardens near Philadelphia and the Fairchild Gardens in Coral Gables, Florida, have a wealth of plants for public viewing. The Brooklyn Botanic Gardens and the St. Louis Climatron also have extensive collections, and almost any conservatory in a large city has a sampling of plants. The worth of the former private collections was no doubt staggering; on a lesser scale, for example, at an orchid auction in Belmont, California, about four thousand plants (a small number for a collection) sold for $27,000.

The American Orchid Society, with headquarters at the Botanical Museum of Harvard University in Cambridge, Massachusetts, has some eighteen thousand registered members and over two hundred and fifty local orchid societies affiliated with them. There are chapters in most large cities, and some states have several orchid groups. Amateur collectors number in the thousands.

There are shows, exhibits, and awards for growers in most cities at various times of the year, and of course new hybrids are being added to the official registered list every year.

Conservation and Orchids

About fifteen years ago I saw a vast stand of native cypripediums in Wisconsin. On a recent visit to the same place, I found no trace of these plants. Whether environmental conditions had changed so they could not survive or whether the plants had been collected is hard to determine, but they were gone.

Generally, the situation of native orchids throughout the United States is the same: the plants are fast disappearing. Some states have passed laws protecting the plants, and other states will no doubt follow suit, but laws do not guarantee the survival of these wonderful plants. If the environmental conditions are altered by pesticides and other pollutants, no restrictions against gathering the plants can save them.

Although we cannot legislate against parking lots and building developments—in general, the clearing of land for man's use—some restraints will have to be put into effect to preserve what we have. The answer may in part lie in the licensing of certain plant collectors, to reduce the danger of excessive collecting by individuals. Yet, to be fair, the responsible person who occasionally takes a few plants for his garden cannot in years do the damage to plants that one bulldozer can do in a few hours. For the time being, it seems wise to discourage people from collecting native orchids. There is no need for it. Today many suppliers can furnish pot-grown plants, and these generally are easier to grow in our gardens than wild collected species.

In tropical countries where orchids abound, the preservation of native species is a matter of great concern. These are mainly the orchids that are collected for sale to plant hobbyists. Some South American countries—Colombia, Peru, and Venezuela—have already put restrictions on native plants. In the African national parks for wildlife, native plants are given protection, too. Yet it must be remembered that plants can survive only *if the total ecological environment remains stable.*

For the most part, commercial cut-flower growers cultivate their own plants from seed or from the meristem process. Species orchids are also now being grown under cultivation. Although orchids are still collected in many tropical countries to supply growers, I see no real danger in this practice. Most commercial collectors in foreign countries are conscientious people who realize that only intelligent collecting will ensure plants for the future. And the recipients of these plants know how to care for them properly.

But the noncommercial harvest of orchids in foreign countries by tourists should, in most cases, be stopped. It is rare that the plants survive, since getting them established is one of the most difficult aspects of orchid growing. Conversely, the importation of wild species by the average hobbyist in the United States should also be stopped; the hobbyist may not know how to establish them, and this practice leads to wanton destruction of orchids.

In the 1930s the American public took African violets to its heart, and they became the number-one houseplants. By 1960 orchids had made inroads with plant hobbyists, and today the number of amateur orchid growers is fast surpassing African violet collectors.

The myth that orchids had to be sealed under glass to survive has finally been shattered. The misinformation that they needed elaborate equipment to help them grow has been erased. We now know that orchids can be grown as easily as many familiar houseplants. Their wealth of bloom and the drama of the flowers' growth entices people of all ages.

There is something very rewarding in having blooming orchids from faraway lands at your windows. Like the armchair traveler, the orchid hobbyist travels great distances without leaving his home—the magic of orchids gives him a small window to the world.

So the lore and legends about orchids have dissolved as the cultivation of the plants has been understood. Yet the allure of orchids will always be there to capture the eye of the seeker of beauty.

Plates

PLATE 145
Anguloa
A. ruckeri
Colombia

The genus name is in honor of Don Francisco de Angulo, director general of mines in Peru and a student of the local flora. The plant first bloomed in the collection of a Mr. Rucker at West Hall, Wandsworth, England, in the summer of 1846. Like most anguloas, it is a difficult orchid to bring into bloom. (Photograph courtesy of Joyce R. Wilson.)

PLATE 146
Anguloa
A. cliftonii
Andes mountains.

This superb species grows in the Andes at 5,000 to 7,000 feet and in flower structure seems to fall somewhere between the genera *Lycaste* and *Stanhopea*. It is a difficult orchid to bring into bloom because too much water rots it and too little harms it. Almost total shade is required. (Photograph courtesy of Joyce R. Wilson.)

PLATE 147 ▶
Anguloa
A. clowesii
Colombia, Venezuela

This species flowered for the first tim in England in 1844. It is a dramatic plant with tulip-shaped flowers. Nativ to high elevations, this terrestrial orchid requires shade and coolness. (Photograph courtesy of Guy Burgess.

PLATE 148
Anguloa
A. ruckeri
Colombia

Another close-up of the flower. See plate 145 for description. (Photograph courtesy of Joyce R. Wilson.)

PLATE 149
Zygopetalum
Z. mackayi
Brazil

This species grows to 40 inches tall and bears exquisite 4-inch blue-and-green flowers. Botanists once assigned over fifty species to this genus, but many are now classified in other genera. These species are distributed throughout the South American continent from the cooler parts of southern Brazil to the Isthmus of Panama, as well as Central America, southern Mexico, and the West Indies. (Photograph courtesy of Hermann Pigors.)

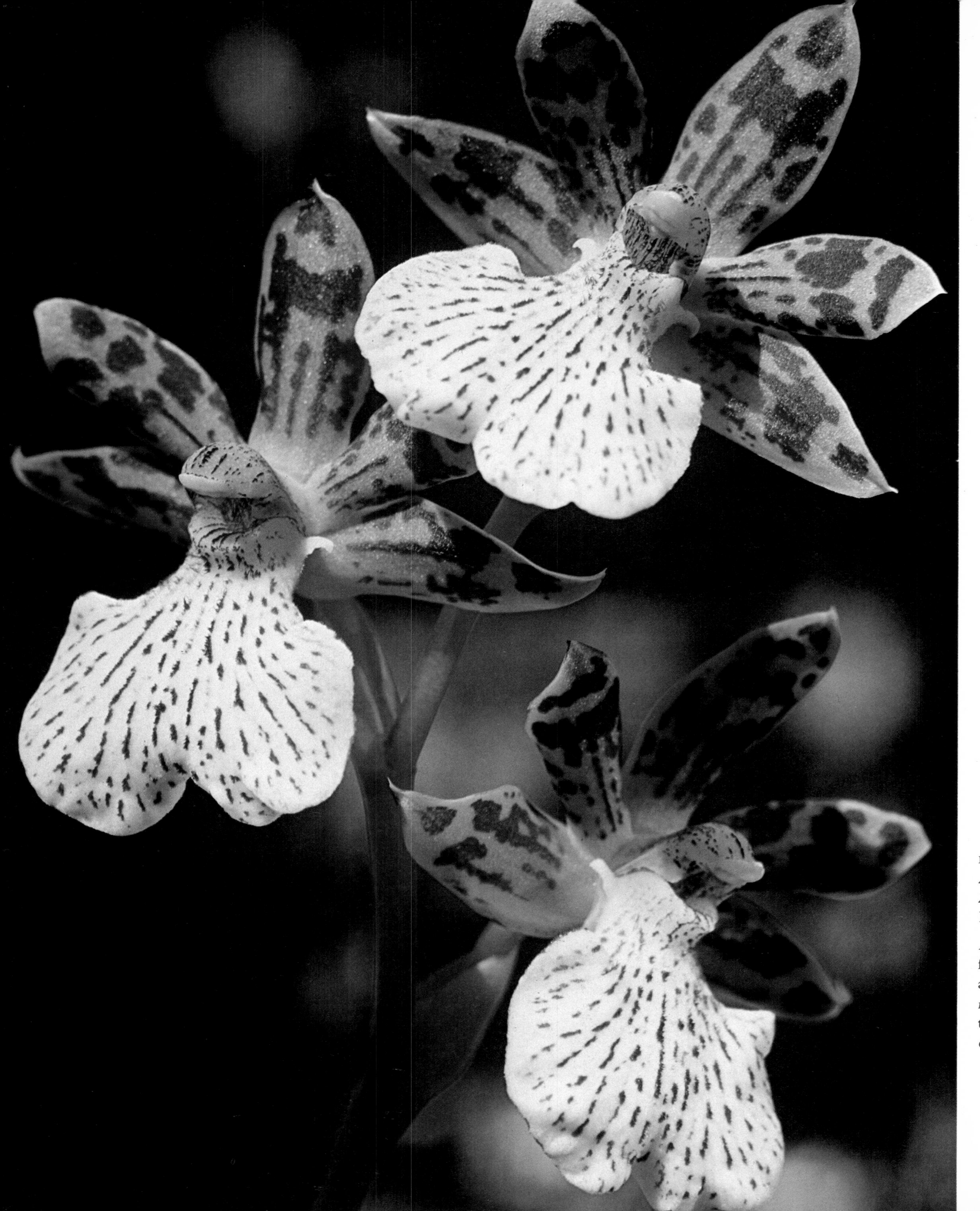

PLATE 150
Zygopetalum
Z. intermedium
Brazil

A species of singular beauty, it was first discovered by Conrad Loddiges and is sometimes classified as *Z. mackayi,* which it resembles. It grows to 24 inches high. (Photograph courtesy of Joyce R. Wilson.)

PLATE 151
Warscewiczella
W. discolor
Costa Rica

Often classed in the genus *Zygopetalum,* this medium-size plant has 2-inch white flowers tinged with purple; the lip is violet-purple. (Photograph courtesy of Hermann Pigors.)

PLATE 152
Pescatorea
P. cerina
Costa Rica, Panama

Snowy whitish-yellow flowers, 3 inches across, adorn this plant, which has leafy fan-shaped foliage. It is attractive even when not in bloom. (Photograph courtesy of Andrew R. Addkison.)

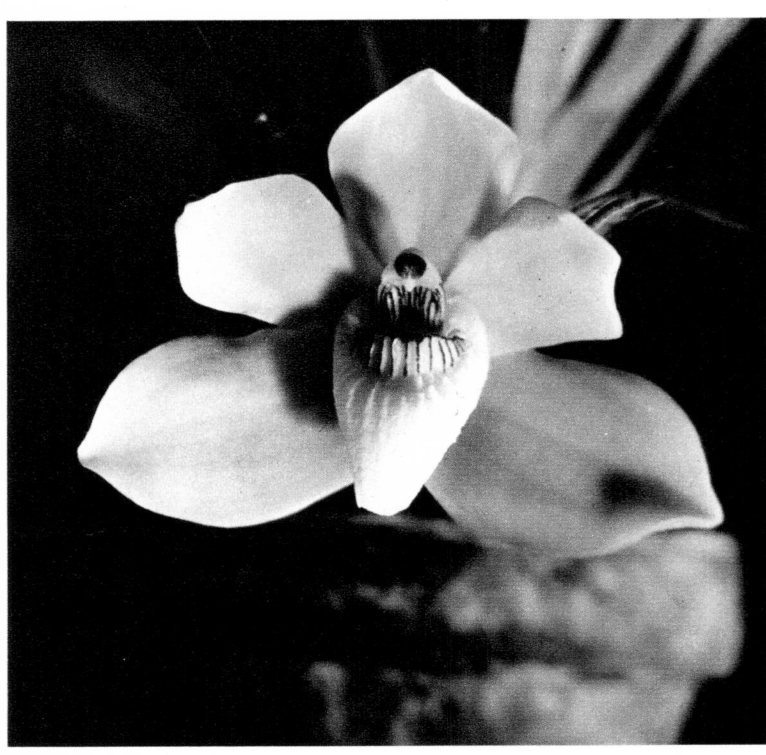

PLATE 153 ▶
Bollea
B. lawrenceana
Colombia

This striking orchid produces fan-shaped foliage up to 10 inches high, with 4-inch flowers of violet-purple. The combination of shape and color makes this species a most desirable one. (Photograph courtesy of Joyce R. Wilson.)

PLATE 154
Huntleya
H. meleagris (burtii)
Costa Rica, Colombia, Brazil, Panama

An unusual orchid, it has apple-green fan-shaped foliage and bears waxy 7-inch brown-and-purple star-shaped flowers. This species is perhaps the most unorchidlike of the entire Orchidaceae. (Photograph courtesy of Andrew R. Addkison.)

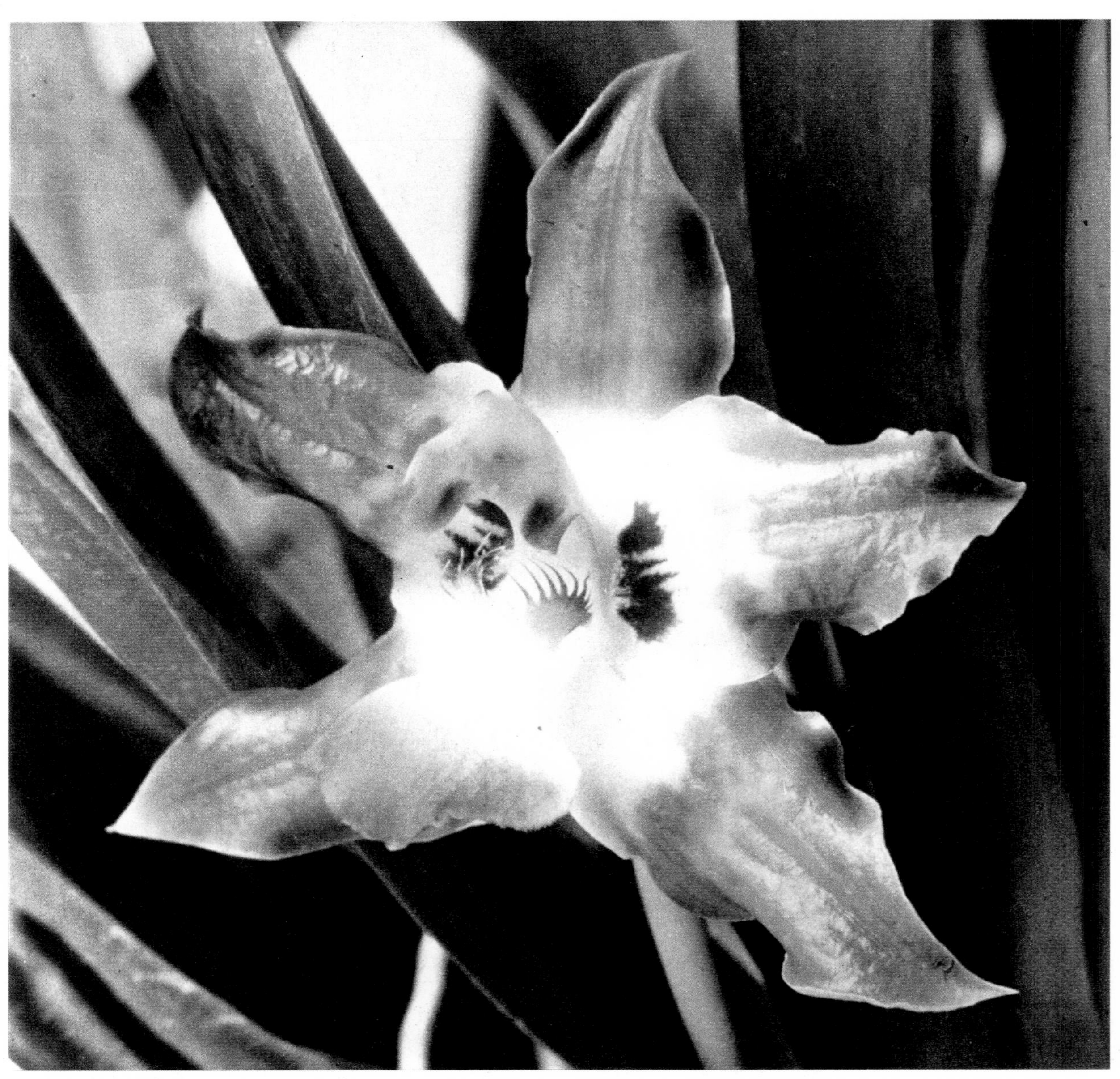

PLATE 155 ▶
Maxillaria
M. luteo alba
Costa Rica, Panama, Colombia, Venezuela, Ecuador

Graceful 2-inch flowers, tawny yellow with purple markings, adorn this 12-inch plant. It was discovered by J. J. Linden in 1842 on the Cordillera of Venezuela, near Mérida, at an elevation of 5,000 to 7,000 feet. (Photograph courtesy of Joyce R. Wilson.)

PLATE 156
Maxillaria
M. picta
Brazil

Small red-and-yellow flowers accent this 10-inch-high orchid. A plant was sent to Mrs. Arnold Harrison of Liverpool in 1831 by her relative William Harrison, who had gathered it on the Organ Mountains near Rio de Janeiro. It was later imported by Messrs. Loddiges of Hackney, England. (Photograph courtesy of Joyce R. Wilson.)

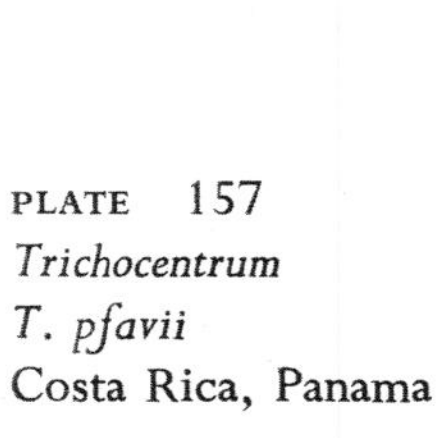

PLATE 157
Trichocentrum
T. pfavii
Costa Rica, Panama

A miniature orchid 2 inches tall with bright 1-inch flowers, it was discovered in Central America by Richard Pfau and introduced in 1881 by the English firm of Messrs. Sander and Co. (Photograph courtesy of Guy Burgess.)

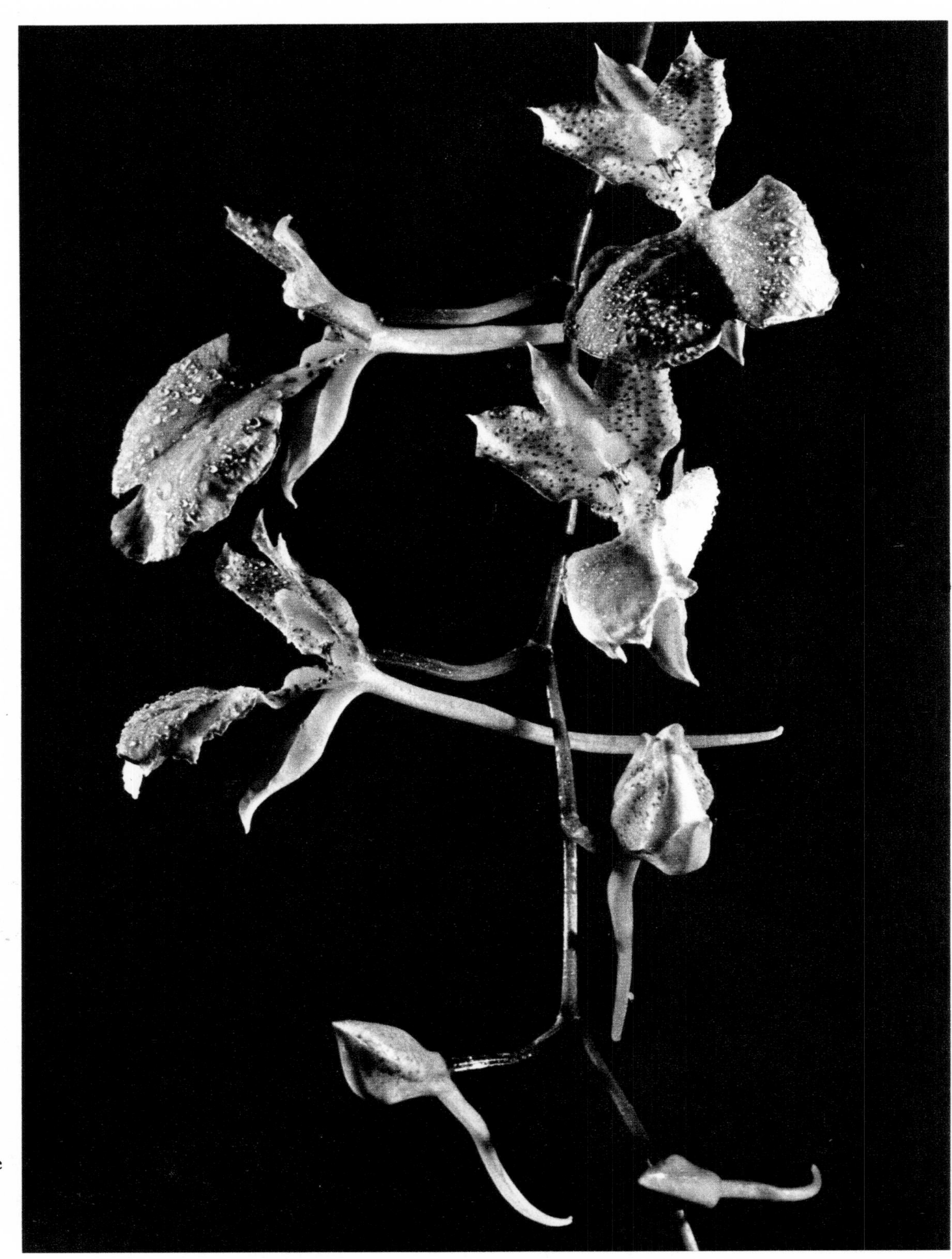

PLATE 158
Comparettia
C. macroplectron
Colombia

This lovely, almost miniature plant bears 1- to 2-inch pink flowers on arching scapes. The genus name commemorates Andreas Comparetti (1746–1801), Professor of Botany at the University of Padua and one of the most eminent vegetable physiologists of his time. (Photograph courtesy of Joyce R. Wilson.)

PLATE 159
Rodriguezia
R. fragrans
Brazil

This small orchid has lovely scented white blooms. The genus was dedicated by its founders to Emanuel Rodriguez, a Spanish physician and botanist of the nineteenth century. The genus is composed of about thirty very attractive species of epiphytes and lithophytes, which are found in the Central and South American tropics, from Costa Rica and Nicaragua to Peru and Brazil. (Photograph courtesy of Guy Burgess.)

PLATE 160
Trichopilia
T. suavis
Costa Rica, Colombia, Panama

This orchid was supposedly first discovered in 1848 by Jósef Warscewicz in Costa Rica in the Cordillera at an elevation of 5,000 to 8,000 feet. It bloomed for the first time in England in 1851. The plant has clustered pseudobulbs, leaves up to 12 inches long, and bears flowers 7 inches across that hug the rim of the pot. (Photograph courtesy of Joyce R. Wilson.)

PLATE 161
Trichopilia
T. tortilis
Mexico, Guatemala, El Salvador, Honduras

Colorful 5-inch flowers characterize *T. tortilis*—the species on which the genus was founded by Dr. John Lindley in 1836. A specimen had been taken to England the year before by George Barker of Springfield. Shortly afterward a plant was sent by John Parkinson, the queen's consul in Mexico, to the Woburn Collection, where it flowered in 1839. (Photograph courtesy of Andrew R. Addkison.)

PLATE 162
Odontioda
O. Redcliff (hybrid)

A close-up of the flower. See plate 165 for description. (Photograph courtesy of Joyce R. Wilson.)

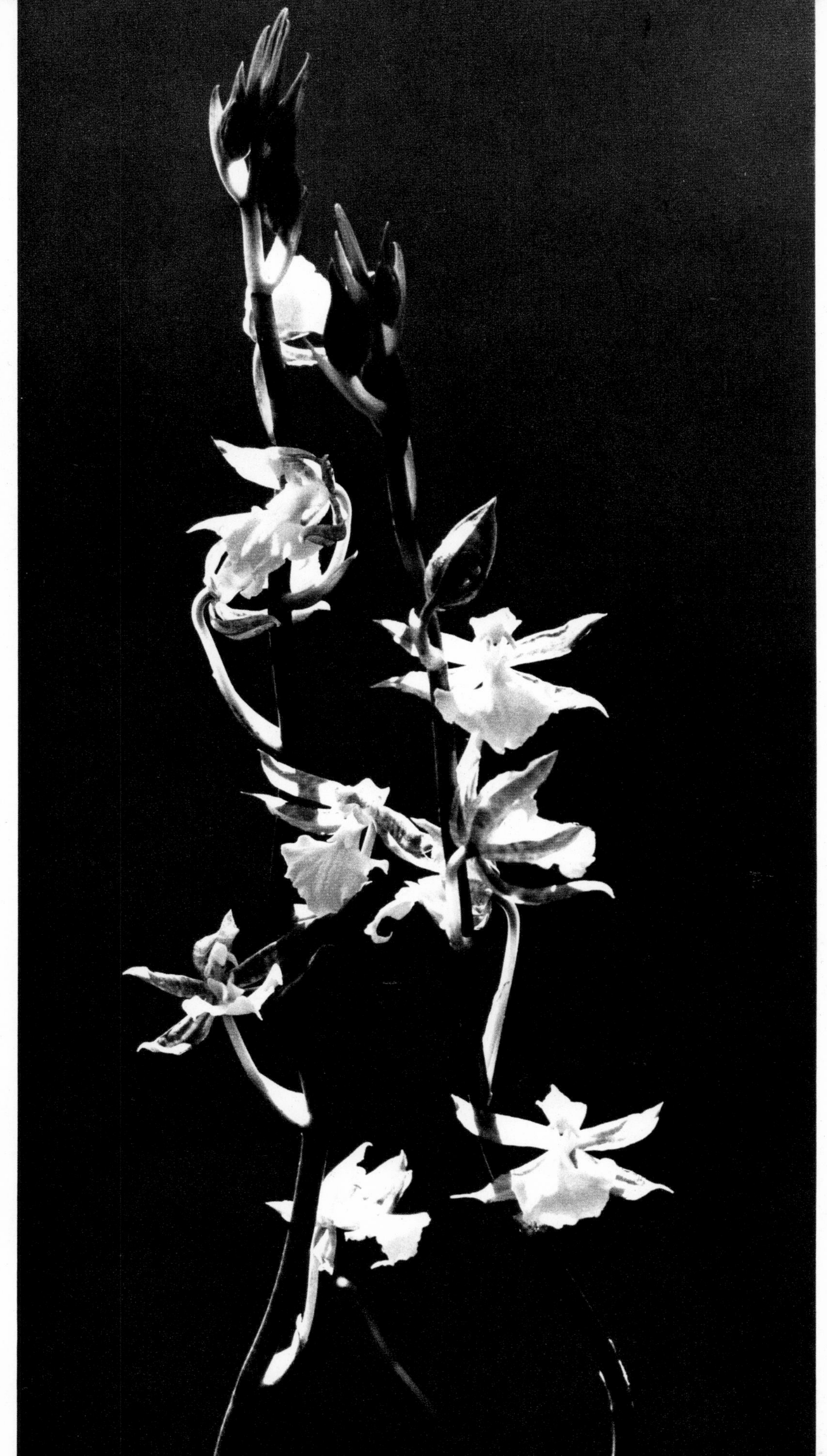

PLATE 163
Odontoglossum
O. bictoniense
Mexico, Guatemala, El Salvador

One of the first odontoglossums to reach England alive, it was discovered in Guatemala by G. Ure Skinner, who sent it in 1835 to James Bateman, at Knypersley. It flowered for the first time in the collection of Lord Rolle in the spring of 1836. (Photograph courtesy of Joyce R. Wilson.)

PLATE 164
Odontioda
O. Guinea Gold (hybrid)

Odontioda is a bigeneric hybrid between the genera *Cochlioda* and *Odontoglossum*. A dazzling cluster of rust-red and yellow flowers on a slender stem, O. Guinea Gold was produced from subsequent secondary crosses. (Photograph courtesy of Joyce R. Wilson.)

PLATE 165
Odontioda
O. Redcliff (hybrid)

Large frilly white-and-red flowers, many to a stem, create a fusion of delicacy and riotous color that gives this orchid star status. It grows best in cool temperatures. Occasionally, it is used for corsages. It is a cross between Odontioda Sensation and *Odontoglossum crispum*. (Photograph courtesy of Joyce R. Wilson.)

PLATE 166
Odontoglossum
O. citrosmum
Mexico, Guatemala

This highly prized orchid has 3-inch snow-white flowers of elegant form. It was discovered in the early 1800s by Pablo de La Llave and Juan Martinez de Lexarza, but its identification remained in doubt for many years. The species was introduced into England about 1838 by George Barker of Birmingham, after a plant was sent by his collector, John Ross. (Photograph courtesy of Hermann Pigors.)

PLATE 167 ▶
Odontoglossum
O. crispum: hybrid
Colombia

The species *O. crispum* was discovered by Theodor Hartweg in the province of Bogotá at an elevation of 7,500 to 8,500 feet. This is one of the many crispum hybrids introduced in recent years. (Photograph courtesy of Joyce R. Wilson.)

PLATE 168
Odontoglossum
O. bictoniense
Mexico, Guatemala, El Salvador

A close-up of the flower. See plate 163 for description. (Photograph courtesy of Joyce R. Wilson.)

PLATE 169
Odontoglossum
O. grande
Mexico, Guatemala

This is the largest flowered of all known odontoglossums—7 inches across. Discovered by G. Ure Skinner in 1839 near the city of Guatemala, it flowered for the first time in England in the collection of the Duke of Bedford at Woburn Abbey in 1841. (Photograph courtesy of Andrew R. Addkison.)

PLATE 170
Odontoglossum
O. Gavotte (hybrid)

This hybrid, a cross between O. Nabab and O. Alorcus, is a relatively new introduction and is becoming successful in the cut-flower trade. Each blossom is 3 inches across. A spray bears from ten to fourteen separate flowers. (Photograph courtesy of Joyce R. Wilson.)

PLATE 171
Odontoglossum
O. schlieperianum
Costa Rica, Panama

Though a small plant, up to 16 inches high, it produces large flowers. First cultivated about 1856 and still widely grown, it is hardly an outstanding orchid but is a favorite with hobbyists. (Photograph courtesy of Joyce R. Wilson.)

PLATE 172
Odontoglossum
O. Tees (hybrid)

This hybrid was named after a river in Scotland by Ellen Low of Sussex, England. It is a cross between O. Amita Emperor of India and O. Pescatorei (Cookson's). This specimen is from the Beall Greenhouse Company, Vashon, Wash. (Photograph courtesy of Joyce R. Wilson.)

PLATE 173
Brassia
B. maculata
Cuba, Jamaica, British Honduras,
Guatemala, Honduras

One of the unusual spider orchids, it has large flowers of pale greenish-yellow, irregularly spotted with brown. The genus was founded by Dr. Robert Brown and named in commemoration of William Brass, a skilled botanical draftsman who collected seeds, plants, and dried specimens on the Guinea Coast and in South Africa for Sir Joseph Banks and others in the early 1800s. (Photograph courtesy of Andrew R. Addkison.)

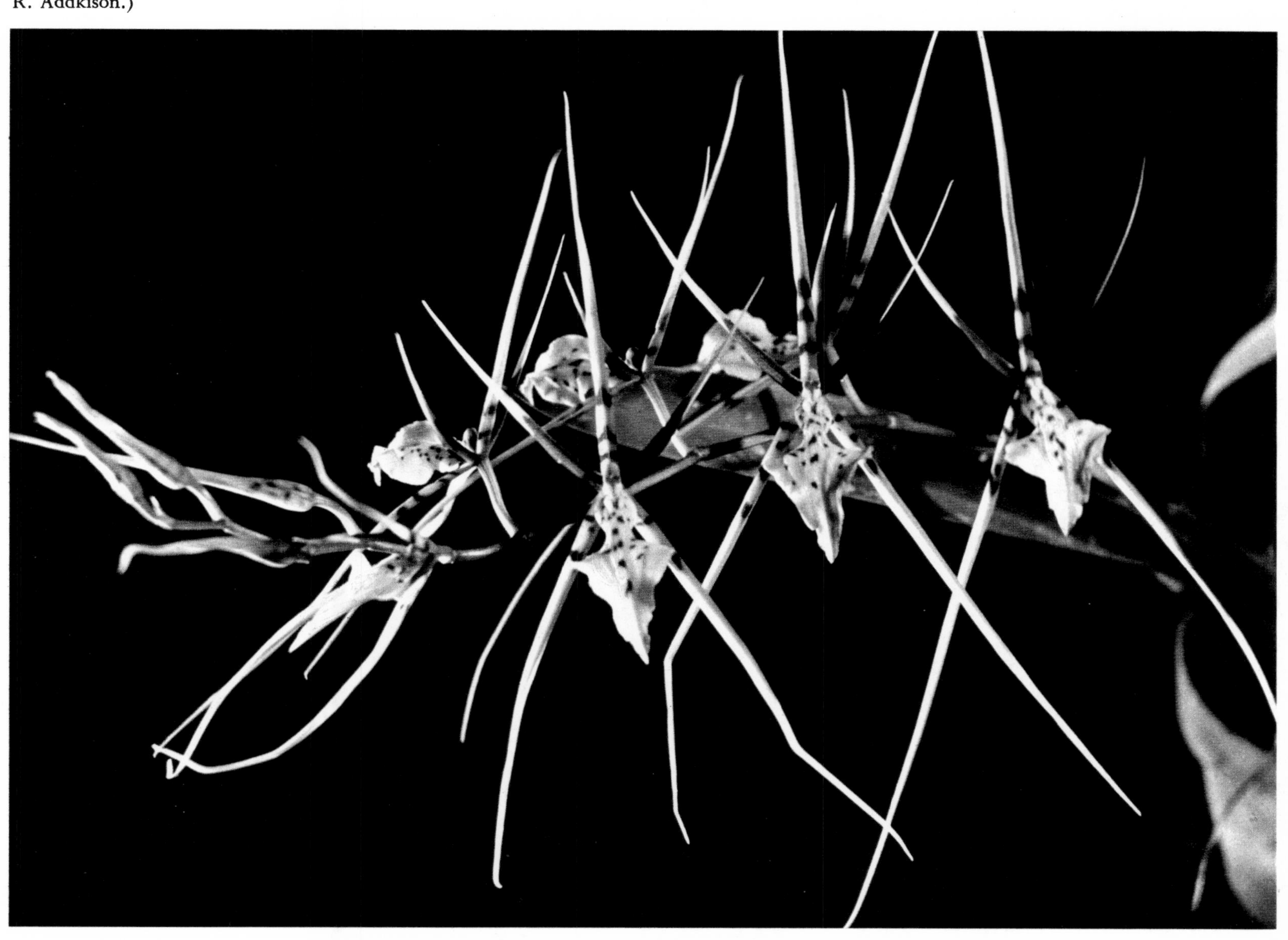

PLATE 174
Miltonia
M. Dearest (hybrid)

Commonly called either pansy orchid or ballerina orchid, this lovely hybrid has dramatic flowers borne on pendent scapes. It is a cross between M. Dolores Hart and M. Champagne. (Photograph courtesy of Joyce R. Wilson.)

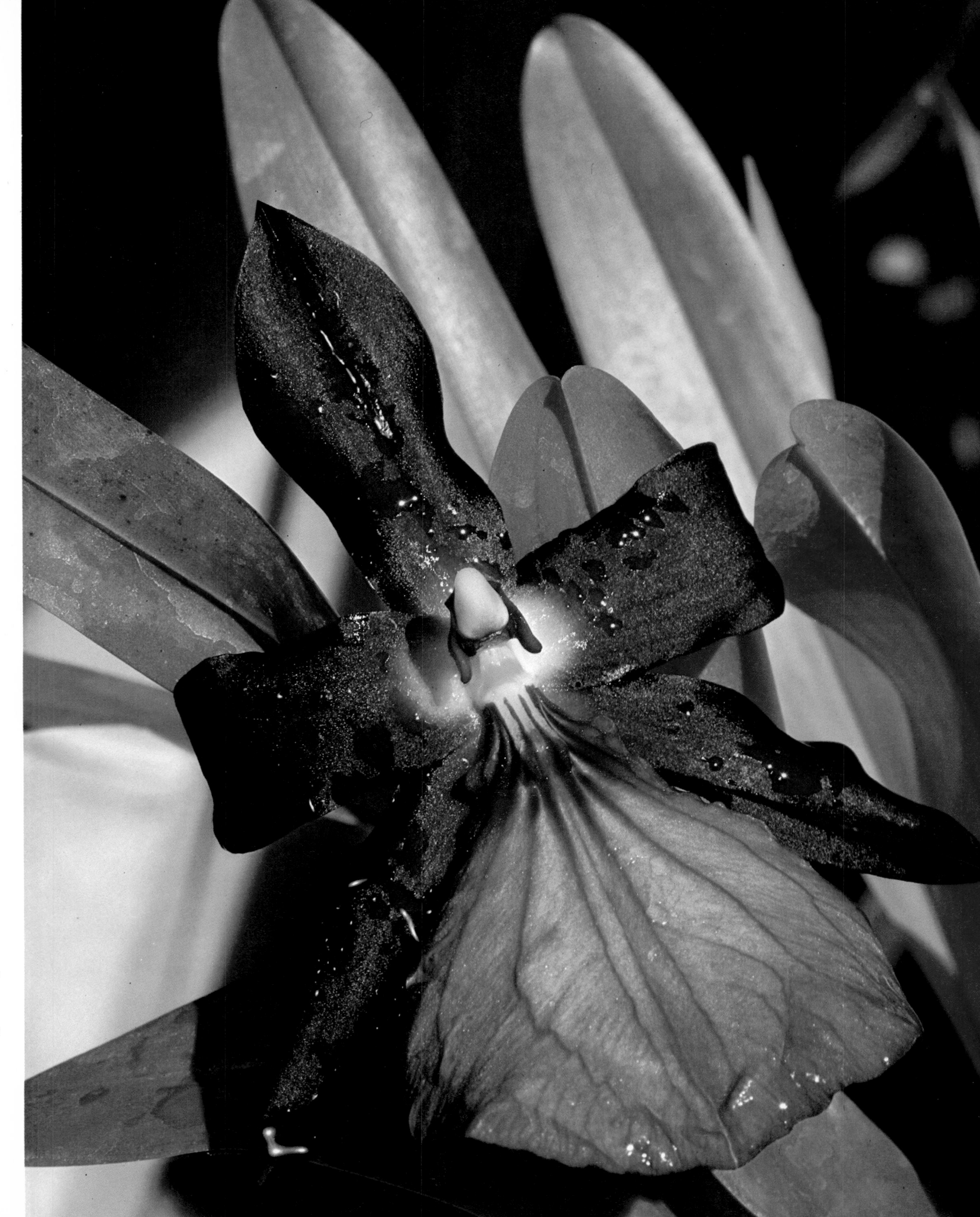

PLATE 175
Miltonia
M. spectabilis var. *moreliana*
Rio de Janeiro, southern Brazil

M. spectabilis is the species on which the genus was founded. The variety *moreliana* (darker in color) was first sent to Charles Morel of Saint-Monde, near Paris, in 1846. The plant grows to 20 inches high and has grassy foliage. (Photograph courtesy of Joyce R. Wilson.)

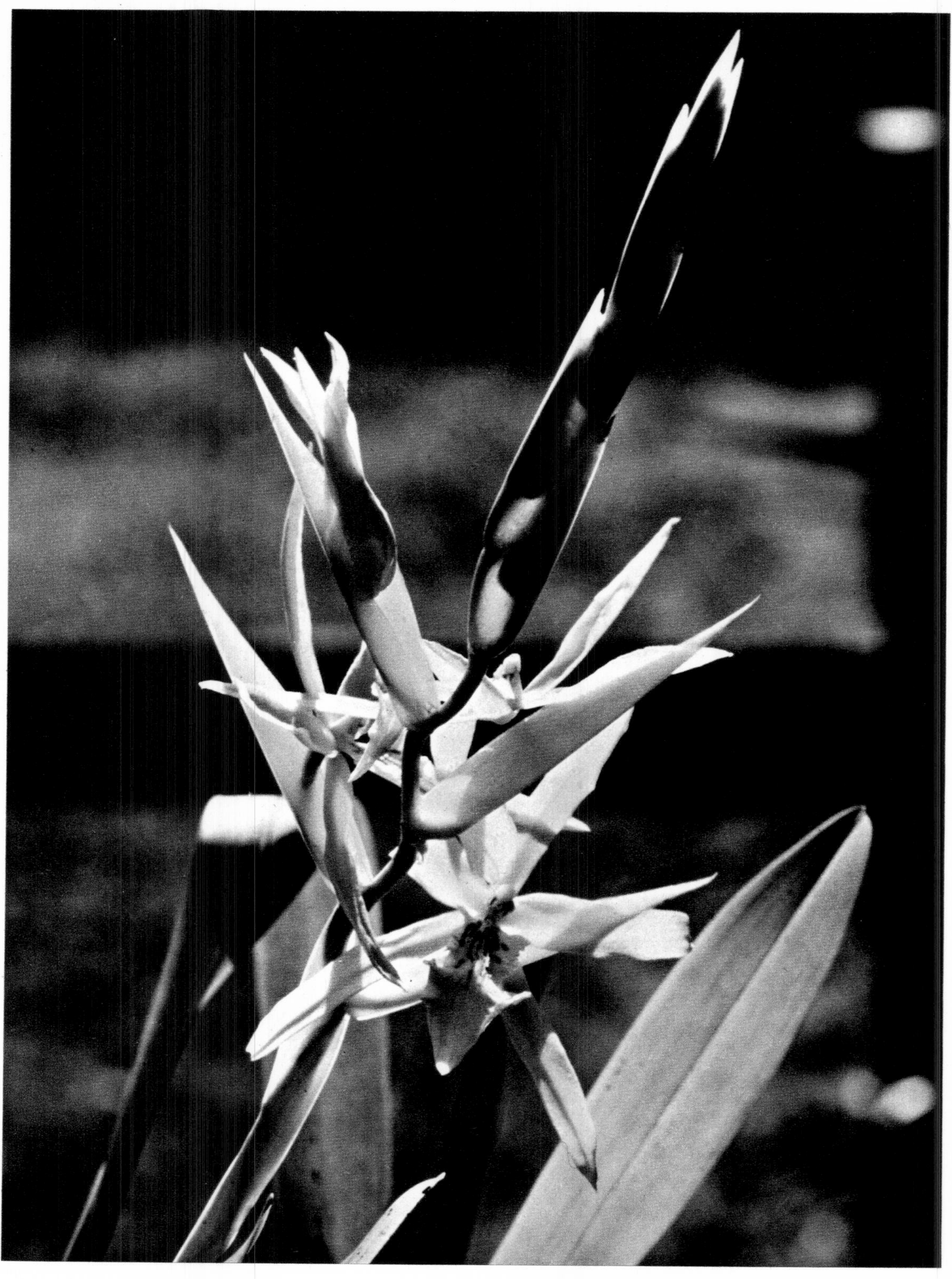

PLATE 176
Miltonia
M. flavescens
Brazil, Paraguay

A medium-size plant with lovely flat-faced 5-inch blooms, it was discovered by Michel Descourtilz, in the early nineteenth century near Banaval in the Brazilian province of Minas Gerais. William Harrison introduced it into England in 1832. (Photograph courtesy of Joyce R. Wilson.)

PLATE 177 ▶
Miltonia
M. vexillaria
Colombia

Basically a cool orchid from the mountains of Colombia, this species was grown for years as a hothouse subject and thus never flowered. It has grassy leaves and is sometimes called the pansy orchid because of its flat-faced flower. Although it was known in England in 1866, it did not bloom there until 1873. Around 1880 it was considered one of the outstanding orchids in Europe. (Photograph courtesy of Andrew R. Addkison.)

PLATE 178
Oncidium
O. ampliatum var. *majus*
Central America

Discovered about 1831 and gathered by G. Ure Skinner and Jósef Warscewicz in Central America, it grows in partial shade and produces tall wandlike stems covered with bright yellow blooms. It is called the turtle orchid because of the shape of the pseudobulbs. (Photograph courtesy of Joyce R. Wilson.)

PLATE 179
Oncidium
O. macranthum
Tropical America, Ecuador

The earliest evidence of this species was a single flower in the herbarium of the Spanish botanists Hipólito Ruiz Lopez and José Antonio Pavon. It was probably introduced about 1780; the locality given was Guayaquil, in Ecuador. (Photograph courtesy of Hermann Pigors.)

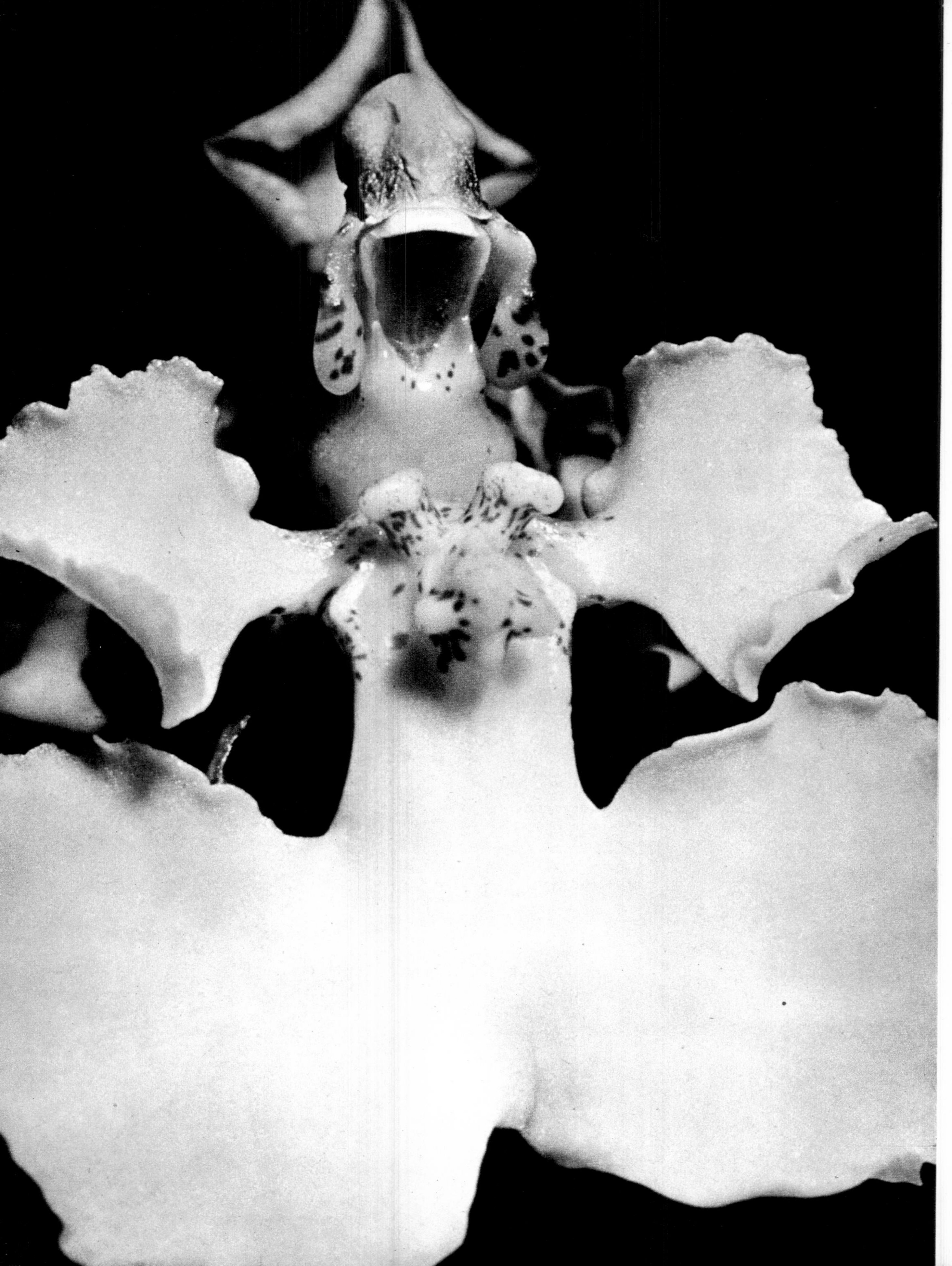

PLATE 180
Oncidium
O. macranthum
Tropical America, Ecuador

A close-up of the flower. See plate 179 for description. (Photograph courtesy of Joyce R. Wilson.)

PLATE 181
Oncidium
O. concolor
Brazil

This orchid has 1-inch bright yellow flowers on a dwarf plant, to 10 inches tall. Discovered by G. Gardner on the Organ Mountains in 1837, it was sent by him to the Woburn Collection, in England, where it flowered in 1840. (Photograph courtesy of Eric Chaney.)

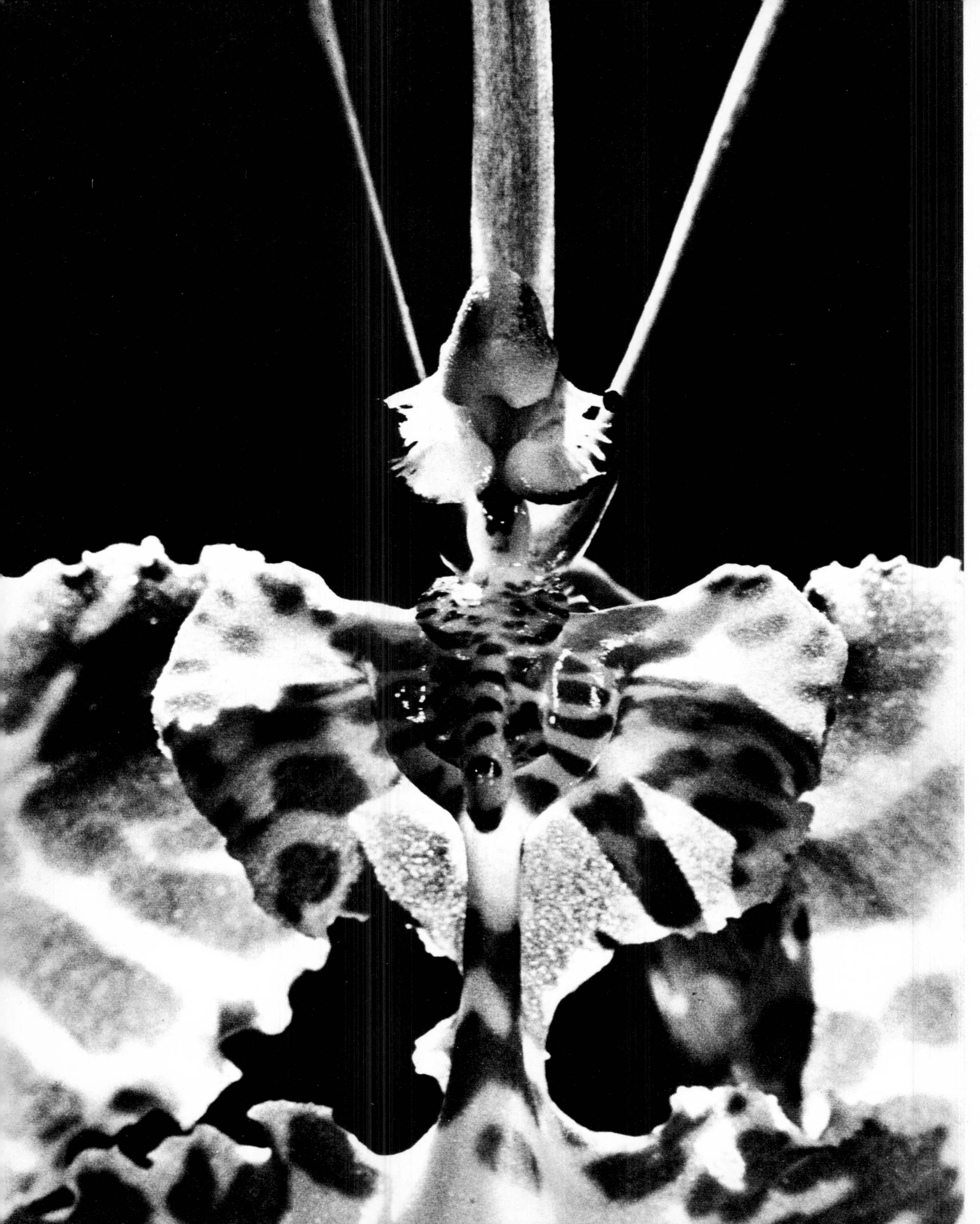

PLATE 182
Oncidium
O. papilio
West Indies

A close-up of the flower. See plate 183 for description. (Photograph courtesy of Joyce R. Wilson.)

PLATE 183 ▶
Oncidum
O. papilio
West Indies

The "butterfly orchid," with 2-in flowers on tall stems, is a choice plant. It was introduced from Tri in 1824 by Sir Ralph Woodford, t governor, who sent living plants t several collections. One flowered the first time in the nursery of a M Colville at Chelsea, England, in th spring of the following year. (Photograph courtesy of Joyce R. Wilson.)

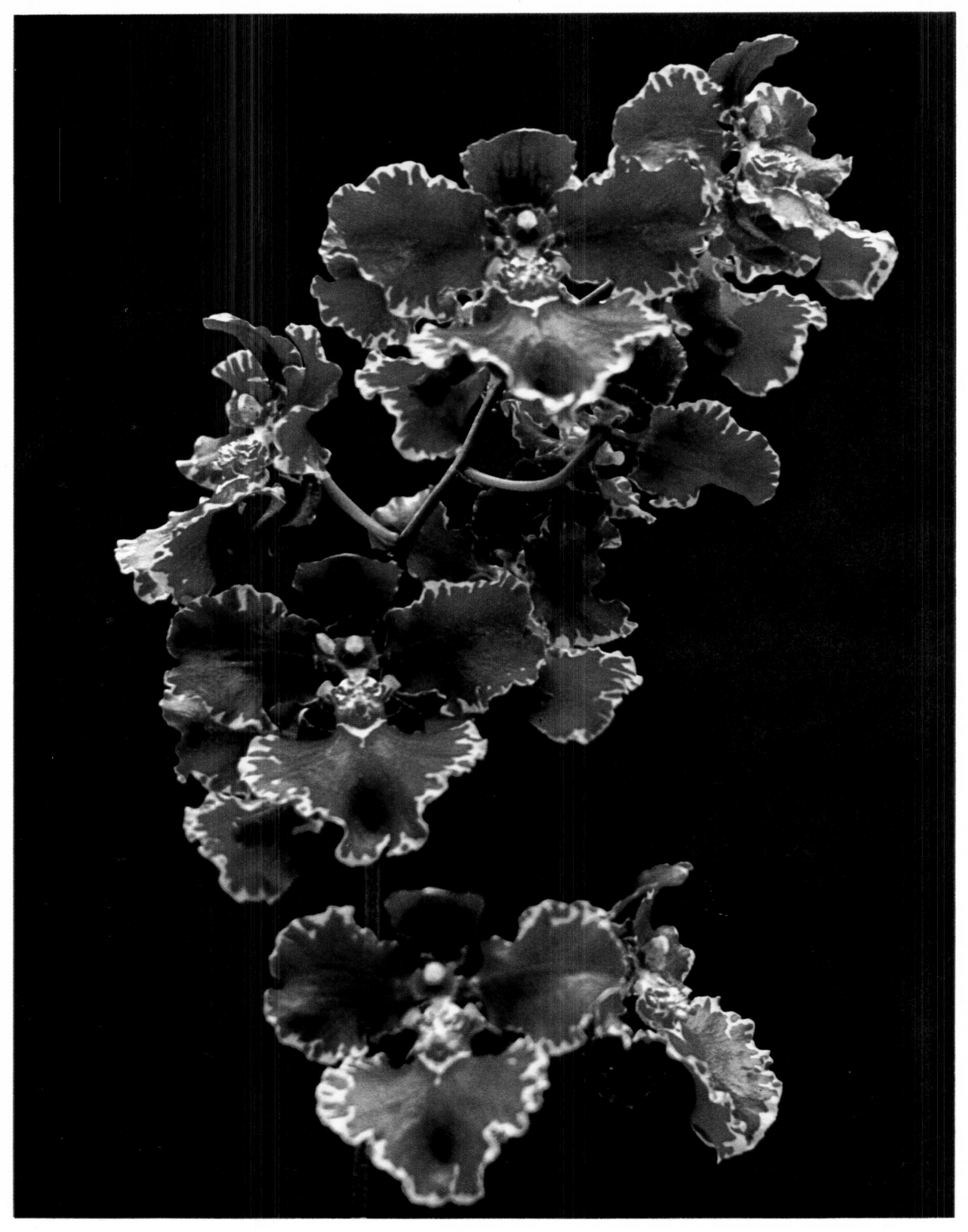

PLATE 184
Oncidium
O. forbesii
Brazil

This orchid was discovered by G. Gardner on the Organ Mountains in 1837 and sent to the Duke of Bedford, whose gardener, John Forbes, cultivated the plant at Woburn Abbey. Later, it was named in his honor by Sir William Hooker. (Photograph courtesy of Hermann Pigors.)

PLATE 185
Oncidium
O. lanceanum
Colombia, Venezuela, Trinidad

A handsome species that grows to 24 inches tall, it has succulent leaves making it look more like a cactus than an orchid. The flowers have a lovely spicy scent. The genus name refers to the warty calluses on the lip of the flower. It was first introduced to cultivation about 1834. (Photograph courtesy of Andrew R. Addkison.)

PLATE 186
Oncidium
O. splendidum
Guatemala, Honduras

A popular orchid with cactus-like leaves and long scapes bearing many flowers, it grows to 24 inches high and is an amenable plant. (Photograph courtesy of Guy Burgess.)

PLATE 187
Oncidium
O. cavendishianum
Mexico, Guatemala

Discovered by G. Ure Skinner near the city of Guatemala, this was one of the first orchids sent to England by him. It was included in his first consignment to James Bateman at Knypersley in 1835. (Photograph courtesy of Joyce R. Wilson.)

PLATE 188 ▶
Ornithocephalus
O. grandiflorus
Brazil

A miniature, this orchid has 1-inch-long leaves and greenish-white flowers about ½ inch across. It was originally discovered by G. Gardner on the Organ Mountains in Brazil in 1837. (Photograph courtesy of Joyce R. Wilson.)

PLATE 190 ▶
Sarcochilus
S. luniferus
North India

One of the numerous discoveries of the Rev. C. Parish near Moulmein, this species was introduced into England by the firm of Messrs. Low & Co. in 1868. (Photograph courtesy of Hermann Pigors.)

PLATE 189
Trichoceros
T. parviflorus
Colombia, Peru

A shy bloomer, this orchid cannot be counted on to blossom with any regularity. The flowers are green with purple-and-brown spots and bars and the foliage is sparse and leathery. *T. parviflorus* is known as the bee orchid because it mimics the bee, thus attracting these insects for the purpose of pollination. This specimen was photographed at the University of California Botanical Gardens. (Photograph courtesy of Andrew R. Addkison.)

PLATE 191
Sarcochilus
S. pygmeus
India, Malaysia, Indonesia

With tiny flowers, about ½ inch in diameter, this orchid is a true curiosity. (Photograph courtesy of Eric Chaney.)

PLATE 192
Ornithochilus
O. fuscus
The Himalayas, Burma, Thailand, Laos, Vietnam, Hong Kong

The genus name means "resembling a bird in flight." The flowers are small, about ½ inch long, and greenish-yellow with a red stripe. (Photograph courtesy of Joyce R. Wilson.)

PLATE 193
Rhyncostylis
R. gigantea: Sagarik's 'Orchidglade' AM/AOS

A magnificent orchid with a sweet fragrance, it has magenta-red flowers on pendent scapes. The plant has straplike leaves. The plum-red types of *R. gigantea* are rare in nature. Such select forms, however, can be obtained by seed methods of growing; Sagarik's 'Orchidglade' is a notable example. (Photograph courtesy of Joyce R. Wilson.)

PLATE 194
Rhyncostylis (*Saccolabium*)
R. gigantea
Burma, Thailand, Laos

This genus was founded by botanist Karel Lodewijk Blume on the beautiful species commonly known as *Saccolabium blumei*. The genus name refers to the beaked column of the original species. A popular orchid with hobbyists, it has straplike leaves and pendent scapes of small scented flowers. (Photograph courtesy of Joyce R. Wilson.)

PLATE 195
Rhyncostylis
R. gigantea
Burma, Thailand, Laos

A close-up of the flower. See plate 194 for description. (Photograph courtesy of Joyce R. Wilson.)

PLATE 196
Rhyncostylis
R. retusa
India, Ceylon, Burma, Thailand, Laos, Vietnam, Java, Borneo, Philippines

The first notice of this species appeared in 1831 in *The Botanical Register* under the name *Sarcanthus guttatus*. The plant grows to 20 inches across, has straplike leaves, and bears rather small pendent flowers, as many as 200 to a spike. It is commonly called the foxtail orchid and has an especially wide distribution. (Photograph courtesy of Andrew R. Addkison.)

PLATE 197
Aerides
A. multiflorum
The Himalayas, Burma, Thailand, Laos, Cambodia, Vietnam

A plant with straplike leaves and pendent scapes of 1-inch white-and-purple blooms. The flowers are especially fragrant. *A. multiflorum* first became known toward the end of the eighteenth century, when it was discovered by Dr. William Roxburgh, the first director of the Botanic Gardens at Calcutta. (Photograph courtesy of Joyce R. Wilson.)

PLATE 198
Phalaenopsis
P. amabilis
Indonesia, northern Australia, New Guinea, New Britain

This popular moth orchid has 4-inch white flowers and straplike leaves. Hundreds of hybrids have been made with *P. amabilis* as a parent. (Photograph courtesy of Joyce R. Wilson.)

PLATE 199
Phalaenopsis
P. amabilis
Indonesia, northern Australia, New Guinea, New Britain

This close-up shows the exquisite spotting and form of this superb orchid. See plate 198. (Photograph courtesy of Joyce R. Wilson.)

PLATE 200 ▶
Phalaenopsis
P. Judith Hausermann (hybrid)

Perfected by Hausermann Orchids of Elmhurst, Ill., this lovely phalaenopsis has brilliant colored flowers. It is a cross between *P. lueddemanniana* and *P. Mariposa*. (Photograph courtesy of Joyce R. Wilson.)

PLATE 201
Phalaenopsis
P. fasciata (*lueddemanniana* var. *ochracea*)
Philippines

This species, with 2-inch flowers of excellent form, is used extensively for hybridizing. (Photograph courtesy of Joyce R. Wilson.)

PLATE 202
Phalaenopsis
P. violacea
Sumatra, Malaya, Borneo

Many hybrids of this species are grown in great quantities for the cut-flower trade. White-blossomed forms especially are utilized for wedding bouquets and the like. (Photograph courtesy of Joyce R. Wilson.)

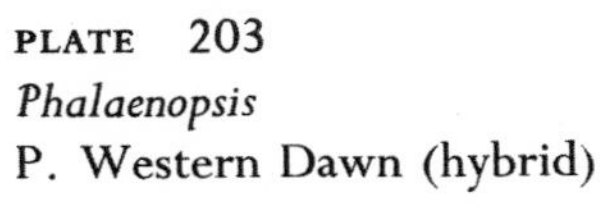

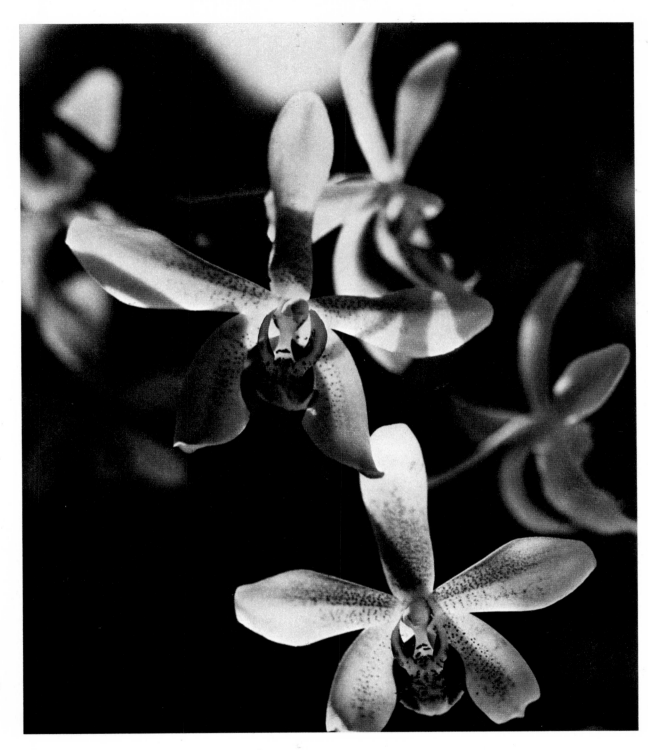

PLATE 203
Phalaenopsis
P. Western Dawn (hybrid)

This charming orchid has lovely flat open-faced flowers, peach or pink in color, with many to a stem. An amenable plant, it also has good keeping quality. P. Western Dawn is a cross between P. Dawn Mist and *P. manii*. (Photograph courtesy of Joyce R. Wilson.)

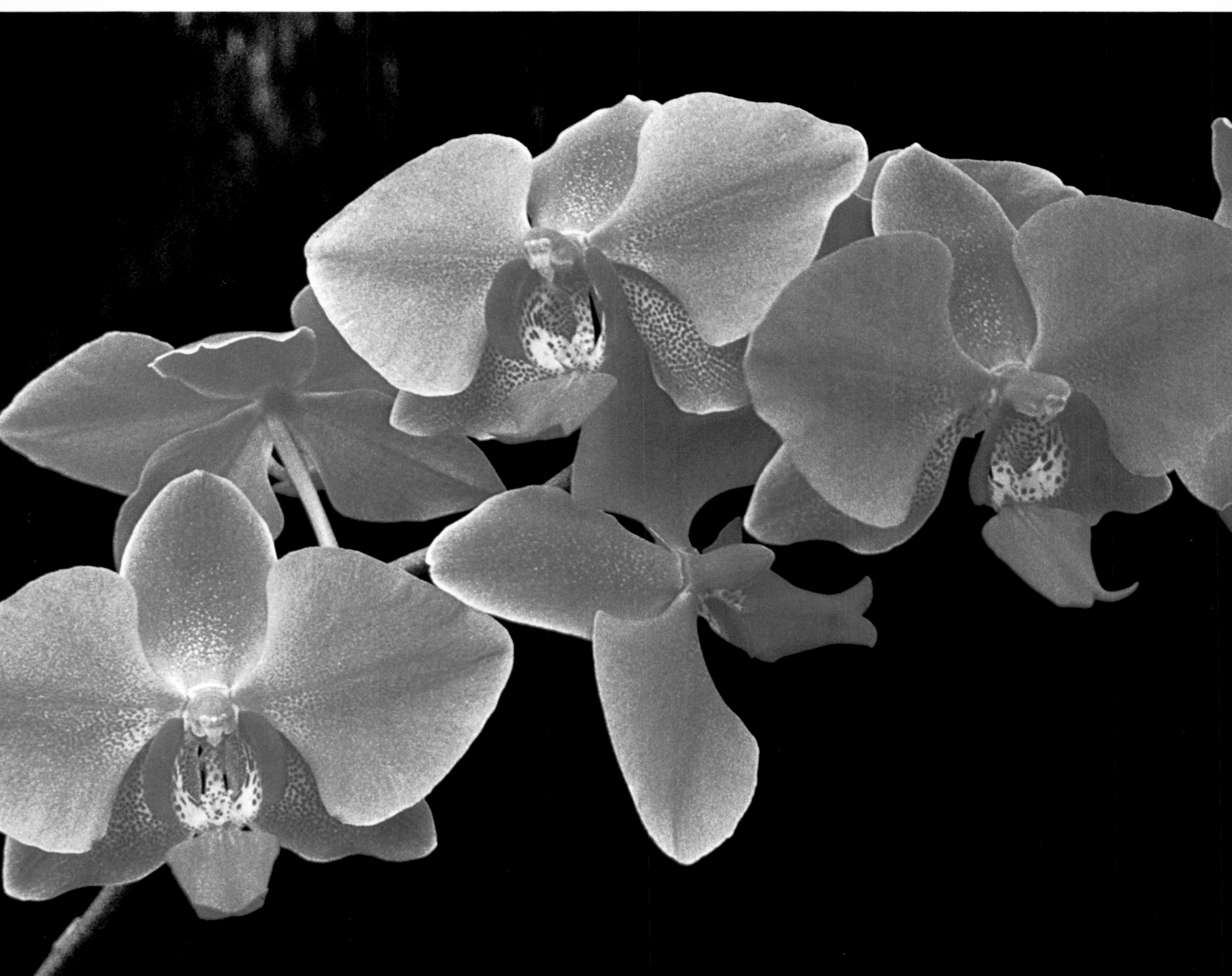

PLATE 204
Doritaenopsis
Dtps. Ravenswood (hybrid)

As startlingly dramatic in its coloring as a neon light, this purplish-pink hybrid is quite easy to grow. It is a cross between Dtps. Mem. Clarence Schubert and Phalaenopsis Zada. (Photograph courtesy of Hermann Pigors.)

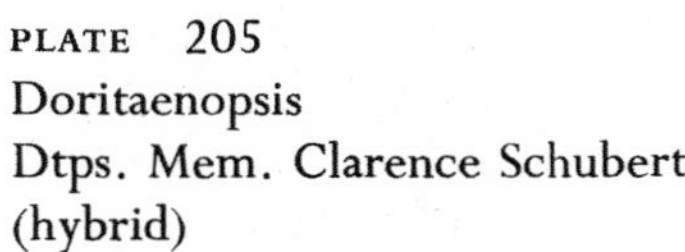

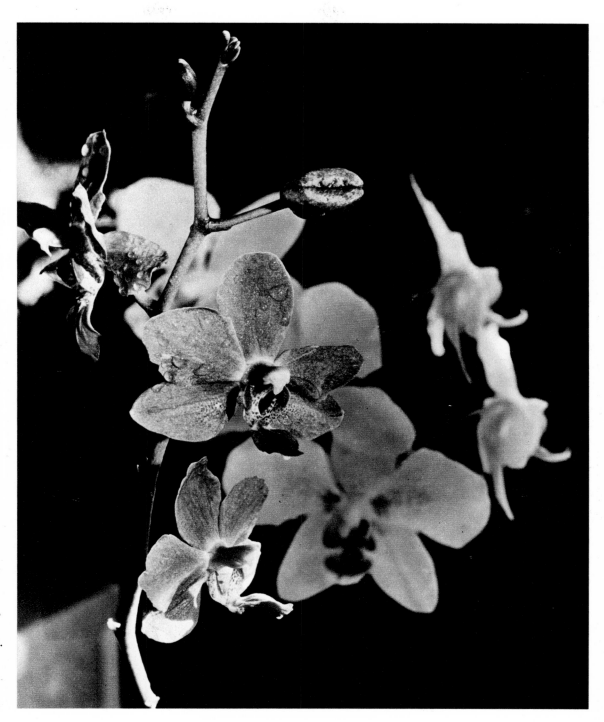

PLATE 205
Doritaenopsis
Dtps. Mem. Clarence Schubert (hybrid)

An excellent cross, it is distinguished by the color of its flowers—luminous, deep violet. The plant blooms for months, one flower following another. Its parents are *Doritis pulcherrima* var. *buyssoniana* and Phalaenopsis Zada. (Photograph courtesy of Joyce R. Wilson.)

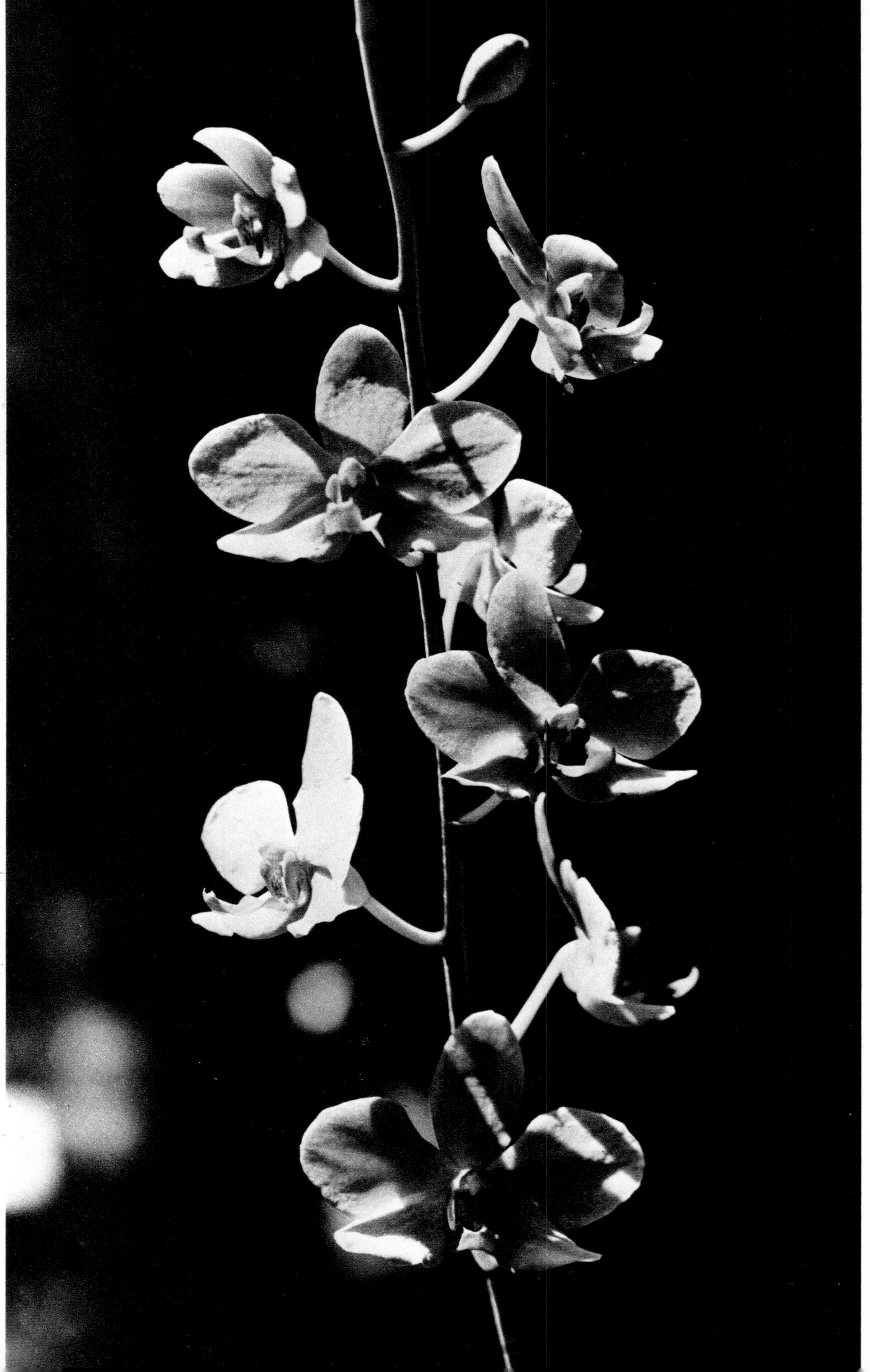

PLATE 206
Doritaenopsis
Dtps. Kenneth Schubert (hybrid)

This lovely orchid bears delicate rose-pink flowers that bloom asymmetrically along a short spike. It is a cross between *Doritis pulcherrima* and *Phalaenopsis violacea*. (Photograph courtesy of Joyce R. Wilson.)

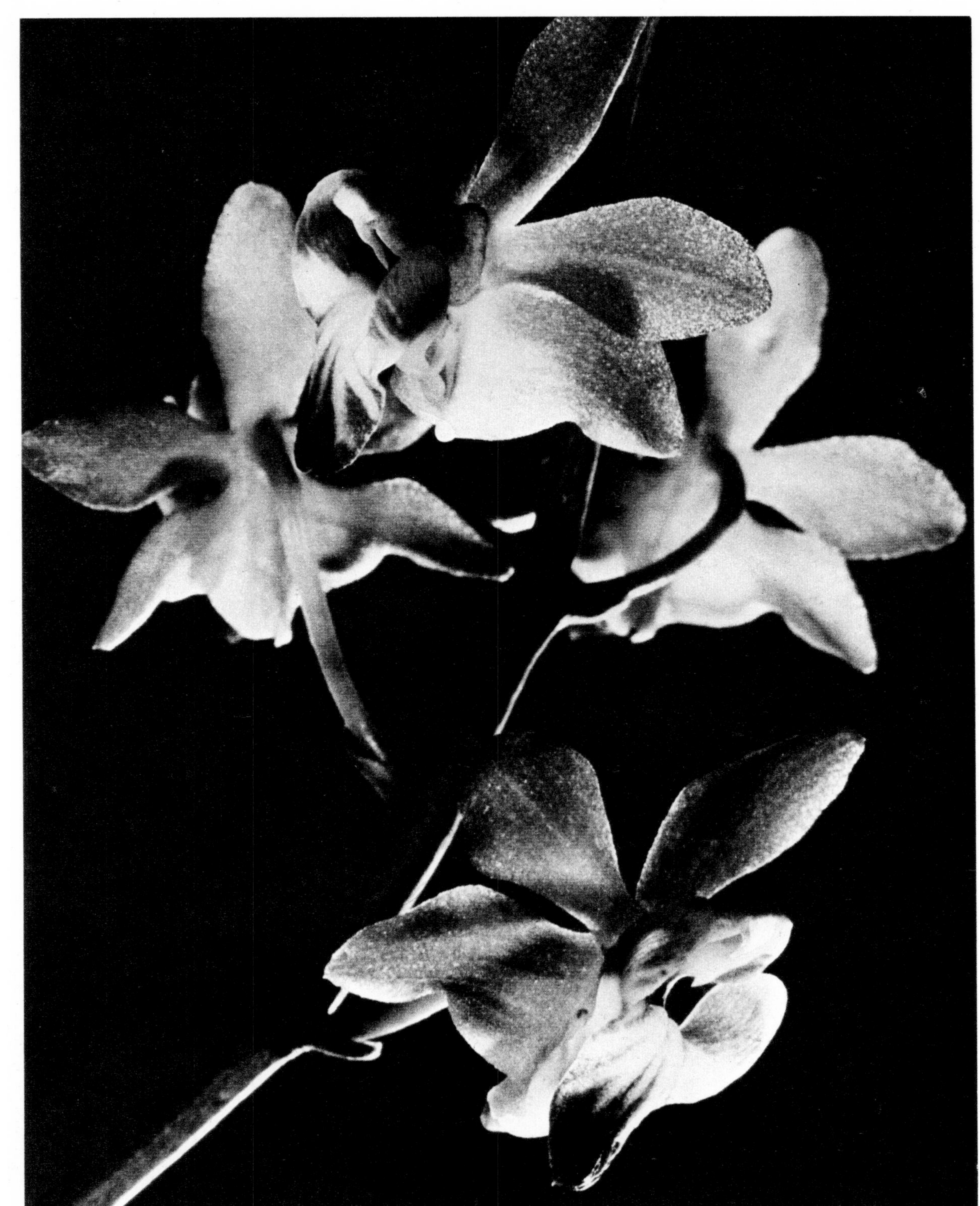

PLATE 207
Doritis
D. pulcherrima
Burma, Thailand, Laos, Cambodia, Sumatra

Until recently assigned to the genus *Phalaenopsis,* this species has been reclassified. It has, however, been successfully hybridized with orchids in that genus. The flowers, usually about 2 inches across, are either pale rose-purple or magenta-rose, with pale lavender veining. (Photograph courtesy of Joyce R. Wilson.)

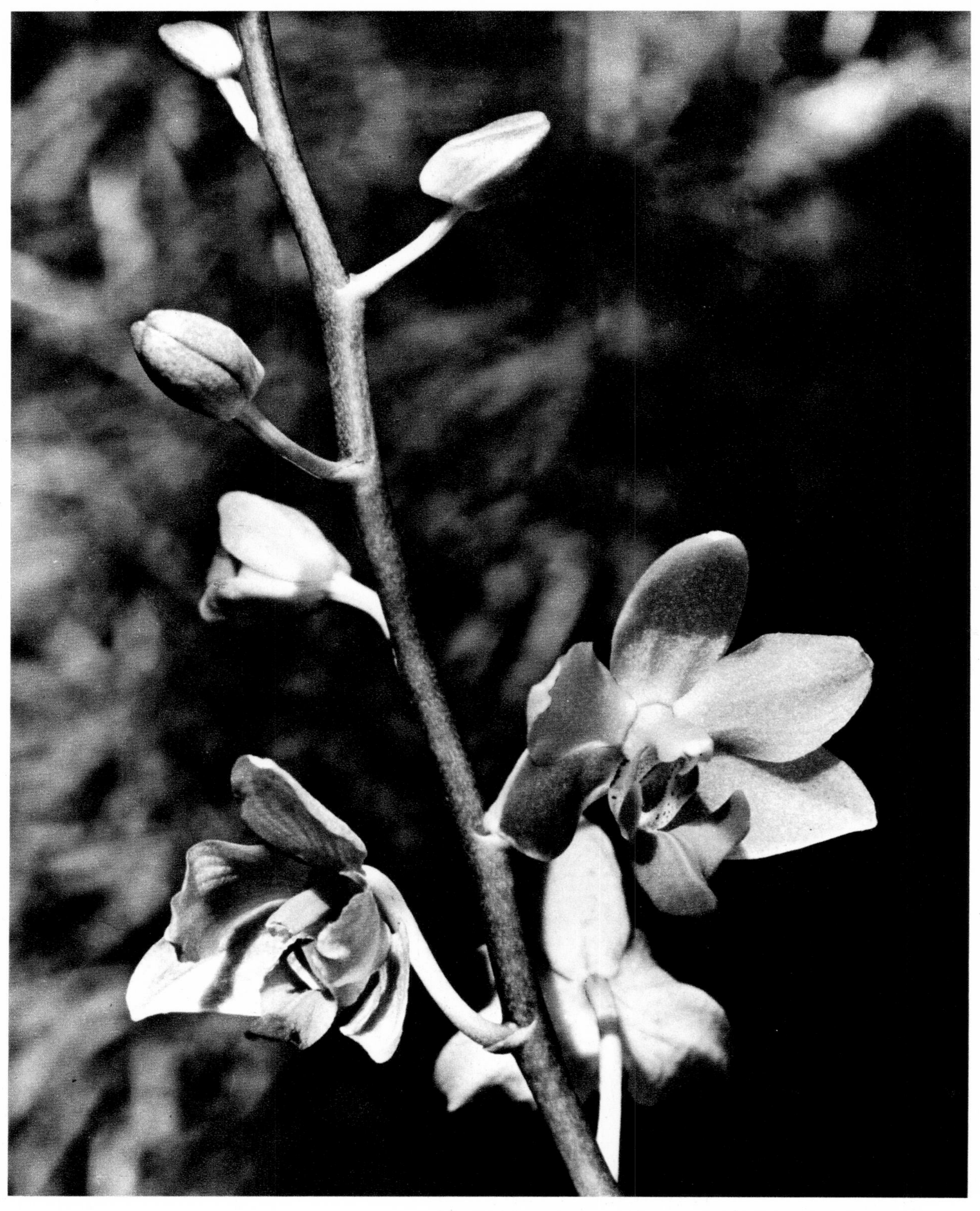

PLATE 208
Doritis
D. pulcherrima var. *buyssoniana*
Burma, Thailand, Laos, Cambodia, Vietnam, Sumatra

This delicate orchid is a natural variety of *D. pulcherrima*. See plate 207 for a description of the species. (Photograph courtesy of Joyce R. Wilson.)

PLATE 209 ▶
Aeranthes
A. arachnites
Madagascar

The genus name refers to mist—or air—flowers. The blooms are indeed ethereal in appearance; the plant grows up to 16 inches high. This is an unusual and lovely orchid. (Photograph courtesy of Joyce R. Wilson.)

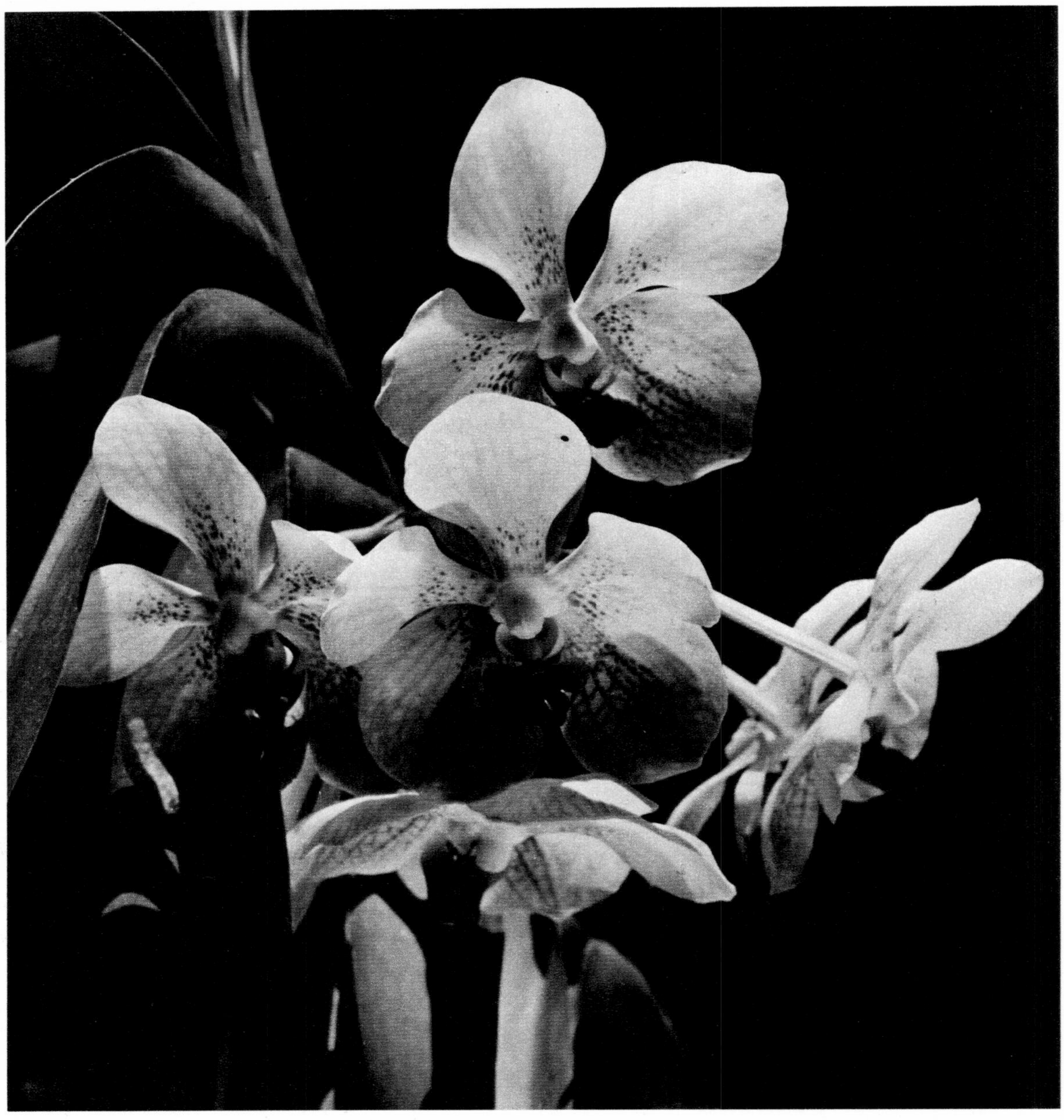

PLATE 210
Vanda
V. hybrid

Today, there are countless vanda hybrids, all exquisite in color and form. The plants are floriferous and sometimes bloom twice a year. The exact parentage of this particularly lovely one is unknown. (Photograph courtesy of Joyce R. Wilson.)

PLATE 211 ▶
Vanda
V. caerulea
The Himalayas, Burma, Thailand

This orchid was discovered by William Griffith in 1837 on the Khasia Hills. One of the first specimens sent to England flowered in 1850 at the Royal Horticultural Society of London. The color of the flower varies from pale blue to pink-blue (see plate 214) to almost dark blue, as in this specimen. An incredibly beautiful flower. (Photograph courtesy of Andrew R. Addkison.)

PLATE 212
Vanda
V. cristata
Nepal, Sikkim

First gathered by Dr. Nathaniel Wallich in 1818 at high elevations in Nepal, this orchid bloomed at the Royal Botanical Gardens at Kew sometime later. (Photograph courtesy of Joyce R. Wilson.)

PLATE 213 ▶
Vanda
V. Evening Glow (hybrid)

This winsome orchid, whose delicate coloring is a subtle mixture of flesh, pink, and other pastel tints, blooms twice a year. It is a cross between V Alice Fukunaga and V. Clara Shipma Fisher. (Photograph courtesy of Joyce R. Wilson.)

◀ PLATE 214
Vanda
V. caerulea (with *Phalaenopsis amabilis*)
The Himalayas, Burma, Thailand

The pale blue orchid, *V. caerulea,* bears several to many flowers on one raceme. The lip is one third the length of the adjacent sepals. The white orchids, *P. amabilis,* are from tropical Asia, Malaysia, and the Philippines. This species is one of the best of the hothouse orchids. It is mostly white with overcolors; and some, as this one, have odd appendages colored with brown-purple and yellow. This photograph was taken in the greenhouse of Klaus Abegg, Colorado Springs, Colo. See plates 211 and 198 and 199. (Photograph courtesy of Guy Burgess.)

PLATE 215
Vanda
V. sanderiana: hybrid

This is one of the large-flowered vanda hybrids of *sanderiana* origin. The exact parentage is unknown. (Photograph courtesy of Joyce R. Wilson.)

PLATE 216
Vanda
V. Rothschildiana (hybrid)

One of the most prized blue orchids, V. Rothschildiana—the middle plant in the picture—is a cross between *V. caerulea* and *V. sanderiana*. Scarce in collections at this time, it is perhaps the most famous blue vanda of all. The orchids on either side are *V. caerulea*. (Photograph courtesy of Hermann Pigors.)

PLATE 217
Vanda
V. suavis
Java

Discovered by Thomas Lobb and introduced into England in 1846, this species has been used extensively for hybridizing. A large plant up to 60 inches tall, *V. suavis* is a star-burst-blooming climber. The flowers are stiff and fleshy, and the lip petal has an exceptionally intricate formation. (Photograph courtesy of Guy Burgess.)

PLATE 219
Renanthera
R. monachica
Philippines

Growing to about 12 inches in height, this orchid bears 2-inch bright orange flowers dotted with red. The genus distribution ranges from China and the Himalayas, throughout Southeast Asia, the Philippines, and from Indonesia to New Guinea. (Photograph courtesy of Joyce R. Wilson.)

PLATE 218
Renanthera
R. imschootiana
Burma

An epiphytic dwarf species, it is distinguished by its dramatic flowers, which are borne on an erect stem with short leaves. (Photograph courtesy of Hermann Pigors.)

PLATE 220
Ascocentrum
A. curvifolium
The Himalayas

A dwarf orchid with bright 1-inch cinnabar-red flowers, it was at one time classified both as *Saccolabium curvifolium* and as *Gastrochilus curvifolius*. (Photograph courtesy of Joyce R. Wilson.)

PLATE 221
Ascocentrum
A. ampullaceum
China to Java, Borneo

This handsome dwarf species has ½-inch flowers of bright cerise. Four of the nine known species in the genus are in contemporary collections, almost always classified erroneously under the genus name *Saccolabium*. (Photograph courtesy of Joyce R. Wilson.)

PLATE 222
Ascocentrum
A. ampullaceum
China to Java, Borneo

A close-up of the flower. See plate 221 for description. (Photograph courtesy of Joyce R. Wilson.)

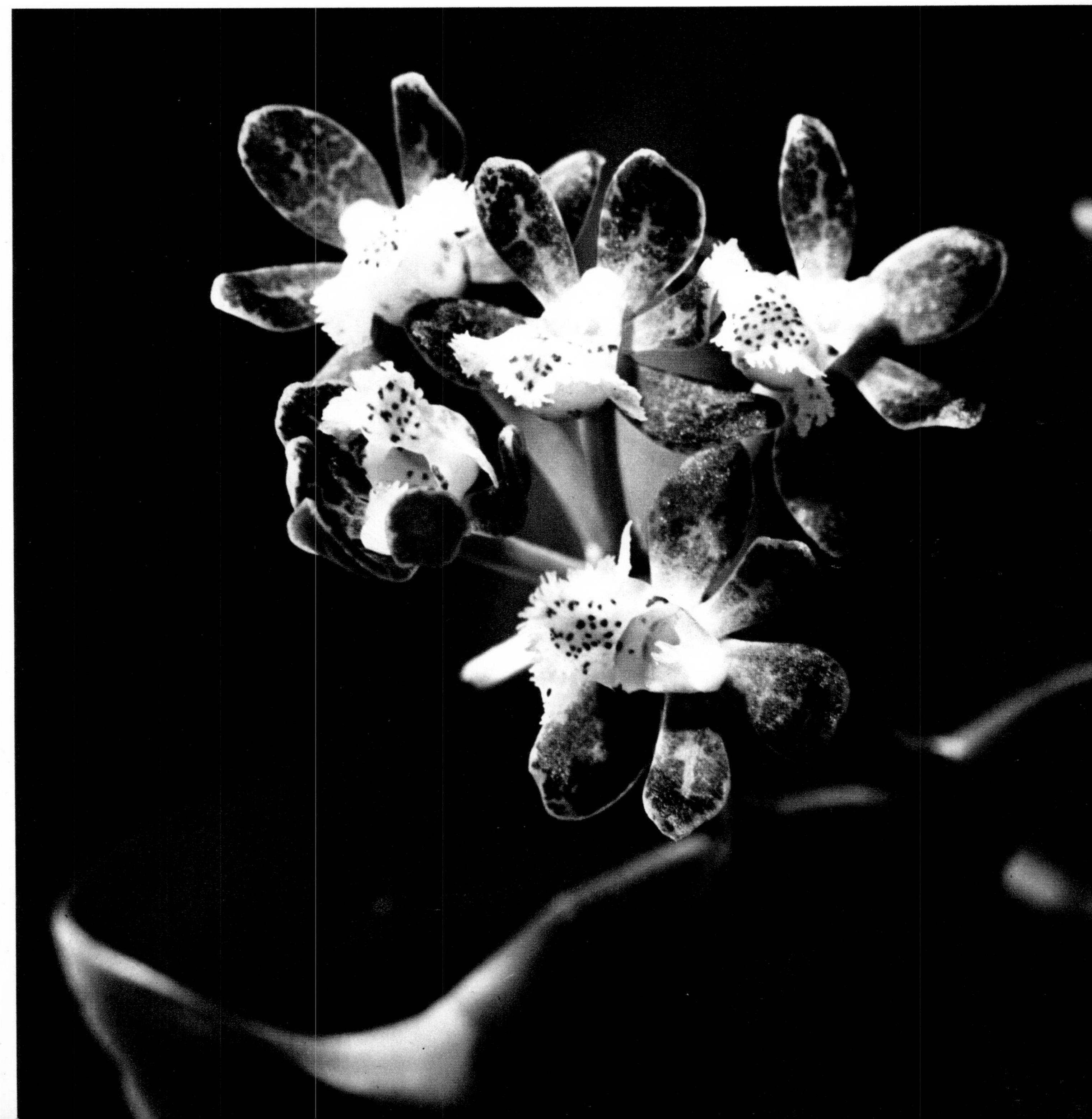

PLATE 223
Gastrochilus
G. calceolare
The Himalayas, Burma, Sumatra, Java

Usually a dwarfish monopodial plant, with only a few leathery leaves, it has small but rather spectacular flowers. (Photograph courtesy of Joyce R. Wilson.)

PLATE 224
Cyrtorchis (Angraecum)
C. arcuata
South Africa

Fine, graceful white flowers give distinction to this medium-size plant. One of the numerous segregates from the genus *Angraecum,* Cyrtorchis is a group containing about fifteen known species, all native to the African tropics. (Photograph courtesy of Guy Burgess.)

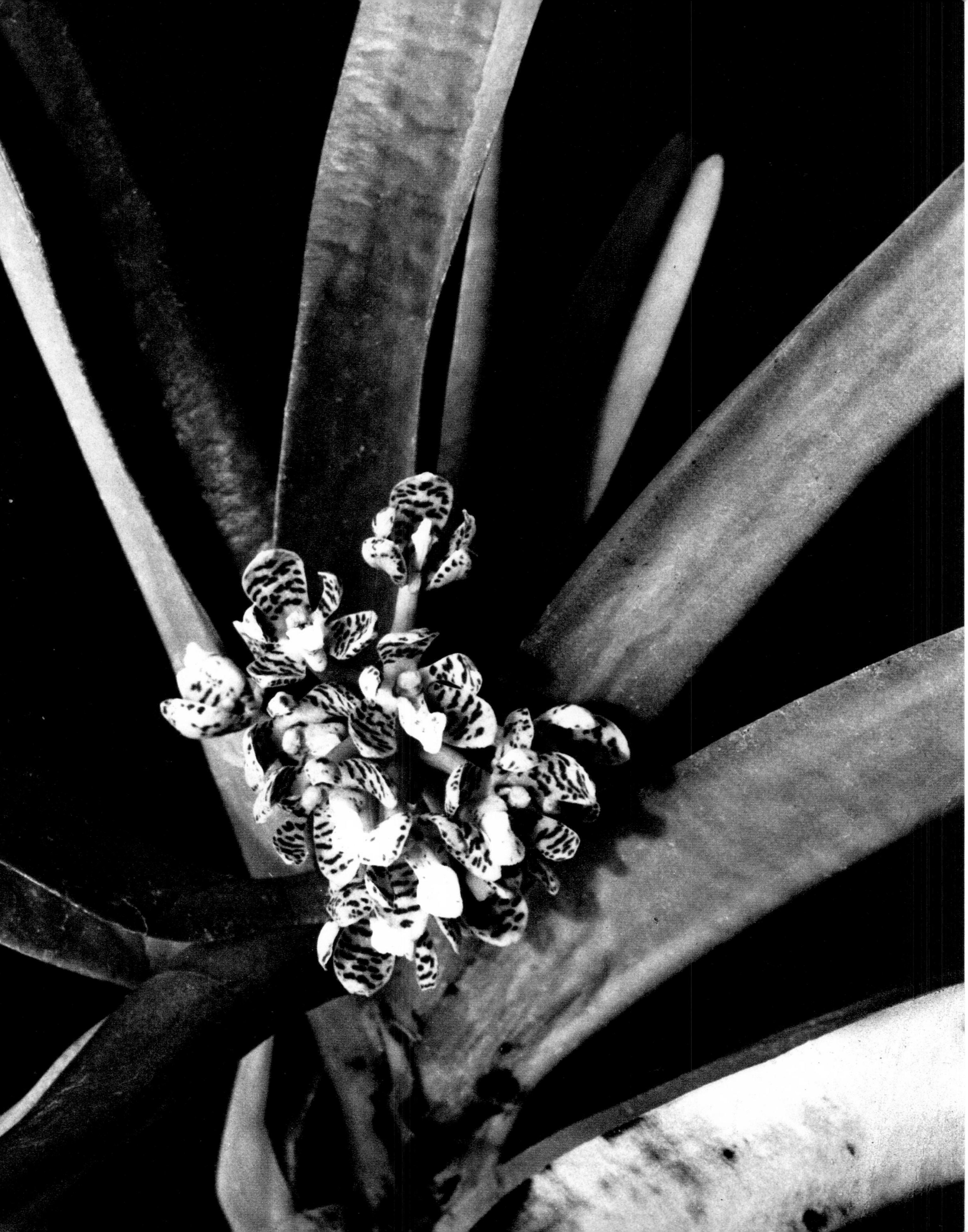

PLATE 225
Acampe
A. pachyglossa
African and Asiatic tropics

Classed as a miniature, this species grows over 18 inches high and bears clusters of fleshy yellow-and-red blooms. It is widely dispersed throughout the above regions. (Photograph courtesy of Joyce R. Wilson.)

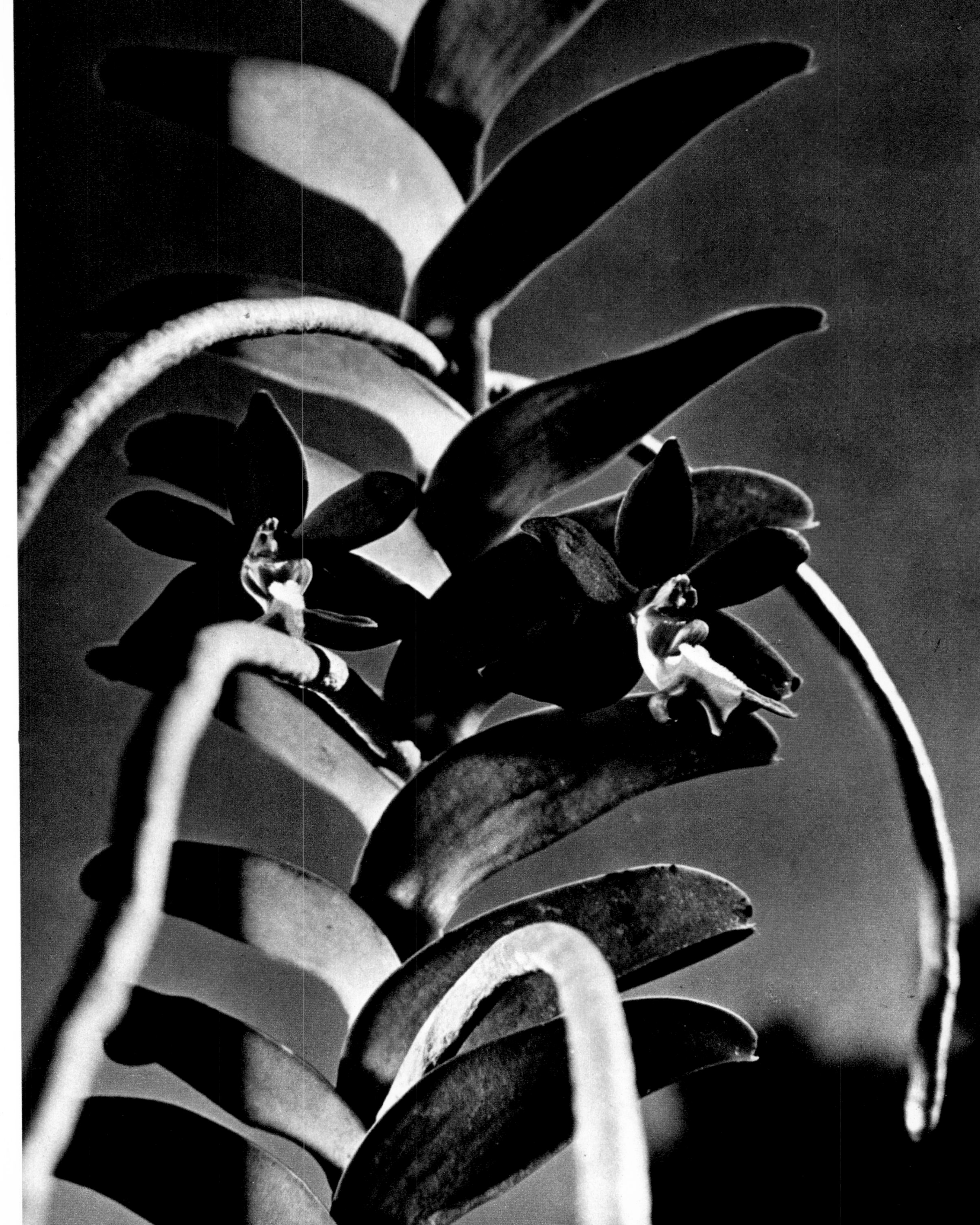

PLATE 226
Trichoglottis
T. philippinensis var. *brachiata*
Philippines

This exotic orchid has 1-inch flowers of purple and red on a vining plant. Though ranging from the Himalayas, throughout the Asiatic tropics, to New Guinea, it is most abundant in the Philippines. (Photograph courtesy of Joyce R. Wilson.)

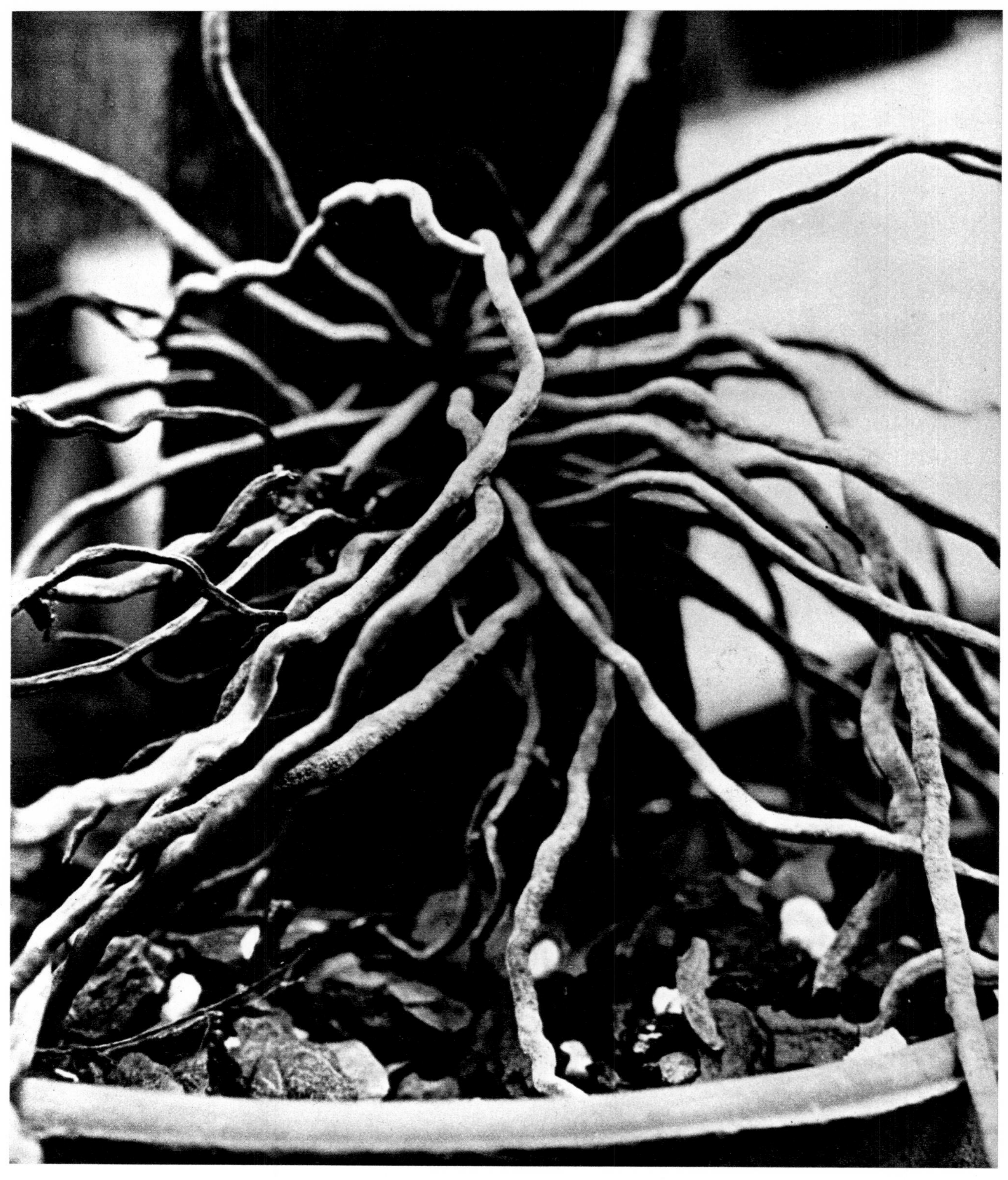

PLATE 227
Microcoelia
M. smithii
Kenya

When mature, this incredible plant is totally leafless and forms a cluster of fleshy roots surrounding a woody stem. During the blooming stage, it has dainty white bell-shaped flowers, produced in profusion. *M. smithii* is the most bizarre orchid in this book. (Photograph courtesy of Joyce R. Wilson.)

Orchid Genera

In the orchid family, allied groups of genera and their component species are called subtribes. Each known plant has been given a place in the scheme of things. Classification, however, is not yet final in all cases so research continues. I do not wish to take sides in the various conflicts about orchid classification. To best serve the purpose of this book, I have chosen to arrange the photographs following the system set up by Rudolf Schlechter in 1915. This system proposes some 660 genera, which contain 88 subtribes. In all possible instances genera are placed so that their relationship one to another is clearly shown. They appear in sequence according to their degree of development, beginning with the ancient cypripediums and ending with the leafless orchids.

Acampe. An African and Asian genus of epiphytes with about twelve species. Leaves are leathery and flowers, borne in clusters, are fleshy.

Acanthophippium. Closely allied to the genus *Phaius,* this genus consists of mostly terrestrial orchids. Plants are somewhat large, growing to 40 inches tall, and have broad, plicate leaves and bear colorful tulip-shaped blooms.

Acineta. With more than twelve species, this genus of epiphytes ranges from Mexico to South America. Like the genera *Gongora* and *Stanhopea, Acineta* has flower spikes that grow straight downward from the base of the pseudobulb. Plants have decorative apple-green leaves and 2- to 3-inch flowers.

Aeranthes. From Madagascar and adjacent islands comes this genus of about thirty species. Plants produce unusual flowers; some are small, others large. Green is the prevailing flower color.

Aerides. From Japan to India and Malaysia, this epiphytic genus has some sixty species. Plants can grow to 6 feet tall, producing arching stems of small, handsome, usually scented flowers.

Anguloa. A fine terrestrial genus of ten species from the Andean region of South America. The fragrant flowers are large, colorful, and somewhat tuliplike in appearance. Not easily grown under cultivation, but worth the extra time and trouble.

Ansellia. Fine spotted orchids, epiphytic or semiepiphytic, from tropical Africa that produce large handsome flowers on medium to large plants. Only a few species are known (according to some authorities, only one species).

Ascocentrum. A genus of small plants with nine species. Ascocentrums grow in southern China and in Java and Borneo. These are brilliant orchids, worthy of space in any collection.

Barkeria. (included in genus *Epidendrum*.)

Bifrenaria. From Panama and Brazil come about twenty species of this epiphytic genus. Most of these orchids have showy flowers and a solitary shiny green leaf. Closely related to the genera *Maxillaria* and *Lycaste, Bifrenaria* produces flowers in racemes rather than singly.

Bletia. A genus of terrestrial species found from Florida to Peru. Plants have grasslike deciduous or nearly deciduous foliage and attractive small flowers.

Bollea. A south American epiphytic genus with about six species represented. Plants have loose fans of apple-green foliage and bear handsome 2- to 4-inch flowers marked with blue. Extremely desirable plants.

Brassavola. With about fifteen tropical American species, this epiphytic genus is known for its white or whitish-green flowers. *B. glauca* and *B. digbyana* have been used extensively in hybridizing with species of the genus *Cattleya*.

Brassia. About fifty species make up the epiphytic genus *Brassia,* found from south Florida and the West Indies to Mexico, Brazil, and Peru. These leafy green plants have lately become popular with hobbyists. The flowers, about fifty to a mature plant, have long sepals and are produced on arching stems. Brassias are commonly called spider orchids.

Calanthe. A genus of over 150 species of terrestrial orchids widely distributed from South Africa to Asia and the Pacific Islands; in the West Indies and Central America it is a single species. Some calanthes are evergreen; many are deciduous. Most of the cultivated hybrids bloom at Christmas. The plants, therefore, are very desirable.

Calopogon. A genus of hardy North American terrestrials common in Florida and the Bahamas. Leaves are grassy; flowers are small but handsome. Plants rarely exceed 20 inches in height.

Catasetum. Epiphytic or occasionally semiterrestrial, this genus has over a hundred species found in the American tropics. Flowers are large and showy; some are beautiful, others grotesque in appearance. Many are deciduous; others hold leaves until blooms appear.

Cattleya. The best-known genus of orchids. Plants are generally epiphytic; a few grow on rocks. The sixty-five species extend from Mexico to Argentina and Peru. They are characterized by prominent pseudobulbs, and have one or two leaves. Cattleyas are the major orchids of commerce; countless important hybrids have been produced by crossing cattleyas with related genera.

Chysis. A beautiful genus of epiphytic orchids with six or eight species found throughout tropical America from Mexico to Peru. Leaves are thick and fleshy; flowers are always showy.

Coelogyne. This genus has over 120 greatly varied epiphytic and terrestrial species in wide distribution over the Eastern Hemisphere. Plants have one or two leaves and generally showy flowers. Most prefer cool growing conditions.

Comparettia. From Mexico to South America, this small genus of epiphytic orchids has solitary leathery leaves and pendant scapes of showy flowers. Some species are lovely, others hardly worth cultivation.

Coryanthes. This epiphytic genus has fifteen species distributed from British Honduras and Guatemala to Brazil and Peru. The plants are called bucket orchids and have an intricate structure. Generally more bizarre than beautiful, coryanthes are rarely seen in cultivation.

Cycnoches. A genus of about eleven species from tropical America. Most of the cultivated species are called swan orchids because they bear some resemblance to the neck of a swan. Generally deciduous, these epiphytic, occasionally terrestrial, orchids produce mammoth flowers having intense fragrance.

Cymbidium. A genus of about seventy species (epiphytic, semiepiphytic, and terrestrial) from the Asiatic tropics and subtropics. Foliage is grassy and ornamental. Species flowers are generally small and hardly showy, but many thousand horticultural hybrids excel in flower form and size. Grown outdoors in most parts of southern California.

Cypripedium. This is the well-known lady's-slipper orchid. The genus contains about fifty species found in temperate and subtropical parts of the world. Plants are attractive with broad leaves and mostly showy flowers. There are about twelve species in the United States.

Cyrtorchis. Sometimes called *Angraecum,* this genus of epiphytic orchids is from Africa and produces star-shaped white flowers.

Dendrobium. A large genus with over 1,500 species growing throughout the Asian tropics and subtropics eastward to the Fiji Islands and south to Australia. The hybrids are important. Plants may have bulbous or reedlike pseudobulbs. Some are evergreen; others are deciduous: leaves fall from the plant before it blooms. There is wide variation in size, flower form, and plant structure. Some plants require heat, others like coolness.

Dendrochilum, see **Platyclinis.**

Diacrium (also called **Caularthron**). An epiphytic genus having four species, with two variable ones from the West Indies and Central America. All usually have hollow pseudobulbs. Flowers look somewhat like epidendrums; plants are usually dwarf.

Doritis. An epiphytic genus closely allied to the genus *Phalaenopsis.* The plants produce small but charming flat-faced flowers.

Epidendrum. With over a thousand species, this genus is found from North Carolina to Argentina. The majority are epiphytic, though some grow in soil, others on rocks. Plant form and flowers vary greatly. There are two major groups of species: those with pseudobulbs and those with reed stem growth. Some botanists have reclassified many epidendrums into other genera: *Encyclia, Barkeria,* and *Nanodes.*

Eria. A genus of epiphytic orchids found chiefly in India and Malaysia. There are more than 550 species. Plants are closely related to those of the more popular genus *Dendrobium.* Flowers are generally small and not as showy as those of other orchids.

Eulophidium. A genus of about ten species, usually terrestrial, the majority from Madagascar and Africa. The leaves are dark green and ornamental. Some species produce small but very handsome flowers; others bear insignificant blooms.

Galeandra. A genus of twenty-five terrestrial and epiphytic species from tropical America. Leaves are grassy and folded.

Gastrochilus. A small genus of dwarf orchids, formerly called *Saccolabium.*

Gongora. With twenty epiphytic species from tropical America, this is a genus of incredible orchids that produce fragrant flower spikes from the base of the pseudobulbs. The blooms, intricate in structure, are usually called Punch-and-Judy orchids.

Grammatophyllum. Native to Asia and the Pacific, this epiphytic genus includes eight species. Leaves are long and strap-shaped; flowers are spotted and have incredible lasting power. Generally huge plants, up to 10 feet high.

Huntleya. An epiphytic genus with about four species. Plants bear waxy flat-faced flowers that hardly appear to be orchids.

Laelia. A genus of mostly epiphytic orchids closely related to the genus *Cattleya,* and found from Mexico to Argentina. One species is the national flower of Brazil. Pseudobulbs are of several shapes (round, oval, or elongated), and flowers resemble cattleyas but have narrower sepals and a less showy lip.

Leptotes. From Brazil and Paraguay, this epiphytic genus has four small species. Plants are well worth cultivating, having large, long-lasting flowers.

Lycaste. A terrestrial and epiphytic genus with about twenty-five species found in tropical America and the West Indies. These popular plants are deciduous; flowers are always showy, and last from six to eight weeks on the plant.

Macodes. This is one of the groups whose members are sometimes called jewel orchids for their exquisite foliage. There are seven species in this genus, mostly from Malaysia or Indonesia. Plants require exacting care.

Masdevallia. About three hundred tropical American orchids compose this genus. Usually epiphytic, the brightly colored, often oddly shaped flowers are borne singly, or occasionally on short spikes. Most of the flowers have long-tailed sepals and are sometimes called kite orchids.

Maxillaria. A widely scattered genus of over three hundred epiphytic orchids; some are small, others quite large. Plants are rarely cultivated. Color range of blooms is extensive.

Miltonia. There are about twenty species in this important epiphytic genus, which is native to Brazil, Peru, and Costa Rica. Some are from high elevations, others from warm lowlands; thus plants may require differing conditions. Generally called the pansy orchid, *Miltonia* has lovely flat-faced flowers and is now used extensively for hybridizing with the genera *Oncidium, Odontoglossum,* and *Brassia*.

Mormodes. An epiphytic genus of about twenty species from the American tropics. Plants are deciduous or nearly so, and flowers appear on leafless stalks. Most of the species resemble birds in flight and are occasionally called flying-bird orchids.

Odontoglossum. A large epiphytic genus of three hundred species from Mexico and South America, the majority from high elevations. Plants and flowers come in many sizes and shapes; some have showy flowers, others insignificant blooms. A most important genus.

Oncidium. The majority of this important genus of 750 epiphytic orchids are from South America and Central America. Flower form and plant structure are varied; blooms may be small or large. Many species produce long stems dotted with hundreds of small brown-and-yellow flowers, and are called dancing ladies.

Ornithocephalus. A genus of thirty-five species, mostly epiphytic, from Mexico and Brazil. Leaves are fanlike in arrangement, and the flowers are usually small but attractive. Most species are dwarfish.

Ornithochilus. Two species make up this epiphytic genus from the Himalayas and China. Flowers are small but pretty; plants are rather dwarf.

Paphiopedilum. A genus of about fifty Asiatic species of lady's-slippers. They are mainly terrestrials. Often wrongly called cypripediums, these orchids have waxy, almost artificial-looking flowers. There are numerous horticultural hybrids.

Pescatorea. A genus of about twelve epiphytic orchids from Costa Rica and Panama. The plants are medium-size and grow in leaf fan shape. They bear fleshy, waxy, exquisite flowers 3 inches wide.

Phaius. The thirty species included in this genus range from East Africa to tropical Asia and the Pacific Islands. A terrestrial genus, it does, however, have one epiphytic species. Not often grown by hobbyists, these robust and lovely orchids have showy flowers that can, if necessary, grow under untoward conditions. *P. tankervilliae* (*grandifolius*) is often called the nun's orchid because the petals and sepals give it a hooded look.

Phalaenopsis. Perhaps the most beautiful orchids belong to this epiphytic genus of some forty species, which are found from Formosa and India to the Philippines, New Guinea, and Queensland. This is known as the moth orchid. All the species have leathery leaves and exquisite flowers. Plants have been extensively hybridized, and there are many fine varieties.

Phragmipedium. Often wrongly classified *Cypripedium* or *Selenipedium,* this genus of lady's-slipper orchids from tropical America comprises about twelve species, which are found from southern Mexico to Peru and Brazil. Plants are characterized by long ribbon-like petals.

Platyclinis (Dendrochilum). A genus of about 150 epiphytic orchids distributed in a vast region from Burma and Sumatra to New Guinea; many are found in Borneo and the Philippines. Flowers are generally small.

Pleurothallis. A genus of tropical American epiphytic orchids with almost a thousand species. Some plants are large, others small. Some have desirable flowers; the blooms on others are insignificant.

Pterostylis. This genus contains about seventy species of terrestrial orchids, known as greenhoods. Most are from Australia; some are from New Zealand, New Guinea, and New Caledonia. Plants are deciduous and flowers small, usually green or greenish with red-brown markings.

Renanthera. An epiphytic genus of showy plants from tropical Asia and some Pacific islands. Famous for their brick-red colors.

Rhynchostylis. With only four species, this epiphytic genus, formerly included in the genus *Saccolabium,* is a floriferous group. The plants have straplike leaves and bright scented blooms; a single plant may bear 200 flowers.

Rodriguezia. A genus of about thirty dwarf epiphytic species from Costa Rica to Brazil and Peru. These are dainty orchids with pendant scapes of colorful flowers.

Sarcochilus. A genus of epiphytic orchids containing about thirty species. They are distributed over India, Malaysia, Australia, and the Pacific Islands. Some do not have leaves but are rather a tangle of roots. Flowers are generally handsome.

Schomburgkia. Closely related to the genus *Laelia,* this genus extends from Mexico and the West Indies to South America. These epiphytic orchids may have two leaves and spindle-shaped pseudobulbs, or larger hollow-shaped pseudobulbs with three or more leaves. When found in nature, ant colonies often live in the hollow bulbs.

Selenipedium. With four tropical American species, this genus contains generally tall reedy plants with slipper-like flowers at the top. Most of the plants cultivated under this name are classified *Phragmipedium*. According to some authorities no true selenipediums are in cultivation.

Spiranthes. A genus of American terrestrial orchids found in grasslands and woods; they are widely distributed. There are almost three hundred species, divided among a number of other genera by many authorities.

Stenocoryne. From Brazil, this is a genus of twelve species closely allied to the genus *Xylobium*. Flowers are small, usually bell-shaped, and brilliantly colored.

Stenoglottis. Terrestrial orchids from South Africa. The tuberous roots produce a rosette of leaves; the flowers are small but attractive. Plants grow and bloom for four or five months and then rest for a few months before starting to grow again and repeat the cycle.

Trichocentrum. A genus of eighteen species from tropical America. The plants are mostly dwarf. Flowers, generally small, are appealing.

Trichoceros. This is a genus of small epiphytic orchids from Colombia, Peru, and Bolivia. There are about six species, which are rarely grown in cultivation.

Trichoglottis. A genus of thirty-five epiphytic species from Asia and Indonesia. Handsome flowers decorate these vinelike plants.

Trichopilia. With about thirty species, this epiphytic genus is found in Mexico, Central America, and Colombia. Plants are undistinguished without flowers, but in bloom several species make a magnificent show, with large 7-inch flowers that hug the rim of the pot.

Vanda. An epiphytic genus of seventy species extending from China and the Himalayas to New Guinea and northern Australia. Plants vary in form and flower, having strap-shaped or cylindrical leaves and long-lasting flat-faced blooms. Hundreds of hybrids have been made within the genus.

Warscewiczella. Generally included in genus *Zygopetalum*.

Xylobium. From tropical America, this genus of twenty species is usually epiphytic but sometimes terrestrial. Flowers are generally small and pale in color.

Zygopetalum. An epiphytic genus of some twenty species from tropical and Central America. The group once included other genera since reclassified. The highly fragrant flowers are an incredible combination of spots and stripes of blue, green, and brown.

Sources of Plants

Alberts and Merkel Bros., Inc., P.O. Box 537, Boynton Beach, Fla. 33435

Armacost and Royston, Inc., 2005 Armacost Ave., West Los Angeles, Calif. 90025

Black and Flory, Ltd., Slough, Bucks, England

Charlesworth and Co., Ltd., Haywards Heath, Sussex, England

Creve Coeur Orchids, 12 Graeser Acres, Creve Coeur, Mo. 63141

Dos Pueblos Orchid Co., P.O. Box 158, Goleta, Calif. 93017

Fennell Orchid Co., Homestead, Fla. 33030

Arthur Freed Orchids, Inc., 5731 S. Bonsall Dr., Malibu, Calif. 90265

G. Ghose and Co., Orchids, Town-End, Darjeeling, West Bengal, India

R. H. Gore Orchids, Box 211, Fort Lauderdale, Fla. 33315

Hausermann's Orchids, see Orchids by Hausermann

Hilo Vanda Nursery, Dr. H. Nishimura, 10–11 Young Bldg., Hilo, Hawaii 96720

Gordon M. Hoyt, Orchids, Seattle Heights, Wash. 98063

Margaret Ilgenfritz, Ilgenfritz Orchids, P.O. Box 665, Monroe, Mich. 48161

J. and L. Orchids, Chestnut Hill Rd., R.D. 2, Pottstown, Pa. 19464

Jones and Scully, Inc., 2200 N.W. 33rd Ave., Miami, Fla. 33142

Wm. Kirsch Orchids, Ltd., 2630 Waiomao Rd., Honolulu, Hawaii 96816

Oscar M. Kirsch, 2869 Oahu Ave., Honolulu, Hawaii 96822

Lager and Hurrell, 426 Morris Ave., Summit, N.J. 07901

Marcel Lecoufle, 5 rue de Paris, 94 Boissy–St. Léger, France

Lines Orchids, Taft Highway, Signal Mountain, Tenn. 37377

Stuart Low Co., Jarvisbrook (Crowborough), Sussex, England

McBean's Cymbidium Orchids, Cooksbridge, Lewes, Sussex, England

Rod McLellan Co., 1450 El Camino Real, S. San Francisco, Calif. 94080

Oak Hill Gardens, P.O. Box 25 Rt. 2, Binnie Rd., Dundee, Ill. 60118

Orchids by Hausermann, P.O. Box 363, Elmhurst, Ill. 60126

Orquideario Catarinense, P.O. Box 1, Corupa, Santa Catarina, Brazil

Joseph R. Redlinger, Orchids, 9236 S.W. 57th Ave., Miami, Fla. 33156

Rivermont Orchids, Signal Mountain, Tenn. 37377

David Sander's Orchids, Ltd., Selsfield, East Grinstead, Sussex, England

T.M. Sanders, 12502 Prospect Ave., Santa Ana, Calif. 92705

Santa Barbara Orchid Estate, 1250 Orchid Dr., Goleta, Calif. 93105

Walter Scheeren Orchids, Poestenkill, N.Y. 12140

Shaffer's Tropical Gardens, Inc., 1220 41st Ave., Santa Cruz, Calif. 95060

Sign of the Coon, Powderville, Mont. 59345

Earl J. Small Orchids, Inc., 6901 49th St., Pinellas Park, Fla. 33565

Fred A. Stewart, Inc., 1212 E. Las Tunas Dr., San Gabriel, Calif. 91778

Tradewinds Orchids, Inc., 12800 S.W. 77th Ave., Miami, Fla. 33156

Maurice Vacherot, 31 rue de Valenton, Boissy–St. Léger, France

Weeki Wachee Orchids, Rt. 4, Box 65, Brooksville, Fla. 33512

Wilkins Orchid Nursery, 21905 S.W. 157 Ave., Goulds, Fla. 33170

Books on Orchids

Ames, Blanche. *Drawings of Florida Orchids,* with explanatory notes by Oakes Ames. 2d ed. Cambridge, Mass.: Botanical Museum of Harvard University, 1959.

Ames, Oakes, and Correll, Donovan S. *Orchids of Guatemala.* 2 vols. Chicago: Field Museum of Natural History, 1952–53. (*Fieldiana: Botany,* vol. 26, nos. 1, 2.) Supplement by Donovan S. Correll, 1966.

Blowers, John W. *Pictorial Orchid Growing.* Published by the author (96 Marion Crescent, Maidstone, Kent, England), 1966.

Boyle, Louis M. *Growing Cymbidium Orchids and Other Flowers.* Ojai, Calif.: El Rancho Rinconada, 1953.

Cady, Leo, and Rotherham, T. *Australian Orchids in Color.* 107 color-plates. Sydney, Australia: A. H. and A. W. Reed, 1970.

Correll, Donovan S. *Native Orchids of North America, North of Mexico.* (*Chronica Botanica.*) New York: The Ronald Press, 1950.

Cox, J. Murray. *A Cultural Table of Orchidaceous Plants.* Sydney, Australia: The Shepard Press, 1946.

Craighead, Frank S. *Orchids and Other Air Plants of the Everglades National Park.* Coral Gables, Fla.: University of Miami Press, 1963.

Curtis, Charles H. *Orchids: Their Description and Cultivation.* London: Putnam & Co., Ltd., 1950.

Curtis, Charles H. *Orchids for Everyone.* New York: E. P. Dutton & Co., 1910.

Darwin, Charles. *The Various Contrivances by Which Orchids Are Fertilised by Insects.* New York: D. Appleton & Co., 1892.

Davis, Reg S., and Steiner, Mona Lisa. *Philippine Orchids.* New York: The William Frederick Press, 1952.

de Oca, Rafael Montes. *Hummingbirds and Orchids of Mexico.* Reproductions of watercolor paintings. Mexico City: Editorial Fournier, S. A., 1963.

Dienum, Dick. *Orchideen van Nederland.* Text in Dutch. 1944.

Dockrill, A. W. *Australian Indigenous Orchids.* Sydney, Australia, 1969.

Dodson, Calaway H., and Gillespie, Robert J. *The Biology of the Orchids.* Nashville, Tenn.: Mid-American Orchid Congress, 1967.

Dunsterville, G. C. K. *Introduction to the World of Orchids.* New York: Doubleday and Co., 1964.

Fennell, T. A., Jr. *Orchids for Home and Garden.* New York: Rinehart and Co., 1956, rev. 1959.

Garrard, Jeanne. *Growing Orchids for Pleasure.* South Brunswick, N.J.: A. S. Barnes and Co., 1966.

Ghose, B. N. *Beautiful Indian Orchids.* 2d ed. Town-End, Darjeeling, Indian Union: G. Ghose and Co., 1969.

Graf, Alfred Byrd. *Exotica 3. Pictorial Cyclopedia of Exotic Plants.* Includes 901 illustrations and descriptions of orchids. Rutherford, N.J.: Roehrs Co., 1963.

Grubb, Roy, and Grubb, Ann. *Selected Orchidaceous Plants.* Parts 1, 2, and 3. Drawn and hand-printed by the authors (62 Chaldon Common Road, Caterham, Surrey, England), 1961–63.

Harvard University. *Botanical Museum Leaflets.* By subscription, or separately from American Orchid Society, Cambridge, Mass.

Hawkes, Alex D. *Orchids: Their Botany and Culture.* New York: Harper and Bros., 1961.

Heohne, F. C. *Flora Brasilica: Orchidaceae.* In parts, incomplete. São Paulo: Instituto de Botanica, 1940–43.

Hogg, Bruce. *Orchids: Their Culture.* Melbourne and Sydney, Australia: Cassell and Co., Ltd., 1957.

Hooker, Sir Joseph Dalton. *A Century of Orchidaceous Plants.* London: Reeve & Benham, 1851.

Kramer, Jack. *Growing Orchids at Your Windows.* New York: Hawthorne, 1972.

Kupper, Walter. *Orchids.* New York: Thomas Nelson and Sons, 1961.

Lecoufle, Marcel, and Rose, Henri. *Orchids.* English ed. London: Crosby Lockwood and Son, Ltd., 1957.

Logan, Harry B., and Cosper, Lloyd C. *Orchids Are Easy to Grow.* Chicago: Ziff-Davis Publishing Co., 1949.

Moulen, Fred. *Orchids in Australia*. 100 colored figures. Sydney: Australia Edita Pty., Ltd., 1958.

Noble, Mary. *You Can Grow Cattleya Orchids*. Published by the author (3003 Riverside Ave., Jacksonville, Fla., 32205), 1968.

Osorio, L. F. *Colombian Orchids*. Medellin, Colombia: F. de Bedout e Hijos, 1941.

Richter, Walter. *Die Schönsten Aber Sind Orchideen*. 64 colorplates. Radebeul, Germany: Neumann Verlag, 1958. English tr. and rev. by Edmund Laurent under title *The Orchid World*. New York: E. P. Dutton & Co., 1965.

Rittershausen, R. R. C. *Successful Orchid Culture*. London, 1953. Published in New York by Transatlantic Arts., Inc.

Sander, C. R., F. K., and L. L. *Sander's Orchid Guide*. Reprint. St. Albans, England, Rev. ed., 1927.

Sander, David. *Orchids and Their Cultivation*. Rev. ed. of earlier book by the Sanders of St. Albans. London: Blandford Press, 1962.

Sander, Henry Frederick Conrad. *Reichenbachia*. Plates are now collectors' items. 4 vols. St. Albans. England, 1888–94.

Sanders. *Complete List of Orchid Hybrids*. Compilation of hybrids to 1946 in first volume. Addenda: 3 vol, 1946–48, 1949–51, 1952–54. *One Table List of Orchid Hybrids,* 1946–60. Addenda, 1963, 1966. Published in England. Available from American Orchid Society, Inc., Botanical Museum of Harvard University, Cambridge, Mass. Addenda published from time to time will be available from American Orchid Society.

Schelpe, Edmund. *An Introduction to the South African Orchids*. London: MacDonald and Co., Ltd., 1966.

Schlechter, Rudolf. *Die Orchideen*. 2d ed. Berlin: P. Parey, 1927.

Schweinfurth, Charles. *Orchids of Peru*. Chicago: Field Museum of Natural History, 1958–61. (*Fieldiana: Botany,* vol. 30, nos. 1–4.)

Summerhayes, V. S. *Wild Orchids of Britain*. London: Collins, 1951.

Thomale, Hans. *Die Orchideen*. Ludwigsburg, Germany: Eugen Ulmer, 1954.

Watkins, John V. *ABC of Orchid Growing*. 1948. 3d ed. Englewood Cliffs, N.J.: Prentice-Hall, 1956.

Watson, W., and Chapman, H. J. *Orchids: Their Culture and Management*. Rev. ed. New York: Charles Scribner's Sons, 1903.

White, E. A. *American Orchid Culture*. Rev. ed. New York: A. T. De La Mare Co., 1942.

Williams, B. S. *The Orchid-Grower's Manual*. 7th ed., rev. by Henry Williams, 1894. Reprint. Darien, Conn.: Hafner Publishing Co., 1961.

Withner, Carl L. *The Orchids: A Scientific Survey*. New York: The Ronald Press, 1959.

Wright, N. Pelham. *Orquideas de Mexico*. Bilingual text. Mexico City: Editorial Fournier, S. A., 1958.

Bibliography

BOOKS

Baker, Herbert G. *Plants and Civilization*. Belmont Calif.: Wadsworth Publishing Co., 1965.

Boyle, Frederick. *The Woodlands Orchids*. New York: The Macmillan Co., 1901.

Cleveland Museum of Art. *Chinese Art Under the Mongols: The Yuan Dynasty*, nos. 235, 236, 245 (1968).

Cox, J. Murray. *A Cultural Table of Orchidaceous Plants*. Sydney, Australia: The Shepard Press, 1946.

Curtis, Charles H. *Orchids*. London: Putnam & Co., Ltd., 1950.

Darnell, A. W. *Orchids for the Outdoor Garden*. Ashford, Kent, England: L. Reeve & Co., Ltd., 1930.

Darwin, Charles. *The Various Contrivances by Which Orchids Are Fertilised by Insects*. New York: D. Appleton & Co., 1892.

Foley, Daniel. *The Flowering World of "Chinese" Wilson*. London: Macmillan Ltd., 1969.

Graf, Alfred Byrd. *Exotica III. Pictorial Cyclopedia of Exotic Plants*. Rutherford, N.J.: Roehrs Co., 1963.

Grieve, M. *A Modern Herbal*. 2 vols. 1931. Reprint. Darien, Conn.: Hafner Publishing Co., 1970.

Hawkes, Alex D. *Encyclopedia of Cultivated Orchids*. London: Faber & Faber, 1965.

Kerner von Marilaun, Anton Joseph, and Oliver, F. W. *Natural History of Plants*. vol. 1. New York: Henry Holt & Co., 1902.

Kramer, Jack. *Orchids for Your Home*. New York: Cornerstone Library, 1974.

Li, H. L. *The Garden Flowers of China*. New York: The Ronald Press, 1959.

Manual of Orchidaceous Plants. vol. 1. London: James Veitch & Sons, 1887–94. Reprint. Amsterdam: A. Asher & Co., 1963.

Richter, Walter. *The Orchid World*. Tr. from the German and rev. by Edmund Laurent. Ed. by P. Frances Hunt. New York: E. P. Dutton & Co., 1965.

Sanders. *One Table List of Orchid Hybrids*, 1946–60. Addenda, 1963, 1966. Published in England, available from American Orchid Society, Botanical Museum of Harvard University, Cambridge, Mass.

Schultes, Richard Evans, and Pease, Arthur Stanley. *Generic Names of Plants*. New York: Academic Press, 1963.

Swinson, Arthur. *Frederick Sander: The Orchid King*. London: Hodder & Stoughton, 1970.

Tergit, Gabriele. *Flowers Through the Ages*. Chester Springs, Pa.: Dufour Editions, 1962.

Whittle, Tyler. *Plant Hunters*. Radnor, Pa.: Chilton Book Company, 1970.

Williams, B. S. *The Orchid-Grower's Manual*. 7th ed., rev. by Henry Williams, 1894. Reprint. Darien, Conn.: Hafner Publishing Co., 1961.

Withner, Carl L. *The Orchids: A Scientific Survey*. New York: The Ronald Press, 1959.

PERIODICALS

American Orchid Society Bulletin. Cambridge, Mass.: Botanical Museum of Harvard University.

Australian Orchid Review. Sydney, Australia: Shepard and Newman Pty., Ltd.

Orchid Digest. La Canada, Calif.

The Orchid Review. Caterham, Surrey, England.

Index of Illustrated Orchids

Numbers in italics refer to colorplates